HARLEQUIN
VALENTINE™

Neil Gaiman
WRITER

John Bolton
ARTIST

For Lisa Snellings

Diana Schutz
EDITOR

Cary Grazzini
BOOK DESIGN

Richard Starkings &
Comicraft's Jason Levine
LETTERING

Mike Richardson
PUBLISHER

Published by
Dark Horse Comics, Inc.
10956 SE Main Street
Milwaukie, Oregon 97222

First edition: November 2001
ISBN 1-56971-620-6

PRINTED IN SINGAPORE

It is February the Fourteenth,
at that hour of the morning
    when all the children
    have been taken to school and
    the husbands have driven
        themselves to work or
    been dropped, steambreathing
        and greatcoated,
at the rail station
        at the edge of the town
        for the Great Commute,
when I pin my heart
        to Missy's front door.

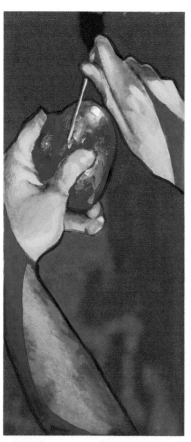
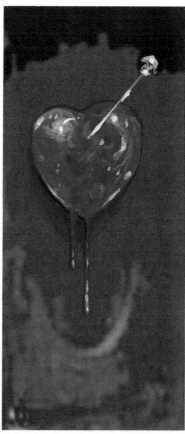

The heart is a deep dark red that is almost a brown, the colour of liver.

Then I knock on the door, sharply, rat-a-tat-tat!

4

And I grasp my wand,
my stick,
my oh·so·thrustable
and beribonned lance,
and I vanish
like cooling steam
into the chilly air...

Missy opens the door. She looks tired.

"My Columbine," I breathe, but she hears not a word. She turns her head, so she takes in the view from one side of the street to the other, but nothing moves.

A truck rumbles in the distance.

She walks back into the kitchen and I dance, silent as a breeze, as a mouse, as a dream, into the kitchen beside her.

Missy takes a plastic sandwich bag
from a paper box
in the kitchen drawer.

She takes a bottle of
cleaning spray
from under the sink.

She pulls off two sections
of kitchen towel
from the roll
on the kitchen counter.
Then she walks back
to the front door.

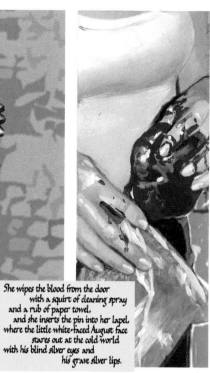

She pulls the pin
from the painted wood--
it was my hat pin
which I had stumbled across...
where?
I turn the matter
over in my head:
in Gascony, perhaps?
or Twickenham? or Prague?

The face on the end
of the hat pin
is that of a pale
Pierrot.

She removes the pin
from the heart,
and puts the heart
into the plastic
sandwich bag.

She wipes the blood from the door
with a squirt of cleaning spray
and a rub of paper towel,
and she inserts the pin into her lapel,
where the little white-faced August face
stares out at the cold world
with his blind silver eyes and
his grave silver lips.

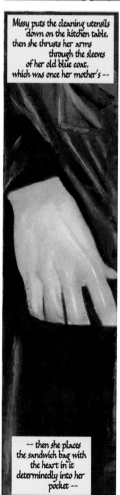

Naples. Now it comes back to me.

Missy puts the cleaning utensils
down on the kitchen table,
then she thrusts her arms
through the sleeves
of her old blue coat,
which was once her mother's --

-- does up
the buttons,
one,
two,
three --

-- and sets off
down the street.

I purchased the hat pin
in Naples,
from an old woman
with one eye.
She smoked a clay pipe.
This was a long time ago.

-- then she places
the sandwich bag with
the heart in it
determinedly into her
pocket --

Secret, secret, quiet as a mouse I follow her, sometimes creeping, sometimes dancing, and she never sees me, not for a moment, just pulls her blue coat more tightly around her, and she walks through the town, and down the old road that leads past the cemetery.

The wind tugs at my hat, and I regret, for a moment, the loss of my hat pin. But I am in love, and this is Valentine's Day. Sacrifices must be made.

Missy is remembering in her head the other times she has walked into the cemetery, through the tall iron cemetery gates:

when her father died; and when they came here as kids at All Hallows', the whole school mob and caboodle of them, partying and scaring each other;

and when a secret lover was killed in a three-car pile-up on the interstate, and she waited until the end of the funeral, when the day was all over and done with, and she came in the evening, just before sunset, and laid a white lily on the fresh grave.

Oh, Missy, shall I sing the body and the blood of you, the lips and the eyes? A thousand hearts I would give you, as your valentine.

Proudly I wave my staff in the air and dance, singing silently of the gloriousness of me, as we skip together down Cemetery Road.

A low grey building, and Missy pushes open the door.

She says *Hi* and *How's it going* to the girl at the desk, who makes no intelligible reply, fresh out of school and filling in a crossword from a periodical filled with nothing but crosswords, page after page of them...

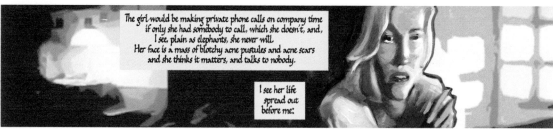

The girl would be making private phone calls on company time if only she had somebody to call, which she doesn't, and, I see, plain as elephants, she never will. Her face is a mass of blotchy acne pustules and acne scars and she thinks it matters, and talks to nobody.

I see her life spread out before me:

She will die, unmarried, and unmolested, of breast cancer in fifteen years' time, and will be planted under a stone with her name on it in the meadow by Cemetery Road, and the first hands to have touched her breasts will have been those of the pathologist as he cuts out the cauliflower-like stinking growth and mutters,

JESUS, LOOK AT THE *SIZE* OF THIS THING. WHY DIDN'T SHE *TELL* ANYONE?

which rather misses the point.

Gently, I kiss her on her spotty cheek, and whisper to her that she is beautiful. Then I tap her once, twice, *thrice*, on the head with my staff, and wrap her with a ribbon.

She stirs and smiles.

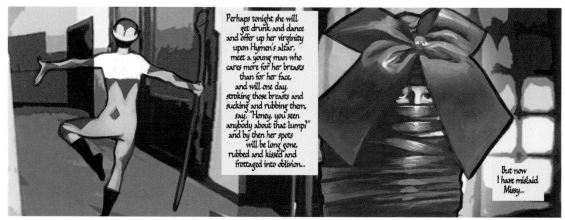

Perhaps tonight she will get drunk and dance and offer up her virginity upon Hymen's altar, meet a young man who cares more for her breasts than for her face, and will one day, stroking those breasts and sucking and rubbing them, say, "Honey, you seen anybody about that lump?" and by then her spots will be long gone, rubbed and kissed and frottaged into oblivion...

But now I have mislaid Missy...

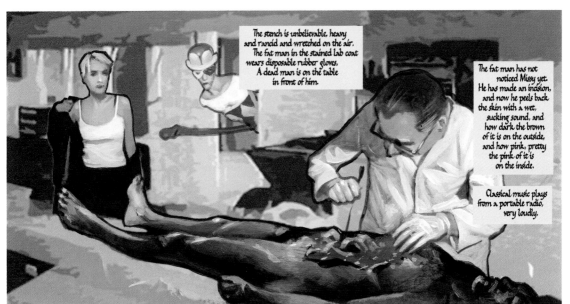

The stench is unbelievable, heavy and rancid and wretched on the air. The fat man in the stained lab coat wears disposable rubber gloves. A dead man is on the table in front of him.

The fat man has not noticed Missy yet. He has made an incision, and now he peels back the skin with a wet, sucking sound, and how dark the brown of it is on the outside, and how pink, pretty the pink of it is on the inside.

Classical music plays from a portable radio, very loudly.

Missy turns the radio off.

HELLO, VERNON.

HELLO, MISSY. YOU COME FOR YOUR OLD JOB BACK?

This is The Doctor, I decide, for he is too big, too round, too magnificently well-fed to be Pierrot, too unselfconscious to be Pantaloon.

His face creases with delight to see Missy, and she smiles to see him, and I am jealous: I feel a stab of pain shoot through my heart (currently in a plastic sandwich bag in Missy's coat pocket), sharper than when I stabbed it with my hat pin and stuck it to her door.

And speaking of my heart...

DO YOU KNOW WHAT THIS IS?

HEART. KIDNEYS DON'T HAVE THE VENTRICLES, AND BRAINS ARE BIGGER AND SQUISHIER. WHERE'D YOU GET IT?

I WAS HOPING THAT YOU COULD TELL ME. DOESN'T IT COME FROM HERE? IS IT YOUR IDEA OF A VALENTINE'S CARD, VERNON? A HUMAN HEART STUCK TO MY FRONT DOOR?

DON'T COME FROM HERE. YOU WANT I SHOULD CALL THE POLICE?

I GUESS *NOT*. WITH *MY* LUCK, THEY'LL DECIDE I'M A SERIAL KILLER AND SEND ME TO THE CHAIR.

LET'S *SEE*... ADULT, IN PRETTY GOOD SHAPE, TOOK CARE OF HIS HEART. CUT OUT BY AN EXPERT.

I smile proudly at this, and bend down to talk to the dead black man on the table, with his chest all open and his calloused string-bass-picking fingers.

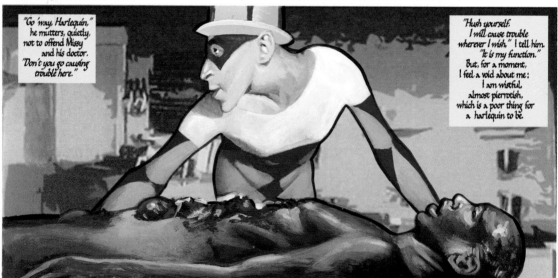

"Go 'way, Harlequin," he mutters, quietly, not to offend Missy and his doctor. "Don't you go causing trouble here."

"Hush yourself. I will cause trouble wherever I wish," I tell him. "It is my function." But, for a moment, I feel a void about me: I am wistful, almost pierrotish, which is a poor thing for a harlequin to be.

Oh, Missy, I saw you yesterday in the street, and followed you into Al's Super-Valu Foods and More, elation and joy rising within me. In you, I recognised someone who could transport me, take me from myself.

In you I recognised my valentine.

My Columbine.

I wonder what she will do with my gift.
Some girls spurn my heart,
others touch it, kiss it, caress it, punish it
with all manner of endearments before
they return it to my keeping.
Some never even see it...

SHALL I *INCINERATE* IT?

MIGHT AS WELL. YOU KNOW WHERE THE INCINERATOR IS. AND I MEANT WHAT I SAID ABOUT YOUR OLD JOB. I *NEED* A GOOD LAB ASSISTANT.

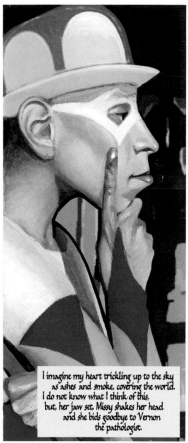

I imagine my heart trickling up to the sky
as ashes and smoke, covering the world.
I do not know what I think of this,
but, her jaw set, Missy shakes her head
and she bids goodbye to Vernon
the pathologist.

She has thrust my heart into her pocket and
she is walking out of the building and up
Cemetery Road and back into town.

I caper ahead of her.

Interaction would be a fine thing, I decide.

Fitting word to deed I disguise myself as a bent old woman on her way to the market, covering the red spangles of my costume with a tattered cloak, hiding my masked face with a voluminous hood,
and at the top of Cemetery Road I step out and block her way.

Marvelous, marvelous, marvelous me, and I say to her, in the voice of the oldest of women.

SPARE A COPPER FOR A BENT OLD WOMAN, DEARIE, AND I'LL TELL YOU A FORTUNE THAT WILL MAKE YOUR EYES SPIN WITH JOY.

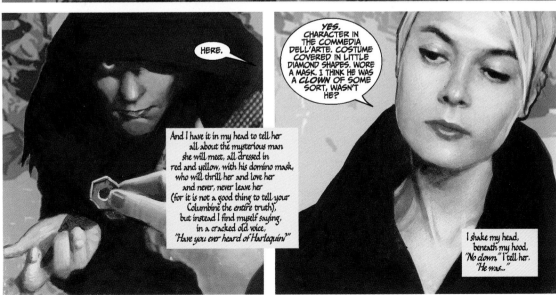

HERE.

And I have it in my head to tell her all about the mysterious man she will meet, all dressed in red and yellow, with his domino mask, who will thrill her and love her and never, never leave her (for it is not a good thing to tell your Columbine the entire truth), but instead I find myself saying, in a cracked old voice, "Have you ever heard of Harlequin?"

YES. CHARACTER IN THE COMMEDIA DELL'ARTE. COSTUME COVERED IN LITTLE DIAMOND SHAPES. WORE A MASK. I THINK HE WAS A CLOWN OF SOME SORT, WASN'T HE?

I shake my head, beneath my hood, "No clown," I tell her. "He was..."

And I find that I am about to tell her the truth, so I choke back the words and pretend that I am having the kind of coughing attack to which elderly women are particularly susceptible.

I squint through old woman eyes at Missy; she is in her early twenties, and she has lips like a mermaid's, full and well-defined and certain, and grey eyes, and a certain intensity to her gaze.

ARE YOU ALL RIGHT?

I cough and splutter and cough some more, and gasp,

FINE, MY DEARIE-DUCK, I'M JUST *FINE*, THANK YOU KINDLY.

I wonder if this could be the power of love.

I do not remember it troubling me with other women I thought I had loved, other Columbines I have encountered over centuries now long gone.

SO, I THOUGHT YOU WERE GOING TO TELL ME MY FORTUNE.

HARLEQUIN HAS GIVEN YOU HIS HEART. YOU MUST DISCOVER ITS BEAT YOURSELF.

I hear myself saying these words, angry at my trickster tongue for betraying me.

She stares at me, puzzled. I cannot change or vanish while her eyes are upon me, and I feel frozen.

LOOK! A RABBIT!

And she turns, follows my pointing finger, and as she takes her eyes off me I disappear -- *pop!* -- like a rabbit down a hole.

When she looks back, there's not a trace of the old fortune-teller lady, which is to say me.

Missy walks on, and I caper after her, but there is not the spring in my step there was earlier in the morning.

Midday, and Missy has walked to Al's Super-Valu Foods and More, where she buys a small block of cheese, a carton of unconcentrated orange juice, two avocados, and on to the County One Bank, where she withdraws two hundred and seventy-nine dollars and twenty-two cents, which is the total amount of money in her savings account, and I creep after her sweet as sugar and quiet as the grave.

'MORNING, MISSY...'

says the owner of the Salt Shaker Café, when Missy enters.

My heart would have skipped a beat if it were not in the sandwich bag in Missy's pocket, for this man obviously lusts after her, and my confidence, which is legendary, droops and wilts.

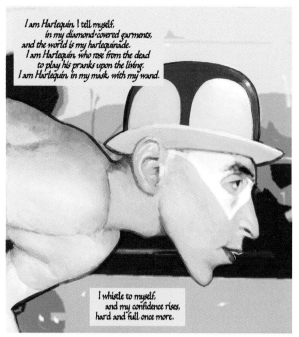

I am Harlequin, I tell myself.
in my diamond-covered garments,
and the world is my harlequinade.
I am Harlequin, who rose from the dead
to play his pranks upon the living.
I am Harlequin in my mask, with my wand.

I whistle to myself.
and my confidence rises,
hard and full once more.

HEY, HARVE. GIVE ME A PLATE OF HASH BROWNS, AND A BOTTLE OF KETCHUP.

THAT *ALL?*

YES. THAT'LL BE PERFECT. AND A GLASS OF WATER.

I tell myself that the man Harve
is Pantaloon,
the foolish merchant that I must
bamboozle, baffle, confusticate,
and confuse.

Perhaps there is
a string of sausages
in the kitchen.

I resolve to bring
delightful disarray
to the world, and
to bed luscious Missy
before midnight;
my Valentine's present
to myself.

I imagine myself kissing her lips.

There are a handful of other diners.
I amuse myself by swapping their plates
while they are not looking,
but I have difficulty finding the fun in it.

The waitress ignores Missy,
whom she obviously
considers entirely
Harve's preserve.

18

Missy sits at the table, and pulls the sandwich bag from her pocket. She places it on the table in front of her.

Harve-the-pantaloon struts over to Missy's table, gives her a glass of water, a plate of hash-browned potatoes, and a bottle of Heinz 57 Varieties Tomato Ketchup.

AND A STEAK KNIFE.

He curses, and I feel better, more like the former me.

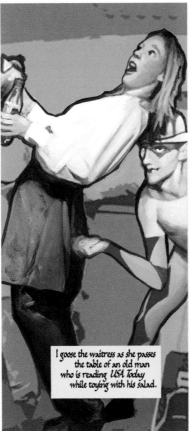

I goose the waitress as she passes the table of an old man who is reading *USA Today* while toying with his salad.

She gives the old man a filthy look. I chuckle, and then I find I am feeling most peculiar.

19

I sit down on the floor, suddenly.

WHAT'S THAT, HONEY?

HEALTH FOOD, CHARLENE. BUILDS UP IRON.

I peep over the tabletop.

She is slicing up small slices of liver-coloured meat on her plate, liberally doused in tomato sauce, and piling her fork high with hash browns.

Then she chews.

And as she finishes eating my heart, Missy looks down and sees me sprawled upon the floor. She nods.

OUTSIDE. NOW.

Then she gets up, and leaves ten dollars beside her plate.

She is sitting on a bench on the sidewalk, waiting for me. It is cold, and the street is almost deserted.

I would caper around her, but it feels so foolish now I know someone is watching.

Missy reaches out and plucks my hat from my head, takes my stick from my hand.

She toys with the hat, her long fingers brushing and bending it. Her nails are painted crimson. Then she stretches and smiles, expansively. The poetry has gone from my soul, and the cold February wind makes me shiver.

IT'S COLD.

NO. IT'S *PERFECT*, *MAGNIFICENT*, *MARVELOUS*, AND *MAGICAL*. IT'S VALENTINE'S DAY, ISN'T IT? WHO COULD BE COLD UPON VALENTINE'S DAY? WHAT A *FINE* AND *FABULOUS* TIME OF THE YEAR.

The diamonds are fading from my suit, which is turning ghost-white, pierrot-white.

WHAT DO I DO NOW?

I DON'T KNOW. FADE AWAY, PERHAPS. OR FIND ANOTHER ROLE... A LOVELORN SWAIN, PERCHANCE, MOONING AND PINING UNDER THE PALE MOON. ALL YOU NEED IS A COLUMBINE.

YOU ARE MY COLUMBINE.

NOT ANYMORE. THAT'S THE JOY OF THE HARLEQUINADE, AFTER ALL, ISN'T IT? WE CHANGE OUR COSTUMES. WE CHANGE OUR ROLES.

She flashes me such a smile, now.

Then she puts my hat, my own hat, my harlequin-hat, up onto her head.

AND YOU?

She tosses the wand into the air; it tumbles and twists in a high arc, red and yellow ribbons twisting and swirling about it, and then it lands neatly, almost silently, back into her hand.

She pushes the tip down to the sidewalk, pushes herself up from the bench in one smooth movement.

Then she leans over, and kisses me, full and hard upon the lips.

Somewhere a car backfired. I turned, startled, and when I looked back I was alone on the street. I sat there for several moments, on my own.

I stared at her. She tossed her pretty hair, and, momentarily, smiled at me.

I adjusted my white clothes, the uniform of the kitchen help, and followed her inside.

It's Valentine's Day, I thought. Tell her how you feel. Tell her what you think.

But I said nothing. I dared not. I simply followed her inside, a creature of mute longing.

Back in the kitchen a pile of plates was waiting for me; I began to scrape the leftovers into the pig-bin.

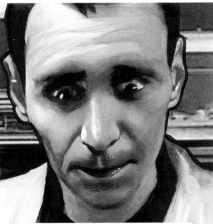

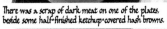

There was a scrap of dark meat on one of the plates, beside some half-finished ketchup-covered hash browns.

It looked almost raw...

...but I dipped it into the congealing ketchup

and, when Harve's back was turned, I picked it off the plate and chewed it down. It tasted metallic and gristly, but I swallowed it anyhow, and could not have told you why.

A blob of red ketchup dripped from the plate onto the sleeve of my white uniform, forming one perfect diamond.

I called, across the kitchen.

HEY, CHARLENE, HAPPY *VALENTINE'S* DAY.

And then I started to whistle.

NOTES ON A
HARLEQUINADE

Harlequin (Har"le*quin) *n.* [F. *arlequin*, formerly written also *harlequin* prob. fr. OF. *hierlekin, hellequin*, goblin, elf, which is prob. of German or Dutch origin; cf. D. *hel* hell. Cf. Hell, Kin.] A buffoon, dressed in particolored clothes, who plays tricks, often without speaking, to divert the bystanders or an audience; a merry-andrew; originally, a droll rogue of Italian comedy.

*A*LL ROADS LEAD TO ROME, AND THIS ONE MAY START THERE, a couple of thousand years ago, with the popular farces known as the *Atellanae Fabulae*, or it may start with the Greeks, five hundred years before that, or earlier, with actors and performances lost to history. The roles of the sixteenth century Italian *Commedia dell'arte*, which became the French *vaudeville*, and, in the eighteenth and nineteenth centuries, the English Harlequinade, go back and go back. And Harlequin goes back further than most.

What would you like to know?

Who is Harlequin?

Harlequin was a stock character in the *Commedia dell'arte*; originally one of many stock characters (even if his roots went back further, deeper, and darker), he soon became one of the principal characters.

Harlequin arrived in England along with his contemporary, Mister Punch, after the Restoration, in the second half of the seventeenth century. By the early eighteenth century, Harlequin's name in the title of a play was already a box office draw — in 1723 the Harlequin Dr. Faustus was produced at Drury Lane, and Harlequin was a star, and the traditions of English Pantomime, and of the Harlequinade, had begun.

(E. Cobham Brewer, writing in his Guide to Phrase and Fable, over a hundred years ago, wrote: "*Harlequin*, in the British Pantomime, is a sprite supposed to be invisible to all eyes but those of his faithful Columbine. His office is to dance through the world and frustrate all the knavish tricks of the Clown, who is supposed to be in love with Columbine.")

Hang on a second here. Is there any difference between an English Pantomime and American Pantomime?

Sure. In America *Pantomime* is another word for mime, or what the English called "dumb-show" — acting without using words. In the British tradition, Pantomime is currently a form of theatrical entertainment popular at Christmas, in which traditional children's stories are acted out as broad comedies with a fixed cast of stock characters (which include the Dame — a grotesque woman played by a man — and the Principal Boy, always played by a leggy young woman). Songs are sung, slapstick is slapped and stuck, and there is often a transformation scene (as when Cinderella transforms from a kitchen girl to a princess).

In Victorian times, Pantomimes were Harlequinades, and all the dialogue was delivered in rhyming couplets.

By the 1930s the British Harlequin-based Pantomime tradition was in a severe decline; and I doubt a real Harlequinade has been produced as a Pantomime for fifty years, except as a curiosity.

These days "Pantos" have their own traditions, including that of casting minor television stars in leading roles.

Harlequin and Pierrot and Columbine went from the stage to the seaside, where Pierrot Shows (Pierrot, the white-faced clown, now topping the bill) were still performed at least until the onset of the Second World War.

And the Commedia dell'arte?

It translates, more or less, as the Comedy of Artisans or Craftsmen. It was a form of theatre without a script as such, but which relied on propelling a set of stock characters through an improvised series of variations on stock situations. Many of the characters had their own "bits" or *lazzi*, funny routines they worked into whatever they were performing.

Commedia dell'arte was performed masked, at least by the male actors, in the beginning, full-faced masks which shrank to half-masks as dialogue became more important, and shrank again as the *Commedia* became the Harlequinade, until the only characters who remained masked were the Harlequin, in his domino mask, and the Pierrot, who, while unmasked, was heavily powdered and worked in whiteface.

So who was Harlequin? And who were Pierrot, and Columbine, and the rest?

They were the stars. Actors playing them attained a certain amount of fame, or no fame at all, but the characters were all. Sometimes actors created versions of the characters who outlasted them. The characters of the *Commedia dell'arte* included:

Harlequin — originally, perhaps, just another one of the "zanies" — a lusty, funny, tricksy fellow. A creature of desire and lust.

By the time of the English Harlequinade, Harlequin had gained magical powers — invisibility, for one. His slap-stick, a noise-making stick, had become a magical staff.

In the earliest plays, his mask was black as soot.

Pantaloon — an elderly miser. If married, his wife is young and pretty, and cheats on him; otherwise he has daughters who need to be married off, but who will ignore his wishes as to the suitability of their suitors; or Pantaloon is in love with a village beauty, and will be disappointed. He is fated forever to be fooled.

The Doctor — a man of vast learning, who knows everything and understands nothing. There is no record of his ever curing anyone of any disease; Doctor, in the Italian, merely indicates a man of learning.

Pulcinella — the hunchbacked, hook-nosed, eccentric old curmudgeon, cruel and violent.

When he reached England, achieving fame a little after Harlequin, it was as a puppet, and a star in his own right: in his story, he kills his wife, first called Joan, then Judy, murders their baby, then sets off on his adventures, killing all who trouble him, until he kills the executioner sent to hang him and murders the devil himself. (Details of his life and crimes can be found in *Mister Punch*, a graphic novel by Messrs. Gaiman and McKean.)

The Captain — a braggart, a coward, a creature of lust and bravado, a brave appearance and a craven nature. He went by many names — Scaramouche was only one of them.

Pierrot — who began in the *Commedia dell'arte* as Pedrolino. When Harlequin plays tricks, Pierrot is the only one caught and punished. He dresses all in white, and his face is white as well. Sometimes he is mute. He loves, and longs, and wants. As the English

Harlequinade progressed Pierrot became more and more the Clown, but his love for Columbine remained unrequited.

Columbine — she went by many names, the Inamorata (or beloved): Isabella, Flaminia, Columbina, Silvia. Columbina, as she gained a distinct personality in the *Commedia*, became a serving girl, often working for Isabella, a witty, self-possessed young lady able to survive even the most involved intrigues.

As Columbine, in the Harlequinade, she became a simpler creature: a ballerina, or a beauty, loved by Pierrot, hopelessly, and by Harlequin, successfully.

The Lover — dapper, engaging, the lover has no character trait other than of being in love. He was Zeppo, in every Marx Brothers comedy. Or worse, he was all the guys who replaced Zeppo in the later Marx Brothers films.

How did the English Harlequinade differ from the Commedia dell'arte?

In the early Pantomime Harlequinade, the story would begin with a folk tale or fairy tale or popular story of the day, which led up to the transformation scene, in which, following a shadowy chase, the characters became the Harlequinade versions of themselves, and the hero would be revealed to the audience as Harlequin. But always there was a sense of archetypal characters performing a drama over and over, and of discovery, of who, in the Harlequinade, they truly were.

And who was Harlequin?

That depends whom you believe.

There are those who trace Harlequin back to the *phallophores* in the Roman comedies, clutching giant phalluses, their faces blackened with soot. There are others who point to his name for clues as to his true origin: the French *herlequin* was a kind of spirit, a sprite, a will o' the wisp; *arlechino* the name of a devil; and most lexicographers, as you will see from the definition which prefaces this afterword, derive Harlequin straight from Hell …

Neil Gaiman
August 15, 2001

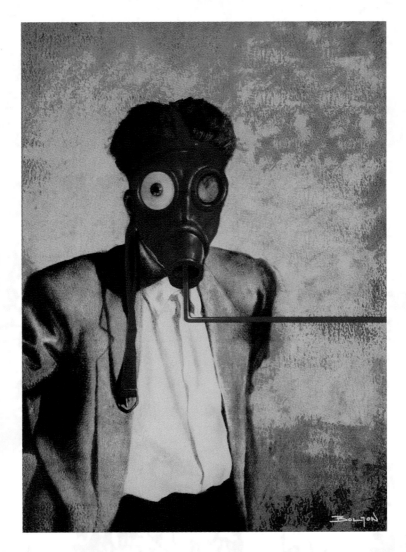

DRAWN IN DARKNESS

LATE IN THE AFTERNOON, JOHN MIRABILIS BOLTON PICKS UP HIS RED LEATHER GAS MASK AND WALKS DOWN THE PATH FROM HIS CROUCH END HOUSE TO THE CONVERTED BOMB SHELTER THAT SERVES HIM AS A STUDIO.

The gas mask, which has been blessed by the Pope, and the Dalai Lama, and the Supreme Sanguifex of the Clinical Brethren, is, Bolton claims, "essential to the process." If he is not wearing it, he cannot paint.

When asked whether it cuts down on his field of vision, Bolton smiles, slyly. "Only in reality," he explains. "I may lose vision, but I can see so much more with it on. It's shamanic, I suppose."

Bolton must be alone while he paints.

He starts each working day, he states, with no ideas whatsoever. "The subjects of the paintings need to come to me," he says, hesitantly. "You see, I have no imagination."

He is being precise here. The subjects of his paintings seek him out. They know where to find him. Bolton sits in his studio, grinding paints, preparing his blank canvases, all alone; when night falls he takes a taper and lights a few of the huge dark candles, melted now, if imagination amends them, into the shapes of fantastic beasts:

turtles and stonefish, dragons and demon-heads, and he waits to see whom, or what, he will be painting that night.

"The candles are my only superstition," says Bolton, who was made a Freeman and Servitor of Crouch End in the 1996 Honours List; if you encounter John Bolton within the bounds of Crouch End, you must remove your hat, and may not, by tradition, speak to him unless he speaks to you first. With the honour comes the right to cull the wild ermine, the small stoat-like beasts that plagued Crouch End long ago, when it was still a tiny village to the northwest of London, but have not been seen in the borough in living memory; even so, Bolton wears a traditional silver ermine knife at this belt. "When they return," he says, with a grin, "I'll be ready for them."

The subjects of his paintings come to him mostly at night. They slip through the shadows and walk down the gravestone steps to his studio, moonlight making their skin glow with a pale luminosity, candlelight glinting in their eyes and on the sharpness of their teeth.

Is he scared of them? The artist shakes his head. "They come to me," he explains. "The process — the making real — is as important to them as it is to me. They need me. Why would they hurt me?" But has he never been scared? He looks down. "You cannot let them see that you are afraid. Who would they find to paint them, if I were gone? Anyway," he adds, patting the silver ermine-skinner on his belt, "I have a knife."

Does he talk to them while he paints them? He does not answer. Instead he begins to light the candles.

How do they find out about him? Is there a grapevine among the naked and undead of London, a word passed along from pale vampire girl to restless satyr to faceless lamia? Bolton declines to speculate. "If they did not come to me, I would have nothing to paint," he says. "I am grateful, and leave it there."

What if he wished to paint something else? Fruit bowls or flowers? What then? He shivers, and shakes his head, and says nothing.

A yellow newspaper clipping, cut from a May 1965 copy of the *News of the World* and taped to the lichen-stained wall of his studio, tells of Bolton's tutelage in painting at the hands of an ancient madman who claimed to have been Richard Dadd, the Victorian painter and parricide, commonly believed to have died in 1886, seventy-five years to the day before Bolton was born. Bolton, however, refuses to discuss it. "It's water under the bridge," he says. "We must let the dead bury the dead. And I am grateful to all my teachers."

The sun is starting to set.

"You must leave now," says John Mirabilis Bolton, placing his red leather gas mask over his face, pulling the straps and buckles tight. "You would not want them to find you here." His voice is muffled, behind the leather and the glass. There are thirteen stone steps up from his studio to the mossy garden. In the trees at the bottom of the garden, something pale moves.

It is wisest not to look too closely.

— Neil Gaiman

NEIL GAIMAN

Born in 1781 in what is now known as Romania, Neil Gaiman, in later life librarian for the Margrave of Ghent, wrote several hundred books and stories in an obscure mixture of Polish and Latin. Unpublished during his lifetime, these manuscripts remained in a local museum until the 1930s, when they were smuggled to England, and were believed lost for good. In 1959, however, the manuscripts were discovered in a bread box in the attic of an abandoned hospital in Kettering, and were offered up for auction. Bought by an anonymous philanthropist, they were donated to the University of Lyme Regis. The "Gaiman translation" project began in 1964, and extracts

from the tales appeared initially in the Philological Digest (Volume 82, Winter 1970).

Commercially available translations of the stories, however, had to wait until 1989 and the ten volumes of *Sandman* (published in America by DC Comics). They have continued with such books as *Neverwhere*, *Stardust*, and the recently published *American Gods*.

Accusations of fraud and forgery have plagued the Gaiman manuscripts ever since their initial rediscovery, and it has recently been suggested that the stories were not, in fact, written by Gaiman but by another man, also in the employ of the Margrave of Ghent in the 1830s, of the same name.

"Yes, I remember. We were talking about that last week."

"No matter what I'm doing—I can be at work or eating dinner or changing my clothes or even having sex, and I get this feeling that if I look up, you'll be standing there. Not saying anything, just watching me. Making your silent judgments." She uses her hands as she speaks and doesn't return them to her purse during pauses but leaves them hanging in midair, above her chest. "Well," she says, "don't you have any response to that?"

"Yes," Will says. "I'm wondering why you think I judge you."

"Because you do. You sit there thinking how purposeless and stupid my life is."

"Why do you imagine me thinking that?"

"Why wouldn't you? After all, whatever I do or feel, I come here and tell you all about it. So you might just as well be there with me. Then you could see exactly how stupid and shallow I am."

"Do you think you might like to have someone with you all the time? Someone to watch over you?"

"Why would I want that?"

"It's not so unusual a wish. People get lonely."

"I'd like to be lonely! I'd like to have a minute to myself. But you make it impossible for me to have any privacy even when I am alone. I told you, it's uncomfortable. It's not something I enjoy. It's like I have a built-in peeping Tom."

"But Maria, it's you who's invented this, the idea of my secretly watching you. And you who imagines that my observations are judgmental."

"Omniscient," she says.

"Omniscient?"

"Yes. Because you're in my head, too, so you can see what I'm thinking."

"Go on," Will says when she falls silent. But she says nothing, and he finds himself feeling impatient. He looks past the couch to the dance studio across the street, through whose windows he sometimes watches the students, children mostly. Today it's a group of little girls about the same age as Samantha, although he can make out a boy or two. Beginners' ballet, he guesses, a lot of antic warming up followed by a halting review of the basics. The teacher, a young woman in black leotard and tights with red leg warmers, stands at the front of the class, holding a position until the three rows of would-be dancers have assembled their limbs in an approximation of her own. Then she goes painstakingly from one child to the next, nudging feet, re-aligning arms, a process that requires her to stoop and squat, pa-tiently doing again and again what she must have done countless times before. From across the narrow street, Will can see her wide smiles of encouragement. Her energy and enthusiasm make him feel tired, even old. What—if anything—distinguishes his work from hers? Does he not spend hours each day nudging and straightening, supporting mostly doomed attempts to approach an ideal from vari-ous points of stubborn individuality? After each position, the teacher has the class jump up and down and shake their arms and legs, pre-sumably in an effort to dispel energy and make them pliable enough to attempt the next.

"You're just," Maria blurts, "I don't know. It's what I said—as long as I'm going to tell you, you might just as well be there. In my bedroom." She stops there, and Will is silent, waiting. "It feels the same as when I used to get in trouble and my mother would make me wait in my room until my dad got home," she says.

"What does?"

"Your watching me."

"How? How does it?"

"Because. It just does, that's all."

"Do you think perhaps you're feeling angry with me and would like to punish me?" Will prompts, unusually direct, but over the past five years Maria has proved herself someone who can get stuck on a topic for weeks, marching the two of them over and over the same territory.

"Angry about what?"

"Well, I remember that you were upset with me last September, after I had been away during August. We spoke about your feeling abandoned."

"But why would that make me want you to see into my private life? Stuff like with my boyfriend—stuff that's intimate. I mean, why would I want you to see me naked or having sex?"

"Tell me if this sounds possible," Will tries. "You'd like to believe that my life is boring, empty, and doesn't include intimacies like those you share with your boyfriend."

Maria lies still on the couch, says nothing.

"Wouldn't it be that much more gratifying if I were to witness your interesting life? And know that my own was comparatively barren?"

She pulls her purse up, hugging it to her stomach. It's one of the few times her handling it doesn't strike him as premeditated. "I think"—she takes a deep breath, starts over. "I think maybe I want you to see me with my boyfriend so I can prove to you that I don't have any . . . any of those feelings for you."

Can it be true that all of Will's patients are consumed by the topic of sex? Getting it. Not getting it. Getting it, but not enough of it. Getting it from the wrong person. Getting it but not It. Coming, not coming, coming too soon, coming too late. Coming, but only under certain highly specific circumstances. Fetishism. Priapism. Frigidity. Bondage, humiliation, latex. Has he done this to them? Communicated his disease?

The last appointment of the day is an intake, a tall young woman, leggy like a teenager and decorated with what he's come to regard as the usual assortment of tattoos. She sits sideways in the armchair, her back against one padded arm, her legs over the other. Two stainless steel studs connected by a post sit on either side of the pinch of flesh just above the bridge of her nose. Placed where they are, the little orbs disturb him as might a smaller, brighter pair of eyes between her own pale blue ones, themselves offset by owlishly smudged eyeliner and mascara. She's attractive in a sulky, ill-kempt way, her hair falling unevenly around her face, appearing to have been hacked rather than styled. More likely, styled expensively to look as though hacked. As she talks she chews one of her nails, all of which are bitten to the quick, and armored with silver rings.

"So," she says, "that's it, I guess."

"Where do you meet these men?"

"Bars mostly. Except the one I'm going to do next will be an art-history professor. So I'll pick him up at the faculty house."

"The faculty house?"

"Uh-huh. It's my work-study gig. I waitress there."

Will tries to picture the young woman in a waitress outfit along with the studs, tattoos, and smudged mascara. She doesn't present herself as a person who would take orders politely. "That's unusual financial aid, isn't it?" he asks her.

"It would be, yeah. But it's not financial aid, per se. See, there's hardly any teaching slots in classics; there's maybe five TA's in the whole department, so if you're a doctoral student, eventually you end up with these funky jobs. Quasi-official. The department secretary will hunt something down for you if you're willing to, like, grovel and curry favor. Which is the definition of higher education, basically, at least as far as I can figure. I'll maybe go into teaching if I ever get out of there. I wouldn't need an education degree to get hired by a private school." Speaking about her future, she looks earnest and sober, not the disaffected slacker who threw herself into the chair but a scholarly disciple whose postmodern finery might peel right off, like a Halloween costume, and reveal one of those laurel-wreathed heads from a Roman coin. "It's not as impractical as it seems," she adds. "Classics are cool again. They're making a comeback."

Will nods. "I guess that's what makes them classics."

She raises her eyebrows, and the two studs ascend slightly as well. "Precisely," she says. Her expression suggests that she's taken his comment to have been sarcastic, which it was not.

"Latin?" he asks. "Greek?"

"Latin and Greek. Latin all the way back to junior high. Greek I began as a freshman."

Will leans back in his chair, hands behind his head, fingers laced. It's a pose, at once relaxed and challenging. "Well," he says. "What would you want from this process? From what you've told me, I assume you're considering weekly therapy rather than analysis, which would be a considerable investment with respect to both time and money—analysis is three to five sessions a week. If we were to meet once weekly, our dialogue would still take a psychoanalytic approach, because that's my training. We'd use dreams, fantasies, free association—whatever means by which we can access unconscious rather than conscious material. But one day a week would imply a distinct, comparatively short-term goal, rather than the less narrowly defined and, some would even say, spiritual quest of a true psychoanalysis. And, as I said, more affordable."

"Spiritual how?"

"Spiritual as in the hope for enlightenment. About the self. The attempt to become a more fully conscious being." She nods slowly, eyebrows raised in a skeptical expression.

"Was I, like, supposed to be answering a question?" she asks after a minute or more has gone by.

"I'm hoping we can figure out how to help you. And to that end, I was asking what you want to accomplish in here, talking with me."

"To get over this bullshit, obviously. To escape from this, this, um, this thing, this whatever-it-is that makes me go after these old guys."

"Old guys," Will says, deciding to defer practical arrangements until the end of the hour. "Tell me what that's like," he says.

"What it's like?"

"Yes. What does it feel like to seduce older men?"

She makes a face. "Well, first off, it's not seducing."

"No?"

"It's collecting."

"Collecting?" Will writes the word down.

"It's more like that than it is like anything else. I mean, it's . . . that's the only way I can describe it."

"How does it feel emotionally?"

"Emotionally? You mean . . ." She trails off, looking genuinely confused.

"I mean, are you happy? Sad? Satisfied when the date is over? Frustrated? Do you feel you're courting danger? Overpowered, or do you feel you control the interaction?"

"They're not *dates*. Dates presume, like, a future. These are just anonymous hookups with old guys."

"Okay," Will says. "Can you tell me how it feels to anonymously hook up with an old guy?"

The girl frowns in concentration, but it's her thumbnail she's working on, not his question. After a moment she looks up. "I feel like I'm collecting them."

"All right. Then what does collecting feel like?"

"I don't know, it's . . . I guess I said 'collecting' because for me it's the same as it was when I was a kid and I had this, like, thing for glass paperweights. There was always one I needed to have, and I'd be like—I couldn't really think about anything else until I got it. So I'd babysit or go through garbage cans for soda bottles to, you know, get the nickel deposits, or I'd do chores. Whatever I had to do, to get the money together to pay for it. And then, when I got it, this dumb thing I'd been, like, frantic to have, I wouldn't be so much satisfied as relieved. Because then I wouldn't have to think about how I needed it anymore. I had it, so I could get on with other stuff."

Will nods. "I'm still listening," he says.

"That's it. There isn't any more."

"Would it be fair to say that adding a paperweight to your collection made you feel as though it was in your power, rather than the other way around?"

The girl studies the freshly bitten thumbnail and returns it, briefly, to her mouth. "I guess," she says.

"Did you enjoy them once you had them?"

"How do you mean?"

"Well, did you spend time looking at them? Were there things to learn about them, like methods of manufacture? Different kinds of glass? Did you get into the history of the glass paperweight?"

She gives him a contemptuous, who's-the-crazy-one-here look. "Nooo," she says, drawing the word out. "I kept them on a shelf in my bookcase. I mean, they were pretty, but what can you do with a ball of glass? I wasn't into, like, dusting."

"So it was all about pursuing the object?"

"I guess, yeah."

"And it's the same with the older men?"

"Pretty much. I have sex with one, move on to the next."

She falls silent under Will's gaze. A low-necked pullover reveals the words tattooed on her chest to be Latin—at least he thinks that's what they are—letters like those that adorn the entablatures of monuments and big civic buildings, *U*'s written as *V*'s—MVSEVM rather than MUSEUM. When she sees his eye hesitate on the tattoo she pulls at the neck of her sweater to reveal another line of text under the first.

"'*Quo usque tandem abutere patientia mea,*'" she reads. "It's from Cicero's first oration against Catiline. Except I edited out the name Catiline and used *mea* instead of *nostra*." She gets up to dig something out of her pocket, then returns to the same position, legs flung over one chair arm.

"What does it mean?"

"'How long, pray, will you take advantage of my patience?'"

Will smiles. He likes this girl. "Is Cicero one of your heroes?" he asks as she unwraps a hard candy. A shred of cellophane sticks to its surface, and she tries to pick it off as best she can without fingernails.

"One of my *heroes*? Do people even have, like, heroes anymore?"

She puts her feet on the floor and sits up straight, shoulders back, chest out. "The culture is posthero," she intones in a low, stentorian rumble, her expression dour and condescending. "Media-saturated, brand-conscious, inclined to mock every virtue from courage to modesty. Posthero and pro-rich-and-famous, heroism representing no more than a few coordinates along the arc of celebrity: conferred, questioned, doubted, debunked."

Watching her performance, Will has to suppress his enjoyment of what seems an effortless caricature. "Skip hero," he says. "Is Cicero a historical figure you admire?"

"I guess."

Will leans back in his chair, hands behind his head. "What about the man?" he asks.

"What about him?"

"I'm wondering if both of you expect the same outcome. Does he—whoever he is—know it's going to be a one-night stand?"

"What else could it be? It's not like we know each other. It's not like we've ever met before." When Will doesn't speak, she goes on. "Usually it seems pretty, you know, equal. They talk about what they do, their jobs. Or they say what they think they have to, what's required by the, the . . . well, the situation makes them feel like they should flatter me, I guess, tell me I have a great ass or they like my hair or my eyes. Whatever. It doesn't mean anything. Compliments are just, whatever, something to say while we're checking each other out and deciding, like, what's it gonna be, hook or book." Will raises his eyebrows. "Meaning," she says, "are we hooking up or booking, as in, like, leaving." Again she sits up straight. "*Book*," she intones, "verb, intransitive, to leave hurriedly as if tardy for a meeting of critical importance." Too bad she didn't choose drama over classics, Will thinks, take the opportunity to act out onstage. "It's not about feelings," she tells him. "It's not about how I feel or how he feels."

"What is it about?"

"Nothing. It isn't *about* anything." Her expression is one of exasperation. "You've heard the expression 'operate on a need-to-know basis'?"

Will nods.

"Generally speaking, I operate on a need-not-to-know basis. So it's not that I don't need to know about how they feel—I need not to know. Get it?"

"If it's not about feelings, what is it about?"

"God, is this what it's like having your head shrunk? You have to answer the same questions over and over? I told you, *collecting*. I collect them."

Will smiles in a way that's meant to be disarming. He's usually pretty quick to get a fix on a new patient, but there's something about this girl that he can't quite pin; she's guarded in a way he can almost feel, as if she's sitting on the other side of a pane of glass. "This is what's called an intake session," he tells her. "We haven't even begun the shrinking yet."

"Intake?"

"I ask questions to help me understand why you've come to me, and, if we decide to work together, to help me establish a treatment plan."

"If we decide to *work* together?"

"Yes. Because it is work, and not only for me. Once we begin, you do most of the talking." She looks at him. "Let's go back to the men," Will says. "Once you've picked one out, then what?"

"You know. We go someplace. His place. If he's single. Or a friend's place—that's happened. Hotel, maybe. But I'm . . . I don't do, like, cars."

Will removes his glasses, cleans their lenses with a handkerchief, replaces them on his nose: a little act to diffuse whatever tension might proceed from his watching her talk.

"So we, uh, you know. I take my clothes off, and I'm, like, probably the youngest person they've had sex with for a while, a long time maybe, and they're, well, they're excited. I mean, you know, my boobs are still where they're supposed to be. I've never been pregnant or anything that would make me, you know, stretched out or whatever. I've never lost or gained a bunch of weight." Having offered the kind of material that takes some patients years to approach, the girl looks directly at Will. "I don't know why, but they kind of turn me on, too. There's this, this aspect to their bodies—like they're not trying so hard, you know? They're not these gym rats lifting weights in the mirror. I guess that in the same way my being young makes them hot, I like that they're older. If they have a little gray hair on their chests, that helps. Chub around the middle, not so much muscle, whatever. It seems weird, even to me, but I do like it. Also, I gotta say, they're better at fucking."

Will remains expressionless and deploys one of his hard-on inhibitors, a picture his father took of a broken fire escape hung with icicles. He doesn't know why—it's not as if the photograph saddens or disgusts him—but it's usually effective.

"They have, well, what they have is technique. Experience. Maybe it's just that they aren't impatient. They last longer—too long sometimes, but that's better than having it end before it begins. Guys my age, for them sex isn't any different from, I don't know, takeout. They're, like, frantic, hardly bother to unwrap me. Older guys, they take their time, pay attention to what's going on. Ask—beg—to go down on me. They are, no kidding, total, I mean total, carpet munchers. I mean, like, all of them." Will stops writing. He puts his elbows on his desk, fingers together, tip to tip, looks at her. She's disclosing frank sexual material to distract him from her emotional absence. Either that or she's trying to bait him.

"I've done thirty-seven," she says after another leisurely examination of her bleeding thumbnail. "Thirty-seven so far. I have one picked out for Friday."

"I thought you said you were determined to quit."

She snorts. "Quit? Like with cigarettes?"

"Maybe like with cigarettes. Or any other addiction."

The girl shoots him a look. "Did I, like, miss something here? Did anything happen that might make it easier, or even possible, for me to, what, abstain by Friday?"

Will puts down his pen, folds his hands on his blotter. "For some patients, those who can be honest with themselves and commit to change, the process of articulating that they have a problem and identifying the behavior they want to stop is enough to begin to change."

"Would that be me, do you think?"

"I don't know. I just wondered if you were actively struggling to quit."

"This is my 'active struggle.' You. A shrink."

"Yes," he says, picking up his pen. "Perhaps together we'll figure out what it is you get from these experiences with older men, so that you can discover a different source for whatever it gives you. A source you can live with, satisfy more easily. And less expensively."

"What's that supposed to mean? It's not like I'm paying for anything."

"I was referring to the psychic cost."

The girl returns the problematic thumb to her mouth.

"Doesn't that hurt?" he asks her.

"They're kind of numb, actually." She puts her feet on the floor and leans forward, holding her hands out. A fresh line of blood has formed at the thumb's tip, and other fingers are bitten to the point of injury, as well. What's left of her nails is surrounded by flesh so enflamed that it puffs up around the nail beds. "Pretty, huh?" she says. Looking at her hands, Will feels a strange leap of sexual excitement, as if he's not just imagining but feeling the heat of those fingers on him, and he has to stop himself from reaching out to touch them.

He has to get her out of there.

"I've gotten these infections," she says. "Paronychia. From the Greek. *Para*—beside, *nychia*—nail. Like, really excruciating. You can't imagine. I had to go on antibiotics."

"Have you tried to stop?" He has an erection. It's instant, not the kind of excitement he can dampen. One second nothing, then, presto, all he's thinking is: the next in her collection of old guys.

"Bunch of times. Nothing works. I've used that bitter stuff that tastes, like, bad enough to make you puke, but I bit them anyway. Tried keeping gloves on all the time, and chewed through them. Behavior mod, where every time I went after a nail I was supposed to snap myself with this, um, punishment thing—this strap around my wrist like a big rubber band—snap it really hard, so it hurt, but no. All three at once, still no good." She shrugs. "Another problem to work on."

Will looks at his watch.

"Okay," she says, quick to pick up on the visual cue. "Same time next week?"

"If you're interested in continuing."

"I guess. I mean, can I just see how it goes?" She stands and pulls on her coat, picks up her backpack. "What about the fee?" she asks. "Do you . . . I read on your policy sheet that you have a, like, sliding fee scale. That for students it can be adjusted, um, down." She settles her backpack into place by flexing and quickly straightening her knees to give it a little bounce. "Because my insurance is student health, and it doesn't cover psychotherapy outside of the university. I'm entitled to ten sessions a year from student mental health, no charge. After that, it's, I don't know, maybe twenty-five an hour. But the therapists are dorks. I mean, worse than. Useless."

"How much can you afford?" Will asks.

"You're asking me what the bill is?" She tips her head to one side and frowns. Her puzzlement makes her look much younger, almost like a child.

"Yes," he says.

"Uh. Could it be . . . how about, um, like, fifty? Forty?"

"All right," he agrees. She digs her right hand into her pocket.

"Here," she says. She puts two twenty-dollar bills on the blotter. He doesn't touch them.

"It's customary to pay with a check," he says. "I send you a monthly statement, you mail me a check."

"Yeah, well, I'm sort of between apartments right now, trying to simplify the whole mail thing. I don't, like, have a forwarding address. Not yet."

Will nods. "All right," he says.

This is the moment when, ordinarily, he would stand and extend his hand to shake hers, but he can't. He doesn't have to look down to know that this isn't the kind of hard-on he can hide with a notebook, at least not subtly enough to risk it. He leans forward, hands folded on his desk, trying to appear as if this is his usual manner of concluding a session. "Next week?" he says.

She steps a few feet back from his desk, her hands shoved in the pockets of her brown suede coat. Around each is a dark ring of what appears to be grease, as if she were in the habit of keeping French fries in her pockets. The stained coat; the unkempt hair; the bitten fingernails; the soles of her boots, past repair: all these conspire to make her look like an orphan, a girl who has been not so much brought up as "dragged up," to use a favorite expression of his mother's. Hers is an unexpectedly sexy squalor, though; it makes her seem as if she's not so particular that she wouldn't be game for . . . well, for almost anything.

"Next week?" he asks again as she's walking toward the door.

"Okay," she says without turning.

t's 2:17 in the morning, 2:12, actually, because the digital clock on the dresser is five minutes fast. Will listens to the sound of water running on the other side of the bathroom door, water from the bathtub's faucet, not the sink's, because it's too loud for the sink's. Probably his wife is sitting in the empty bathtub, using her hands to direct water from the faucet to rinse soap from between her legs. "It's not you I'm washing off," she's told him, and he believes her. He thinks he does. She just doesn't like to get up in the morning smelling of stale sex. He gropes around for his pajama bottoms while he waits for her to come back to bed.

"Here's what I do, Will," Carole says when she's next to him under the covers. "What I do is, I don't think about myself. I think about you and Sam and my clients, and about Luke. But not in a way that makes me sad. Because lately what I've been thinking is this. We—and I don't mean us particularly, I don't mean you and me, but people in general—we are so fixated on this idea of a life span, that everyone should live a certain number of years. And it's maybe helpful to try to focus on something different, like that Luke had a good life, a happy life, when you think about it. Nothing much went wrong for him. He liked school. He had friends. He was a healthy, happy boy. He was. And maybe that's a thing we can be grateful for—that even if it was just ten years, they were these ten nearly perfect years, and, my God, Will, there is so much suffering—we see it all the time. You do, and I do, too. For much of their lives people are not happy. And, well"—Carole sighs here, a long and almost groaning noise— "Luke was. He was. Think how much worse it would have been if he'd died after struggling with some terrible illness. After years of enduring pain or . . ."

Carole stops speaking. Will keeps beginning a sentence in his head, a sentence that begins *But* and goes no further. If he looks into the darkest corner of the bedroom, where the streetlight doesn't penetrate, the blackness there seems to pulse, as if with a pressure like that of blood, something that shoves the blackness up against his eyes. Carole always assumes that in his wakefulness Will is obsessively returning to the accident, punishing himself by reviewing it over and over, but in fact he'd been thinking about his brother. While he hadn't allowed himself to admit this—not consciously—if he didn't really expect Mitch to come to the reunion before he'd seen the class book, once he'd found that his brother had contributed a bio to it, he was sure he would see him there.

It's odd, but ever since their estrangement, Will's thoughts of Mitch have tended to summon a particular scene from Stanley Kubrick's *2001: A Space Odyssey*, a movie the two of them had watched together every afternoon they could for as long as it played in Ravena's one theater, spending all the allowance they'd saved, searching between sofa cushions and under car seats for stray change. It's the opening scene that Will continues to revisit, as if it might hold some means of understanding his relationship with his missing brother. In it, a community of apes—hairy, upright animals that have yet to evolve into *Homo sapiens*—are disturbed by the sudden appearance of a monolith, and it's this monolith itself that compels and sometimes even upsets Will.

More than once during his insomniac rambles he's found himself picturing, almost seeing, the looming slab in their bedroom, not against a wall or pushed back into a corner but smack in the middle of the braided rag rug Carole bought from an antiques shop upstate. Perfect in its blankness, its refusal of feature or detail, the sinister metal slab stands where it is bound to get in their way, to interrupt, block, and impede them. What can it mean, this fantasy? Will assumes the slab, in its inscrutable quality, represents his brother, Mitch's disappearance having become an emotional stumbling block, one right in front of their marriage bed, so large that it doesn't just stumble but blinds, ruining the view. Or maybe the thing is a kind of clock, a massive chunk of a plutonium-like element whose half-life divides and divides the hours, not so much displaying as emitting time: informing them with time, implanting the correct and true time within them. Aligning their mortal coils with its infinite and inexorable measurement. Maybe it's one of Will's clumsy attempts to represent God—a god, at least—who reigns over everyone, as deaf to one petition as to another. If Will can't always believe in God, he can't not believe in Time.

A car passes. Its headlights slide through the windows and over the furniture, the armchair and dresser, the desk piled with clutter: magazines; professional journals; catalogs; a picture of a house made from dried beans glued on blue construction paper; instructions for the assembly of toys long lost or broken.

"When I think of myself at all," Carole says, after what has transcended an awkward silence to become a more pure kind of quiet, the in-out sounds of their breathing joining and then diverging. "When I do think of myself," she says, her voice low and measured, "it's in a little boat on a wide sea. I'm sitting in the boat—I picture myself from high above—and I have to keep my balance. I have to stay right in the center of the boat so I don't tip." She inhales, exhales, an audible, deep exchange of air. "All the things I do, the district work, seeing clients, taking care of Samantha and the house and you, seeing friends, making dinner, weeding the garden, going to yoga, folding laundry, remembering birthdays, calling your parents—all of it, every piece of my life, is about staying there in the center of my little boat."

"But," Will can't help protesting, "but there is such a thing as a life span. An expected life span."

"I know," Carole says. "I know that."

"So your . . . your choice to focus on, well, let's call it the quality rather than quantity of his years—is this one of your ways of remaining in the middle of your boat?"

Carole says nothing. At the foot of their bed, the monolith on the rug fills the room with time, time too big to be contained by their bodies lying small under the sheet, time that is silent and unbearable, time that is a clock too accurate to tick.

"Did you say a river or the sea?" Will asks.

"Did I say what?"

"Your boat, it's on—"

"Oh, the sea, the ocean. Wherever I am, it's all water. There isn't any shore."

Carole turns from her back to her side, facing the window. "Do you remember when we went to see the Edward Hopper show?" she asks. "The retrospective? It was a while ago, at the Whitney. Maybe in 'ninety-eight. There was a painting I kept coming back to, with a woman standing naked in a room. She's that model Hopper used over and over, the woman with straight, thick hair that falls down her back, past her shoulders. A sort of auburn color, almost red. She has a strong, fit body. Muscular in a way that qualifies her nakedness— makes her less naked, I mean. As if she's clothed by her musculature. You know how I mean? Like women at the health club. I see them in the sauna, and they're not naked. Not really. Their clothes are off, but they've created a kind of uniform out of their bodies. They're so aggressively trained and toned that they've conformed to an established, standard shape.

"Anyway, I got off track. There's a door in the room, an open door in front of the naked woman—we see her in profile—and outside the door is the sea. Water, anyway, but it seems endless, there isn't any shore. Blue, flat but not glassy flat, little whitecaps all over. The water fills the doorframe. It's surreal. No context. No path to the beach. No transition. Nothing. Just water.

"We argued about that painting. You said it gave you the creeps, and I understood what you meant. I assumed Hopper probably meant it to be a painting of, I don't know, something existential. Dread, I guess. Like Sartre's moments—crises—of nausea, the times when he apprehends *thing*ness, or whatever he called it. Our material and therefore decaying presence. But this wasn't so . . . it wasn't so stark as that. It was scary but softer. More eternal." She stops.

"Go on," Will says to her back.

"Oh, yeah, I almost forgot—here's the weird part. A while ago I tried to look up the painting in a catalog. I wanted to see it. And you know what?"

"What?"

"It doesn't exist."

"What do you mean?"

"I made it up. Not on purpose, obviously, since I didn't know I had, but in my head I put two paintings together—one of a naked woman standing in a room with an unmade bed and an open window, and a different painting of an empty room with the doorway filled by the sea. I don't know if they were maybe hung next to each other or if I just . . . if I joined them in my head, the woman and the water. Because I needed them together like that."

"I'm not sure I get what you mean," Will says. "Sorry. Am I being dumb?"

"Maybe just that the image—the one I invented—explains something to me, represents something I don't have words for. All I'm trying to say is that when I'm in the little boat, my boat, I'm on the water from that painting."

"Are you the woman?" Will asks her. "The woman who isn't naked when she's naked?" Carole makes an ambiguous noise, one that might be taken as assent. *Please can't you just admit you're angry with me?* he's about to say when another thought stops him.

"That's the reason why—that's why you don't let me touch you anymore, right? Because you have to be alone. Alone in your little boat. The mistress of your own pleasure. You have to mete it out, just so, know when they're coming, your orgasms, so they don't capsize you. Tip you out. That way you won't feel more than you can handle. Because if it were my hand instead of yours, my finger, my tongue, then you'd be taken off guard." Carole doesn't answer. "Right?" Will prompts when the silence has grown long enough to make him anxious.

"I don't know," Carole says to the window.

"But you're not willing—you won't go back to the way we were, the way we were before?"

"No." She shakes her head against the pillow. "Not . . . not now."

"Why?"

"I can't."

"But why? Why, if it's not on account of your little boat?"

"Oh, Will," she says. "Does it really matter why? Or matter that much?"

He sighs loudly in the way that irritates her, one of what she calls his accusatory sighs. "It matters to me, Carole," he says.

"I can't right now." Carole turns onto her back and aligns herself on the mattress. She takes the duvet and gives it a smart shake so that it flies up and then settles slowly and evenly over their two bodies. "Not right now, Will," she says.

"But 'right now'—what does 'right now' mean? It's been three years."

"I know. I know."

"You're angry with me. You don't trust me."

"No."

"Then it's about intimacy. About your wanting to maintain some kind of boundary between us. A kind of sexual cordon sanitaire, invisible, inviolable." Will is speaking with his eyes closed. "You don't want me to get that close to you," Will says. "Close enough to engage you."

"No," Carole says. "I don't know."

"Why not?" he asks. "Why don't you know? We're talking about you, after all. If you'd just admit you're angry, then maybe we could get through this."

"It was an accident, Will."

"But feelings aren't rational. By definition they're irrational. So it doesn't matter whether or not it was an accident."

"It does to me." Carole turns to look at him. "Will?" she says. "If you're going to lie awake, why not remember happy things? Like all the Little League stuff you and Luke did together. Even when you weren't coaching, I don't think you missed one game. Or that summer you taught him to bodysurf, remember how excited he was? And that fort thing you guys made. Or the time—"

"You know what?" Will says. "Before, when I still hadn't fallen asleep, I wasn't even thinking about Luke. You always assume that when I can't sleep it's because I'm thinking about him, but I'm not, not all the time. Not one time in ten. I think about work. Sex. The stuff around the house that I never get to, like the rain gutters. I think about the old wiring upstairs in the apartment and how I have to call an electrician to bring it up to code. And about getting the tree surgeon to come back and take down that maple before it comes down and breaks some windows. Tonight, before we made out, I was thinking about the reunion."

"What about it?"

"I don't know. It was strange. Self-conscious. Uncomfortable, I guess."

Carole makes a told-you-so sound, expelling air from her nostrils in something that isn't, quite, a snort. "Of course it was strange and uncomfortable," she says.

"I guess I really expected—a part of me expected Mitch would be there. Did you think he'd show?"

"No," she says after a moment. Carole yawns and turns in his arms. "Will?" she says. "Can we stop talking?"

Will pulls her body into his, burying his face in the damp nape of her neck, inhaling that smell that, only an hour after they've made love, gets him instantly hard: part shampoo, part sweat, part whatever chemical recipe of pheromones and God knows what add up to his wife. He kisses her, and her skin tastes salty. "We could do it again," he says. "How about making out again?"

W hy did Mitch contribute a page to the Class of '79's reunion book? Perhaps he'd intended to come and then changed his mind? It wasn't as if he needed it for the sake of PR, and yet his bio, organized like a résumé, highlighted all his aquatic triumphs since graduation. No mention of Will or of their parents, and no photographs of a wife or kids; Mitch is unmarried. Will has wondered if his brother has so thoroughly sublimated his libido that he remains a virgin, his poor nuts routinely immersed in water as much as forty degrees below body temperature. Mitch's testicles would do well to permanently relocate somewhere warm, ascend as far as his kidneys, perhaps, or go south to cruise the Caribbean. But this is Will's fantasy. Despite Mitch's awkwardness with girls, it's likely that he enjoys the usual trappings of celebrity, athlete groupies who find his exploits so sexy that he needn't bother to woo them, or even go through the motions of getting to know them.

There's no picture of Mitch in the reunion book, nothing from a family album anyway, nothing that shows his face, just one of him in the water, as well as a small if not exactly modest reproduction of his *Sports Illustrated* cover, a silhouette that reveals how long his torso is, and how comparatively short his legs, especially if measured against arms with a span of more than six feet. "Who is Mitchell Moreland?"

a cover line demands. Mitch has been profiled in *People* and is a routine feature in *Swimming World, Outside,* and some other environmentally concerned magazine, Will can't remember its name. By swimming distances unimaginable to the average person, and selling his exploits to wealthy sponsors and patrons, his brother has raised hundreds of thousands of dollars for the Sierra Club, Greenpeace, Audubon, Flora and Fauna International, World Wildlife Fund, and others, a long list included in small type at the bottom of the page. He endorses products for the Nature Conservancy, and that share of company profits is distributed among charities that benefit endangered marine life. The swimwear company that sponsored Mitch's "Challenge: Bermuda Triangle" pours funds into not-for-profit organizations whose goal is to slow environmental damage, a useful means of diverting attention from this same company's overseas factories that employ children as young as nine and routinely dump pollutants into the Third World's unprotected waterways. The summary of Will's brother's accomplishments makes Mitch seem as if he's his own invention, which, Will guesses, is not far wrong.

In Will's experience, identical twins are either insufficiently differentiated, with a single personality floating, amoebalike, between two bodies, or each goes to great lengths to separate and prove his ascendancy. Through grade school, Will and Mitch were, in retrospect, too close to know where one brother left off and the other began. Like conjoined twins, they shared a vital organ, not the kind filled with blood, but a sensory apparatus that, without substance, processed and secreted emotion. At least this is what Will remembers. Maybe it's a conceit, something he's invented in the wake of his brother's desertion—a fantasy projected backward onto a past that had never held such extremes of intimacy. Odd that the culture would fixate on traumatic false memories, child abuse, sexual assault. In Will's experience, false memories tend to be happy.

He knew he wasn't always or even usually kind to his brother. He used to bait him, looking for a way to shatter whatever it was that connected them. Sometimes Mitch didn't want to fight, and Will would go at him until it was impossible for him to resist. Until it was a matter of losing face. He'd plant himself between his brother and whatever Mitch was doing, knock the book out of his hands, mess up the carefully organized pieces of the model he was building.

"Quit it," Mitch would say.

"Make me."

Around the house they'd run, Mitch on Will's heels. They were evenly matched—of course they were—so it was Will who determined how many laps. Because once they'd begun, once Mitch had lost control and lunged, someone had to win. Finally, Will would slow and then Mitch would get close enough to trip or kick him, to shove him to the ground.

His brother's fists found their mark with enough force that Will heard them from the inside out; the sound they made traveled through his body and arrived on the wrong side of his eardrums. Blows to his back that were so hard they made him cough. Kidney punches he could taste, like metal, a taste that filled his mouth with saliva. He never cried. A couple of times Mitch had gone on hitting him long enough that he thought he was going to puke, but he didn't cry.

Swimming changed all that. Hard to imagine they'd started out with the same measure of raw physical aptitude, which didn't add up to talent, clearly not. Will had never liked swimming, never wanted—needed—it; Mitch swam like someone who anticipated shipwreck. Didn't seem to take pleasure in dominating his opponents, not that Will could see, anyway. Packed his trophies away like dry goods: necessary, uninteresting.

Before Will had completed the course work required for a doctorate in clinical psychology, Mitch, by then an industrial engineer employed by a cranberry-processing plant in Maine, was swimming up to eight hours a day, Saturday through Wednesday. Swimming a forty-hour week. Having qualified for the 1980 Olympics, Mitch didn't get to go to Moscow. In protest of the Soviet invasion of Afghanistan at the end of 1979, the United States boycotted the games. Mitch claimed he wasn't, like all the other athletes, bitterly disappointed. Naturally, he'd wanted the validation of his place among those who qualified, but he was impatient to get on with his single-minded pursuit of a more lonely and remarkable quest, a prize unavailable to ordinary swimmers, swimmers who tested themselves only in the controlled environment of pools.

Sour grapes, Will suspected, but if he was correct in his conclusion, what began as an unconscious strategy to offset dashed hopes became not only vocation but monomania. Without yet knowing what it was he was training for, Mitch began spending entire days in the frigid water off the coast of Maine, so compulsive that he rarely changed his schedule to accommodate bad weather, so focused that he interpreted the loss of his job as an opportunity to devote all his time to what he'd come to understand was his real, perhaps even ordained, purpose. He'd spent so little of his salary over the previous two years that, as he told their parents, he could finance his own sabbatical. And, as though he were blessed by the gods, or by one god— Neptune—before Mitch had run through his own money, the Bar Harbor Oceanographic Society adopted him as a kind of mascot merman whose remarkable stamina they put to use for fund-raising. Sponsors paid by the minute for Mitch to breaststroke, crawl, and butterfly through the cold Atlantic surf. He was a local hero, and then an international one, turned pro after the '84 Olympics, got his Wheaties box, the athlete's emblem of fame, arguably a prize of greater value than the gold medals that buy it. For its part, Post Cereals used his face in profile, concealing much of the purple stain.

For a decade Mitch kept in touch with Will and their parents. Even when he left Maine for bigger, international seas, he came home for holidays, and he continued to correspond with Will, writing him long letters crammed with details of his training schedules, the various diets he undertook to maintain an ideal percentage of body fat. Then, when Will and Carole married, Mitch took off. He came to the rehearsal dinner, and the stag party that lasted into the early hours of the wedding day, but he didn't show up for the ceremony itself.

Since then, something in his parents' voices, or perhaps it was their expressions, always strikes Will as resigned to Mitch's behavior. If asked to describe this quality, he'd say it's a look he'd expect to see on the faces of people who own shares of a company that has tanked, a bought-high-sold-low-let's-make-the-best-of-this-and-move-on kind of look.

"You didn't get a call from him?" Will asked when he and Carole returned from their honeymoon. "A letter? Anything?"

"Nothing," his father said.

At the rehearsal dinner, Mitch, who was to have been the best man, stood to ring his knife against a glass. Once everyone was quiet, he began a toast. "To my brother—older, wiser, and more accomplished than I . . . by eight minutes."

Even in his drunk and overwrought condition, Will was embarrassed by the rancor he heard in his brother's voice. Mitch continued on in the expectable, formulaic vein and made the usual benedictions— he flattered Carole, called attention to Will's undeserved good fortune, recounted boyhood stories. A transcript would show that his words were unremarkable. But his tone stunned Will, who listened closely, straining to catch a note of affection, but there was none. As his brother spoke, Carole looked into her lap. Will reached for her hand and squeezed it.

"You okay?" he whispered, and she nodded, squeezed his hand in return, her face betraying nothing.

Carole was twenty-four when they met, one of those girls, Will is sure, who always seem older than they are. In Carole's case this was because of her serene and unruffled, *unrufflable*, countenance, a look of such profound calm that she still has no need, ever, to hide her feelings—often they don't register on her face. Certainly, they never distort it. Dark brown hair, a distinct widow's peak that imparts a heart shape to a face with a wide forehead and wider cheekbones, large hazel eyes, a straight nose, and a small, if not exactly pointed, chin. Pretty features, but then, as now, what made Carole beautiful was her expression of tranquillity, a calm that didn't partake of late-twentieth-century multitasking, of frantic jabbering on cell phones while scurrying among sidewalk crowds, grimacing down subway stairs, PalmPilot in one hand, *Financial Times* in the other. No, Carole still seems exactly as she used to, as if she's slipped out from between the pages of a Victorian novel, or out of the frame of a centuries-old painting, any wrinkle of trouble or doubt smoothed away by the writer or artist.

Wherever they went together—often as not those grimy, chaotic places where students gather because beer is cheap—her face was immediately distinct from all those around it. Unflushed. Unadamant. She seemed to have nothing to prove, and this made Will want to prove everything; it made him want to fuck her. And immediately, from the first date, they made love a lot. A lot a lot, to the point where dates weren't going out but staying in, and when the Chinese food arrived, or the pizza, or the delivery boy from the market came with eggs and orange juice, whoever answered the door was wearing only a sheet.

From the neck down Carole was lustful and energetic, but Will wonders if on some level he hasn't always been aiming at her face, driving toward it. Not that he wants to rupture her countenance, not at all. He wants to plunge through it, as one would the reflective surface of water. Sees himself come out on the other side knowing what he didn't before. He is changed, while she, she of course remains the same. Like water, Carole's face, where he enters it, comes back together, bearing no trace of him, no more than a ripple that catches the light and then vanishes.

Maybe Will's obsession with sex, his sexual fantasies about his female patients, aren't the formulaic, knee-jerk symptoms he's assumed they are. Maybe they aren't just a manifestation of his guilt over Luke's drowning and his desire to be punished, revealed as a danger, humiliated by his peers. Maybe they're more than an escape route from his hyper-intellectualizing everything. Couldn't it just as easily be that all that sex represents his search for Carole, for the anger that must be there, deep under her skin and therefore something he has to force his way toward, into? Unconsciously, maybe he feels that her refusing to make love face-to-face means he has to reach her, arrive at her anger, through a surrogate twice removed from Carole herself, aggression displaced first into fantasy and then onto an object other than his wife.

And as long as he's training his reductive, psychoanalytical apparatus on himself, wouldn't it all relate to his unflappable mother? As we children of the twenty-first century know, she's the first woman he wanted to enter, or rather reenter, return, regress, revert, relapse, the first whose mysteries he was determined to plumb, whose body was once and ought still to be his.

At the rehearsal dinner Will saw that at last Mitch had become a man with a measure of poise, an ease with people that success had afforded him. But being able to stand, unflinching, before a crowd had required approval that blurred into awe, a counterweight to all that had preceded it. Will listened carefully to his brother's comments, a retrospective that included their years together at camp, their first jobs, and first girlfriends. *Girlfriends*—that word was a surprise. Will was sure Mitch had never had one. Well, perhaps in the context of a twin brother's imminent wedding, he'd needed to invent a romantic history.

Effective therapy for *Nevus flammeus* should be initiated in early childhood, because with time, port-wine stains can darken and thicken, acquiring a pebbly texture. Among birthmarks, they aren't accidents of pigment but vascular abnormalities that affect three of every thousand people. Their cause is unknown; there's no genetic predisposition for these spreading patches of malformed, dilated blood vessels, so close to the surface of the skin that they color it pink or red or, as in Mitch's case, purple.

Used as Will was to his brother's face, it scared him when they were kids. Not during the day when he could see it, but the idea of it would take hold of him at night. In the dark he couldn't stop seeing it grow until it had covered his brother, bled over the beds and into the shadows, splattered the walls and run down the stairs. He'd lie still as a stone, too frightened to go to their parents or even to call out to them. In the morning—he knew this, in his fear he could see it—their house and everything in it, and everyone, their neighborhood, the used-to-be-blue sky, it would all be stained and ruined, and who could stop a thing like that?

Will remembers their parents as having been curiously insensitive about Mitch's disfigurement and can imagine the excuses they might have made about doing nothing in response to the stain, the wound, as he used to think of it, unable to see it as skin-deep. Treatments that existed in the sixties were imperfect. Without the ability to fine-tune or pulse the beam, as doctors can today, lasers were either ineffective or left burn scars. In any case, the cost of what an insurance company would consider an elective, cosmetic procedure was prohibitive; it wasn't as if Mitch were physically endangered by the birthmark.

Although he might have been. Port-wine stains such as Mitch's, which involve the eyelids and forehead, are associated with Sturge-Weber syndrome, which affects vascular tissue in the brain and causes seizures and learning disabilities. But Will doesn't believe their pediatrician entertained such a possibility, if he even knew of it. "Don't borrow trouble," was Dr. Aldrich's favorite expression. He dismissed any fever below 104, interpreted all stomachaches as attempts at truancy, and, most infamously, misdiagnosed a case of appendicitis as stage fright precipitated by the 1965 Christmas pageant. Will and Mitch visited his cluttered office once each year, where they were weighed and measured and where Dr. Aldrich would take Mitch's face in his hands and look at it closely. "Doesn't hurt, does it, Mitchell?" he'd ask, and Mitch would shake his head.

"Not like he's a girl," he'd say to their mother. "If he was, I'd send you to the skin man up in Albany."

Mitch never complained. It was Will who removed the mirror from the back of the closet door in the room they shared, no longer able to stand the sight of his brother's circuitous passage around beds and behind chairs, his face averted from the sight of itself.

According to *Swimming World*, Mitch has participated in scientific studies of cold-water endurance, trials that require him to spend hours in tanks of frigid water, wearing only a swimsuit, his temperature monitored by a "rectal probe." He maintains nearly normal core body temperatures in water that, after several hours, would render the average person hypothermic to the point of shivering incoherence, even cardiac arrest. He's swum in water just a few degrees above freezing and lost remarkably little body heat. So far, the doctors who have studied Mitch don't know what circulatory adaptation allows this, but one researcher's hypothesis is that whatever ontogenic glitch caused the vascular abnormality that resulted in his *Nevus flammeus* is linked somehow to his freakish ability to swim for many hours, even days, in cold water, protected by nothing more than a Speedo, goggles, his own body fat, and a layer of petroleum jelly. If this is true, then Mitch's tragic flaw—his heroic strength that is also a mortal weakness—is an accident not so much of character as of biology.

Twinship was a torment. Will can't remember a time when he wasn't aware of Mitch's discomfort, sometimes even misery, as well as his own. How could it have been otherwise? Mitch could always see how he might look if unmarked, and Will knew what it would be to have his face disfigured. To be de-faced. The birthmark denied them the fun of pranks based on mistaken identity, and saved them the insult of not being recognized as individuals. "War Paint," they called Mitch at school, and "Gobbo," and then, finally, the name that stuck—"Africa."

Irresistible, because there was nothing fanciful about the similarity between the coastline of the continent and the outline of Mitch's port-wine stain. Certain borders, the Atlantic coast of Namibia and South Africa especially, seemed to have been traced onto his face. Cape Town marked the faint cleft in his chin; Angola blanketed his nose. His right eye was at sea, the left was the Democratic Republic of the Congo. His left temple was as pale as Will's, his right was Ethiopia. The purple stain covered 60 percent of his face, leaving

only his left ear, eye, cheek, and the left half of his nose and chin untouched.

It was arresting, Mitch's face. A person of broad and sophisticated
taste might even call it beautiful, in that beauty can terrify and accuse.

There was one teacher who didn't permit Mitch's
classmates to tease him, but this didn't endear him to Will's brother.
Any witness to his plight made Mitch that much less able to pretend
nothing was happening. With his flushed face and ill-kempt black
suits, Mr. Slaughter might have been a drunk, although none of his
students understood this at the time. From U.S. History—the course
he'd been hired to teach—Mr. Slaughter strayed east to Europe,
Palestine, India, Asia, and beyond, circling the globe until he'd
crossed the Pacific and landed back on native soil. He lectured on
all topics with equal fervor, never referring to the stack of note cards
he held in his hands. Every other Friday he handed out lined paper,
and when all the class was sitting at attention, eyes on him, he bowed
theatrically—sometimes he did a Shakespearean flourish, sweeping
an imaginary hat through the air—and then wrote a date on the
blackboard. 1862, 1884, 1918. The test was to summarize what was
happening all over the globe during that particular year, old world
and new: Europe, Asia, and Africa, the Americas, Australia, India,
Russia, Greenland—everywhere.

Not surprisingly, no one succeeded at these tests. No one but
Mitch. He earned the one A among all the other C's and D's. Once,
to honor his achievement, Mr. Slaughter read Mitch's answer aloud,
and what he read wasn't so much an essay as an associative string of
facts, some connections apparent, some not, each detail astonishing

for its accuracy, and the accretion of so many of them more surprising still. At home Mitch was in the habit of reading the *Encyclopaedia Britannica* for entertainment; without trying he'd memorized names and dates that he recycled into his answer. When Mr. Slaughter came to the last line of Mitch's test, he held it up so that everyone could see the large letter *A* on the top of the first page.

At the ceremony marking the class of 1975's graduation from Ravena High, Mr. Slaughter presented Will's brother with a leather-bound book of his tests, arranged chronologically, about two hundred pages' worth of Mitch's hurried block printing, the pressure of his pen so intense that he could use only one side of a sheet of paper. The cover was embossed with gold letters. "The History of the Modern World" by Mitchell Moreland, it read.

"Can I have this?" Will asked his mother when he found it on a shelf in the bedroom he'd once shared with his brother. It was a guest room now; flowered wallpaper covered over the scuffs and grime of boyhood; the *Apollo 11* decals had been razored from the window panes long ago; but the bookshelf remained, and on it the books.

"What is it?" Will's mother asked, taking it from his hands. She sat at the breakfast table and paged through a few tests. "I suppose," she said, closing the cover. "What for?"

Will shrugged, and she didn't press him for what he wouldn't have admitted—that he was going to read it for clues. Somewhere, embedded in the text, there must be some tiny something that Will's training would allow him to pick out and deconstruct, an answer to the riddle of Mitch that Mitch's own unconscious had hidden among references to war and revolution, the invention of the cotton gin, the birth of Mozart, Dr. Livingstone's discovery of Victoria Falls.

There was no such answer, but Will looked for it anyway, wondering if, in the end, his vocation was going to add up to anything more, really, than his ongoing attempt to understand his brother and the way an accident of biology might form—deform—character. 1830, 1843, 1878, 1902 . . . He combed through one year after another, and when he was done he put the book on the table by his side of the bed, not on top but at the bottom of the pile of things he never gets around to reading. Every so often he still pulls it out, but he's found he can't look at it for long without the risk of becoming ensnared in an hours-long spasm of searching through whatever documents he has of his past—snapshots, letters, his own juvenile diaries that embarrass and pain him, and a lot of other detritus packed in boxes but not put far enough away. All of it has the ability to leave him with one of those headachy hangovers peculiar to a nostalgic wallow, and—depending on how long it's been since he's suffered one of these—he usually replaces Mitch's tome within a few minutes of looking inside, sometimes before he's even opened the cover.

Number thirty-eight," says the girl with the bitten fingernails. "Very old-school, very houndstooth tweedy. Like, the leather patches on the elbows of his jacket appear to be genuine, as if it didn't come like that but his wife sewed them on for real after he wore holes in his sleeves. He's so central casting that it's actually cute in a kind of avuncular way. I mean, maybe less than sexy to most girls and even a little too Mr. Chipsy for me, but as we've established, I'm turned on by the musty, old, academic type. Even the slightly askew bow tie does it for me. Still, I'm worrying because he's onto his third glass of pinot noir and, well, you know . . ."

"The faculty club serves alcohol?" Will says, intentionally missing his cue.

"Faculty *house*. Yeah. In the fourth-floor dining room. Elsewhere, administration or whoever turns a blind eye on professors going to the bar and buying drinks to carry back to wherever. Besides, it's not as if I'm underage."

"No, I was just—"

"*Anyway*, so I'm counting glasses of wine, and by the time he orders a third, I'm thinking erectile dysfunction, and I start teasing him a little. I say, I can't remember what exactly, something to the effect that so handsome and distinguished a scholar shouldn't be drinking alone. Or maybe I called him a gentleman and a scholar. Whatever I say, it's direct and it's also kinda generic, you know, not too personal, so that if I've, like, miscalculated—which hasn't ever happened, FYI—but if I did, and he's going to get all offended, I haven't compromised myself by saying something too sort of overt. But he's not offended. Not at all. The point is, I've put out minimal effort and already he's very friendly, very chatty, very ha-ha-ha. By now we're close to closing, and remember, this is the faculty house we're talking about, it's not exactly your happening venue. Anyone who has, like, a life is pursuing it elsewhere. Since he's the only diner left in the room, he says, why don't I sit down, I must be tired, no? Maybe I'd like a piece of cake. I can bring it along with his dessert. So I'm like, sure, that'd be nice, and he asks what's best on the dessert menu, and I say mud pie, and he says too rich, so I say apple brown Betty, and he says too sweet. Pear tarts are not his cup of tea. By now I'm wondering, did I go overboard this time? Maybe he's not just older but *old*, and has to watch his cholesterol or his gallbladder or whatever, because now that I'm thinking about it, he did order an inauspiciously Spartan entrée. Not that I'd imagined he was some sort of sybarite epicure, because anyone of, like, gustatory sophistication would sooner suck down a platter of Chicken McNuggets than a faculty house dinner, but I am hoping for a person of appetite because, you know, sex and food, people who like one usually like the other, and this guy's chosen a meal conceived by a, like, frigid nun—filet of sole without any sauce, meunière, tartar, whatever, only lemon. And on the side a dry, make that desiccated, baked potato, and he didn't touch the dish of creamed onions that automatically comes with everything; you can't get rid of them for some reason.

"So, how about sorbet, I ask, and he says too cold. Pecan pie? Too sweet. So, now that we've established that everything's too this too that, I say, very perceptive here, 'Maybe you don't want dessert?' and he says yes, I'm right, just bring him a cappuccino—which, by the way, suck big-time at the faculty house, I don't know why; it's not exactly rocket science, making coffee. Starbucks should bring in a franchise, since there isn't one in a radius of, like, three feet. Anyway, I bring him one, and another for myself, and neither of us mention the fact that it tastes like shit. He drinks his; I pretend to drink mine."

The girl pauses and, when Will doesn't speak, goes on with her story. "By now we've established that he's a professor of Italian Renaissance architecture, and we've tried to move beyond our own 'disciplines,' as he calls them, to an appreciation of each other's, and while he's asking have I seen the Brunelleschi chapel or the *baldochino* or the—whatever it is, it begins with a *B*—while he's asking, I'm making my standard, hello-nice-to-meet-you gesture, surfing one stockinged foot up his inseam, and when I get there, guess what? He's not fifty, not downtown he isn't. Downtown he's maybe twenty, his hard-on is *hard*. So hard I'm thinking, like, whoa, what's this, a strapon? You know, like a fake one? And my next thought is that it may be cliché but it might also be true that many professors are pedophiles. I mean, why else settle for all that work, plus the academic rat-fuck for tenure, and then there's the crummy salary? Intellectual passion? Maybe. But, come on, there have to be perks. Not that I'm exactly a child, or even underage, but institutionally speaking, we could call me the child whereas he's, um, what's it called, in loco parentis?

"The professor stops talking as my foot starts rubbing, and we have a bit of an uncomfortable moment, and guess what? Not a strapon. A palpable retreat from high-impact, crash-dummy rubber to, say, Dr. Scholl's gel arch supports, but it's temporary, nothing so much as a setback. In a minute we're back to playing chicken, which apparently neither of us is. Mr. Crash Dummy is back in the game."

Will opens the imaginary bag of ice he's been holding in his lap, turns it over and pours ten pounds of cubes directly onto his unsheathed and unsuspecting penis, willing it to freeze in mid-tumescence.

"'Have you been keeping up with the film series at the Thalia?' he inquires, Professor Suave—he has to have said this line about a gazillion times—and I answer, quite on cue and even truthfully, 'Berlin Alexanderplatz?' I nod, he nods, we say incisive things about Mr. Fassbinder and other of our favorite self-destructive artistic geniuses. It's a grim little game, the pathetic penny-ante one-upmanship of academe. They say dentists are more likely to commit suicide than people in any other profession, but I dunno, this whoever-commands-the-most-rarefied-cultural-references-wins audition makes me feel like sawing at my wrist with a steak knife. But finally it's over, he wins by two Japanese directors and a Maori poet no one's ever heard of—he could have made him up for all I know—and goes off to pay, while I head for the lockers to change out of my waitress costume. Which, by the way, is not so much Howard Johnson's as it is French Maid, a genuine asset as far as my motives are concerned, and I guess kind of unexpected in an institutional setting. I mean, we're not talking Hooters, but it does have that naughty, come-hither look. Still, off it goes, except for the tights. I've brought an alluring après-work outfit, a crotch duster, meaning microminiskirt, plus a sweater I've had since ninth grade, a little short so there's navel-ring disclosure, and a redder-than-red swing coat for the sake of high visibility plus modesty while walking in dark alleys.

"The too-brilliant-to-live Fassbinder is playing not far from the faculty house. The Thalia's maybe three quarters of a mile the safe way, a little less if you're late and willing to risk your life for culture. And, guess what, Mr. Crash Dummy is wild for culture, can't get enough stimulation, and the shortcut offers a perfect opportunity for the professor to coax Little Red off the primrose path and into the woods. We cross over the green in front of the library, and, big surprise, Professor Hard-on pushes me against what's holding up some giant dead bronze guy for some very eager and, I have to say, clumsy wet kissing before we move on to this sinister little breezeway near the bookstore. Then it's him leaning against a wall and me on my knees eye-to-eye with his trouser button. How I get there is one of those delicate, wordless negotiations, his hands on my shoulders exerting a faint but not ambiguous pressure, me responding with a gradual, is-this-where-we're-going descent.

"Once I'm where he wants me, everything accelerates. A little friendly attention, and Mr. Crash Dummy speeds through the intersection and whams into the back of my throat. A minor episode of gagging on my part, as, having expected a, like, five- or six-second so-nice-to-meet-you-won't-you-come-in prelude, I've been taken off guard by his impetuousness, but I ignore the fact that I can taste pizza dating back to dinner at six and regain my composure to deliver a perfectly calibrated act of fellatio, meaning great rather than good, great rather than pro forma, a few little touches that would imply erotic creativity plus generosity. Then I stand up, leaving Mr. Crash in the cold autumn wind. 'How about shelter?' I ask, not having to feign eagerness. Forget breezeway, it's 'a nipping and an eager air' tearing at my skirt—that's Shakespeare for arctic blast, if you didn't know. Not only am I just about frozen, with aching knees to boot, but I really want to fuck him, I'm no-kidding-around horny. But he can't take me to his place because—well, just because. Why waste time enumerating complications? But, as his office is on a newly refurbished floor of Barnard Hall, perhaps I'd like to see an etching or a Xerox machine or a box of paper clips?

"We scurry off through Low Plaza, me hoping to arrive before my snatch, like, grows stalactites. He fumbles the electronic key, the regular key, the light switch, the security code. Whatever he can get wrong, he does—testosterone impairing cognitive function, no doubt—and the department phone starts to ring. Good evening, sir, campus police. Would you be so kind as to give us the password? Which, of course, the professor has forgotten, if he ever knew it, that is—his mind was meant for better things—so now he's scrabbling around in the bottom of his briefcase for whatever matchbook or gum wrapper on which he's inscribed the code word or whatever, since the alarm did go off at the station and we wouldn't want to trouble an officer on a Friday night when countless degenerate undergrads are jitterbugging naked in adults-only clubs or topping off their iPods with stolen music or snorting their dead grannies' OxyContin or whatever it is they do for entertainment.

"When he finally finds it, the password is, get this, 'Lily Bart.' Kind of a nice touch, I think at first. Later, lying in my own little bed and reviewing the evening's successes, I remember the plot of *House of Mirth* and think, not so nice after all. I mean, is this how it goes: Barnard Hall faculty calls a meeting and decide that the open sesame for their building should be a reference to illicit and, by the way, fatal promiscuity?

"Anyway, too late for regrets. His office is"—the girl looks around at Will's walls and furniture—"I guess it's well appointed, sort of contemporary intellectual, like yours. Black and beige and chrome, and there's some framed Renaissance print thing on the wall." Her tongue appears and explores her lower lip with seeming interest. Will says nothing, recrosses his legs to adjust his thawed erection.

"We don't undress, not all the way. I peel off my tights, he drops his tweedy trousers. And, I can't believe it, but he is actually, really and truly wearing sock garters. I mean, wow. They almost turn me on, that's how gross they are, black and stretchy and, well, anyway, once I get past the shock, we go at it, we do it three ways. One, standing at his desk, my ass on his blotter, legs around his waist. Seems it's inevitable whenever there's a desk around—you do end up taking cues from the office environment. Two, on the brand-new, itchy, Scotchgarded, stain-and-spooge-repellent, blue-gray institutional carpet. I'm the bottom and it's missionary, so his knees and my ass are getting, like, third-degree carpet burns. Three, I'm on top, standard, liberated, attuned-to-her-physical-self female taking advantage of her partner's still rock-hard cock. Altogether I get off about four times: once on the desk, once on my back, then twice astride before I let him have his.

"He's so close, it's one, two, three thrusts, and that's it. He moans, closes his eyes, I stand up and note with satisfaction that when we did it on the desk I left a big stain of squat juice on his blotter. I do not, do not over my dead body, let myself look at him naked and flaccid and wearing sock garters. This, I know, would make me feel worse than desperate; the whole world and all its nearly four billion human occupants would somehow be implicated by the sight of them. It would be one of those unfortunate moments when I have an unanticipated and very much unwanted awakening to how pathetic and ridiculous and indefensible it is to be an example of this disgusting species."

"Why?"

"Why?"

"Yes," Will says. "Why will seeing the sock garters of an Italian Renaissance architecture professor reveal the pathetic and indefensible ridiculousness of being human?"

"You can't be serious."

"I am serious."

"Do you wear sock garters? Tell me you don't. If you do, you're the one who should be having your head examined."

Will says nothing. Within the parameters of this dialogue he wears whatever she thinks he does.

"Well, you've, like, seen them, right? You do know what they look like?"

He nods.

"So, picture these ultra-ultra-white legs with not so much as one hair because, well, I guess because it all gets, like, rubbed off by his pants or something—or maybe it's his age—and on his glabrous old shins are these pervy black socks that are kept up without a sag or wrinkle by sock garters. *Glabrous* is a good word, don't you think?" She looks at Will pointedly.

"Very descriptive."

"Yeah. I looked it up in the *OED* to be sure it was the one I wanted." She smiles at him.

"You looked up *glabrous* before you came here today?"

The girl nods, still smiling. "When I was rehearsing the story for you."

Will folds his hands on his desk. "This is a story you rehearsed for today's session?"

"Story as in narrative, not make-believe. Swear to God." She holds up her right hand, puts her left on an imaginary Bible.

"Why would you need to rehearse?"

"I'm shy."

Will lets this one go and watches while she bites her nail, taking the finger out of her mouth, examining the damage, putting it back in for another leisurely go before continuing.

"What I've described doesn't make you feel suicidal?" she demands. "Picturing that? Shiny old shins dressed up in serial-killer socks and garters?"

"No."

"Well, okay. Fine. Whatever. There's stuff like sock garters and toupées that don't match the person's actual hair color that are just too depressing."

"Why is that?"

"Because they are! Why do you pretend to be stupid!"

"I—"

"In fact, his sock garters are so inclined to inspire suicidal ideation that I ask him to do me a favor, and he says what, and I say take me to the student center and give it to me in a stall. He sits up, checks Mr. Crash to see he's not all gummy with spooge. 'In a stall?' he says, looking more than willing.

"'Yeah,' I say, 'like the women's room, or the men's, I don't care—just so it's public.'" The girl stops talking. "What are you writing down?" she demands when she sees Will noting her use of the words *suicidal ideation*, a term that only someone with experience of psychiatric texts or treatment might use. She sighs dramatically when he doesn't reply, returns to her story.

"'That would be the lavatory in the basement under Kent—the Starr Library,' he says, and I'm like, 'Why there?' 'Because it's open until midnight and guaranteed to be deserted,' he says. 'Stalls for you. Safety for me.' I tell him I prefer the student center. He shakes his head. 'Student center no, Starr Library yes. Take it or leave it.'

"I take it. We pull up our scanties and head over to Kent. I don't know if you remember last Friday, but like, wow, a record low for November fourth. I'm getting head-to-toe frostbite, and it's not as if I'm a girl who wears sensible shoes, the soles are, like, nonexistent. Anyway, we arrive and, as promised, the library is open and empty. Except for the librarian, who's in a vertical coma of boredom, basically, and the bathroom downstairs is suitably vile. Shocking, really, considering tuition, but a place to keep in mind for the future.

"I don't know what it is, my inner gay man maybe, but I am majorly turned on by public toilets—I love metal stall doors with the enamel chipping off the corners, a little rust, dirty words that won't scrub off—you can see where the poor janitor has scrubbed the thing dull trying to get *cunt* or whatever off the damn door, but it's there forever. Words like that—they have a life of their own, don't you think? Also, I love the fluorescent light and even that gross smell of disinfectant. I get all itchy and sex-starved just walking into a public *loo*. Which is what my mother calls it in certain company. Unbelievably pretentious and irritating. I mean, as if! She's about as British as Oprah." The girl checks her watch and buttons her coat.

"It unfolds according to my script: inside the stall, up against the door so the whole thing kind of squeaks and moves, and despite being taller than me and not so young that I can assume buff thigh muscles, Mr. Italian Renaissance is very good on the tricky upthrust. It only takes a few minutes for us both to get off. No sock garters in view, praise the Lord, so we end on a good note. Polite parting in the corridor, a handshake—quite weird—and we're off in opposite directions."

"Weird?" Will says.

"Don't you think?" She stands and swings her backpack up onto one shoulder. "I mean, we've had sex, what, four times in an hour— thrice in his office and once in the lavatory—and he's holding out his hand to shake mine like we've just been introduced at some dread sherry-and-cheese mixer." She approaches the door—it's exactly ten of three—and pauses, apparently struggling with the knob. "Do you mind?" she says. "I'm having this, like, carpal tunnel flare-up."

Will stands to open the door, notebook casually (he hopes, dear God, he hopes) hiding his erection, the fact of it preoccupying him enough that he doesn't see what's coming. Like a cartoon character who steps into the noose attached to a bent-over sapling, *zoing*, he's flying in the air—What's up? What's down?—Will is without a clue.

She's got him with his back to his office door, a hand on either side of his face, her tongue deep in his mouth. He makes an ineffective noise, something between a gargle and a moan, a noise intended as protest but received as encouragement. The tongue does a little somersault, and one hand leaves his cheek, drops down to his fly.

"I thought you'd like that story," she says, her breath warm on his face and smelling like her tongue tastes, of caramel or toffee, something sugary. She rubs him harder, seals his mouth with hers so he can't respond. But what was he going to say? Already he's forgotten. After months of panic over his own barely controlled lust, he's been—he's *being*—jumped by a patient, forced up against his own door, his tongue sucked so hard that it aches at the root, his cock very aware of each one of her moving fingers.

He's always loved dreams—his own, other people's. With respect to analysis, they're invaluable, like having a wiretap on someone's soul. Even the most cryptic yield to examination, and a mere fragment can get a session going. But, as transparent as Will finds his patients' dreams, suddenly he's become clumsy, even dim-witted, with respect to his own. Take the one he had last night, when at last he fell asleep, having told Carole what had happened with the girl without managing to communicate what really happened, which was not that a patient had pulled some highly inappropriate stunt but that he'd been aroused by it.

He'd refused himself the relief of masturbating to dismiss the erection that popped up shortly after he'd made love with Carole—his traitorous cock stirring even before she fell asleep—because there was no way he could beat off without again reviewing the kiss and the feeling of the girl's avid fingers, their tips that seem less chewed now than burned by corrupt explorations. His memory of what she'd done, what he'd allowed her to do, was—*is*—all too pungent: three parts horror, say, to one part intoxication, a scene highlighted as if by a mental klieg light, a thousand watts of attention issuing from some dark corner of his head, trained on the two of them at the door. Familiar clichés apply: she's caught red-handed, he with his pants down.

When he woke from the nightmare—at least he doesn't have to deal with sweet dreams following upon guilty fantasies—he remembered it in detail. Commented to himself that it was obvious, almost formulaic. But then he couldn't interpret it. The longer he tried, the slipperier it grew, until now he finds it's acquired the quality of a koan, a riddle that confounds as much as it compels.

In the dream, he's engaged a third party, an agent to whom he entrusts a sum of money to hire a private investigator. This detective's assignment is to tail Will—Will himself is the object of the hunt—and the detective is to use whatever powers of surveillance are required to mark Will's passage through each day. Spy cameras, hidden mikes, infrared periscopes—the man is outfitted with all the paraphernalia of male paranoia, an array of absurdly compact devices like those that saturate a James Bond movie: potent, shiny, and impossible.

The dream detective makes notes and tapes and photographs. He captures Will as he sleeps, showers, works, as he has sex with his wife and, as this is a dream, with other women as well. When the report comes back, when Will is shown the evidence collected against him, he's shocked by what he sees.

The detective's photographs and videotapes have an unimpeachable authority. Black-and-white, blurred, grainy, they look illicit, as one expects of images that have been snatched. Will stares at them in loathing. Despite the snow on the video monitor, and despite interfering, vertical lines—as if all the action unfolds in a jail cell—Will sees that it is, in fact, his face that leers at him, his features twisted with malevolence. But can this really be how he appears to other people? The man's face is his own, but the sinister expression, the animosity, even hatred, the intent to wreak havoc: it's a person he can look at for only so long.

The pictures frighten and disgust him; he wants to destroy them;

yet he cannot deny that they render the very thing he's paid to be shown: a monstrous and unredeemable someone who must lurk within him, but whom he couldn't find without the help of a private eye.

It's only after he's fully awake, after he's been awake long enough to have left behind the murk of his unconscious, that Will realizes the face in the dream was never more than half revealed. In every image, a dark swath has fallen across the man's features, leaving the right half of his face black. Shadowed, Will assumed in the dream, but perhaps all along the man in the pictures, the man the detective trailed, was the wrong man.

Not Will. Mitch.

Beside Will, Carole sleeps. It's not yet light outside. She's kicked the covers off and is facedown with her nightgown bunched up around her waist, arms and legs spread, showing him more than enough of herself to summon an erection. Apparently, nothing can kill off lust, not his lust. It's always there, undeterred by illness or by lack of sleep, by mourning, by nightmares. And Carole has an appealing butt, plump and defiant, the arrival of middle age halted with— what else?—yoga. Sometimes he feels like he sees it more often than he sees the rest of her.

Not looking into each other's eyes: wasn't this one of the accommodations they made after Luke died, a tacit one? How could they have risked the chance of recognizing it: the other's anguish? But because it had been an unspoken adjustment, not so much a decision as a reflex, they'd never undone it. Just as no one said *let's*, neither has either of them said *it's time we stopped*.

It used to be that Will considered himself among the self-aware, but something—what?—seems to have taken away some essential knowledge he had of himself, his true character. As if there exists a key—Will's key—to his own psyche, a key he once owned and now has lost. He's misplaced it, or someone has taken it. Is that even possible?

He tries the idea out on Daniel. "Does that make sense?" he asks, and receives the standard analytic riposte.

"It only matters if it makes sense to you." Daniel raises his eyebrows, and Will, reading the expression as a request that he continue, goes on talking.

"Well, there are two possibilities—two that I see. Two points at which I might have, I don't know, lost touch with myself, I guess. First, my brother's disappearance, which, since the reunion, has taken on some new weight of significance. I don't know why. But it feels even more personal than it used to. His rejection or abandonment or whatever you want to call it.

"And second, I'm guessing the loss of Luke, also in the past, but the recent past, relatively speaking. I mean, I didn't even feel as if I'd woken up, as if I were genuinely conscious and aware of my surroundings, until a year or so afterward. And he was my son. Myself projected into the future. Not finite. At least not in any way I had to admit. Because in the natural order of things I would die first. His death would never exist for me. It wouldn't be possible to be abandoned by my child, the person in whom I placed my essential self."

"Without your son you discover mortality? Your mortality?"

Will stands up. He shoves his hands in his pockets and looks at the ceiling and then back at Daniel. "Are you ridiculing me?" he asks.

"Not at all." Daniel shakes his head. "Do you think what you've said is ridiculous?"

"No. But I do find it banal. And I wasn't talking about mortality. At least I don't think I was. Certainly, it's a topic that preoccupies me, but just then I was talking about how I'd managed to lose touch with myself."

"Why banal?"

Will sits back down. "Isn't this the crisis of faith I was supposed to have as a kid, when my dog died? The standard-issue if-my-dog-died-there-is-no-God crisis?"

"Who said anything about God?"

Will laughs, at himself, shakes his head. "Touché. I think it must have been me, the guy with the God problem."

Daniel raises his eyebrows, folds his hands on his desk. Hanging on the wall behind him are so many framed diplomas and citations that he has no more space to put any of the newer ones. Instead, he opens old frames and slips one in front of another so that in a few cases two sets of words appear, ghostly writing from the document on the bottom showing through the paper of the one above.

"Forget the key. The idea of a key or something to unlock me. My secret self. I want to come at this a different way. The context for the dream is, I think, my continuing to dwell on the reunion." *The girl, the girl,* Will prompts himself, *tell him what happened with the girl.* But he goes on without mentioning what he was stewing about when he fell asleep. "The context aside from my knowing we would be meeting today, that is. Because I realize that for the last few weeks I've been remembering what I dream the night before I see you, so I can bring it here, like a cat with a dead bird."

Daniel raises one hand, a signal for Will to stop, but his innate politeness makes it a slightly deferential gesture, tentative, like an uncertain student's rather than the person whose name is presented in all those frames above his chair. "You haven't forgotten to be suspicious of those dreams?" he asks.

"Because of the likelihood of their being a defense?"

Now both of Daniel's hands are in the air, palms up and empty. "What might we talk about if we weren't busy deconstructing your dream?"

Will starts to laugh. "Maybe Carole's right. Maybe analysis does depend on masochism."

"Self-absorption."

"Was that the word she used?"

"I think so," Daniel says. "I could look it up."

In years past, before Daniel's wife died, the four of them—Will, Carole, Daniel, and Jessica—often ate out together, arguing companionably around the window table of a Korean barbecue restaurant, a place none of them had liked particularly but that no one disliked enough to sacrifice the ritual aspect of gathering around the same table time after time. They always shared a couple of bottles of wine, and if anyone said something Daniel found interesting or amusing, he'd inscribe it in a notebook he used for that purpose.

Will shrugs. "Don't bother. The part I liked was her idea that psychoanalysis should adopt a symbol like that used by physicians. You remember, instead of two snakes coiling around a sword, there would be only one, swallowing its own tail."

"Right," Daniel says, and he laughs. "She drew a picture for me. In my journal."

"Anyway," Will says, "admittedly, the reunion is over and done with. Well, no, not done with, actually, because it's had so long a fall-out. Subjected me to what felt like an interrogation. Which was the reason Carole refused to go, and why she didn't want me to go, because of all the questions people were bound to ask. I'd have to talk about Mitch and about Luke. Obvious, right, but I didn't see it coming. I never anticipated it myself, and whatever Carole said, I didn't hear. In fact I was so deliberately unprepared for what happened that I find myself wondering if my being interrogated wasn't the point. Wasn't what I wanted, deep down.

"Of course, once I'd seen Elizabeth's page and read her bio, I did want to ask her about her daughter. And I certainly seem to have been talking from the depths of some unconscious sinkhole when I embarked on that unfortunate line of inquiry. But way before that, as far back as last winter, when the reunion was just an idea rather than a collection of particular individuals, I wonder if I wasn't planning to use it as a . . . a . . . I was going to say crowbar, but a better metaphor would be solvent. If I hadn't wanted, unconsciously, to immerse myself in an environment that would have a caustic effect on whatever defenses I'd built around my psyche, a solvent that would eat away at them and force me to deal with what I've hidden from myself. Issues that need to be examined—or maybe just acknowledged—but that I wasn't ready to approach before now.

"And then in reaction to this—this interrogation or crowbar or solvent or whatever I'm calling what I'm applying to my defenses—I take on too many patients, I run myself ragged chasing down other people's problems, because I'm fearful of my own. Part of me prefers being defended. So I'm conflicted, I'm ambivalent, unresolved conflicts are filling me with anxiety. Anxiety I try to keep at bay with obsessive sex fantasies. Does that make sense?" Will sees Daniel's expression and answers his own question. "Yes," he says, "it does. It does make sense to me."

Daniel smiles. "Well, your interpretation would satisfy my favorite analytic axiom, one I know you must be sick of hearing, that the unconscious . . ." He leaves it to Will to finish the thought.

"Is always on your side," Will says. "My side, in this case."

"Exactly," Daniel says. "I'm afraid you don't really need me, Will. I'm just an old dog whose tricks you already know."

"No, no. I do need you. I need you because it isn't until I'm sitting before you, determined not to disappoint whatever faith you may have in me, that I see myself at all."

The two men are silent until Daniel speaks. "What are you feeling, Will?" he says.

"Not much."

"Care to guess why that might be?"

Will, who is leaning forward with his elbows on his knees, drops his face in his hands. "I imagine," he says without looking up, "that I've successfully protected myself—defended myself—from my feelings by being so hyperanalytical, so . . . so cerebral, in reference to my defenses."

Daniel nods. "You're a good psychoanalyst," he says.

"And a crummy patient." Will looks up. "But I still don't think I'm wrong."

W ill and his father are at La Luncheonette, a little bistro all the way over on the West Side. From where he's sitting, Will can see the red stack of a barge moving slowly up the Hudson through a gray-green slice of the river. "So, how's your love life?" Will asks his dad.

"Not bad. Yours?"

"Never mind. You're the art-world ingénue having an affair with his wealthy patroness." His father smiles, a little wearily, Will thinks.

"Considering my advanced age and modest circumstances, I think it's going well enough. At least my wealthy patroness hasn't voiced any complaints." He holds up one hand to flag down the waitress, a Vietnamese no older than eighteen and very beautiful, her shining hair gathered into a chignon. It's the sort of seemingly artless arrangement of hair that might take a woman hours to pull off; in the case of this girl, Will would bet she really has just slipped down the wine-cellar stairs for a moment, twisted it into a coil, and skewered it with a pencil so that it remains there, at the nape of her neck. The few strands that have escaped look like a painter's finishing touch, highlighting her cheekbones and calling attention to the line of her jaw.

"Not ready to order," his father says, "just wanted to see you close up."

Will braces himself for a tart response, almost closing his eyes so he doesn't have to see his father being rebuffed, but instead, the girl beams at him. She ducks her head so close to his that for a second Will thinks she's going to kiss him.

"*Bonjour, mon ami intéressant,*" she says.

"What did she call you?" Will watches the girl go to the bar for the glass of water his father asked for.

"Nothing scandalous. Her interesting friend, that's all. I eat here every so often."

Will raises his eyebrows; his father shrugs.

"Apparently you've reached the age where you can get away with anything," Will says.

"We'll see." His father picks up his knife and slips its blade between the uneven tines of his fork, straightening them by leveraging one against another. When he's satisfied that the job is done, he polishes the fork on his napkin and replaces it on the table. "We'll see what I can get away with," he says.

"You make it sound as if you're about to be subjected to a test of your not inconsiderable charm."

His father smiles and takes a sip from the water the waitress has put before him. "Charlotte's husband showed up last week."

"I didn't even know she was married."

"I did. But the way she told it, she made it sound like a nonissue. Said they hadn't lived together as man and wife for more than ten years."

"So why's he dropping by?"

"It's all on account of a cockroach. Two cockroaches, in fact."

"What's that supposed to mean?"

"He's having his apartment fumigated. Girlfriend found a roach in her shoe."

"And?"

"And?"

"You said two. Two cockroaches."

"Oh, right. Another bug set up shop in the cheese drawer of the fridge."

"So he just comes back any time he wants?"

"Guess so. Has a key. And a room."

"You never noticed the room?"

"I thought it was a guest room. No personal effects on view, and it's not as if I go around checking closets and drawers."

Will takes off his tie, folds it, and puts it in his jacket pocket. "Was he civil?" he asks his father.

"Very civil. Friendly. Put his hand out to shake mine—this was at breakfast the next morning. All of us sitting down together eating muffins and reading the *Times*. Fancy muffins, size of footballs. He went out for them. And for juice. Strawberries." Will's father shakes his head. "He told me the mayor wasn't even five feet tall."

"What does that have to do with anything?"

"I don't know. Must've been something in the paper, but it stuck in my head. All week I've been thinking, apropos of nothing, 'The mayor's not even five feet tall.' Guess I'm a little discombobulated by the whole setup."

"He'd come in the previous night?"

"Middle of the night. 'Who's that?' I ask Lottie when I hear the door, someone rummaging around in the kitchen. 'Must be David,' she says.

"'David who?' I ask.

"'No one,' she says.

"'No one?' I ask.

"'My husband.'

"'I thought he was an ex-husband.'

"'He is,' she says, 'he is for all practical purposes.'" Will's father takes another swallow of water. "At the word *practical,* she gives me a little goose down belowdecks, sort of pats me there. Then she goes back to sleep. Next morning she wants to, you know, but I can't, uh, can't . . ." Will raises his eyebrows. "Can't muster myself for the job at hand," his father clarifies. "I mean there's the guy sleeping on the other side of the wall."

"I'm sorry, Dad. That must have been weird."

"Guess so. Kind of disorienting, anyway. Can't concentrate. Went to the movies three times in two days." Will purses his lips, shakes his head. Going to the movies has always been his father's response to stress. When Will and Mitch were growing up, if his father had had what he called a "five-flick week" that was reason enough for them to behave very well.

"Also, and here's the worst of it, well, not the worst, maybe. Trying to be polite, I guess, the guy keeps dragging me over to where Lottie's hung my prints. Wants to talk about them. Wants me to talk about them. Asks questions. Not the stupid kind, but still."

"Oh boy."

"You remember which ones she bought."

"Of course. How could I not?" Will thinks of his first look at one of those photographs. Uncharacteristically, his father had mailed him a print, sandwiched between two pieces of cardboard joined with duct tape. "Look," Will had said to Carole, who didn't glance up from the pile of mail she was sorting, pulling out the catalogs to add to the recycling bin. He laid the photograph on the dining table, and she walked around and stood beside him so she could see the image right side up. Briefly, he'd considered keeping it from her; he couldn't say whether this was selfishness or kindness or a murky tangle of both.

"It's sort of . . ." She stopped, her lips together, and sucked inside her teeth, leaving just a line where they'd been, one of her many strategies for suppressing tears. "Beautiful," she managed, nodding.

She had her hands on her hips and her feet were planted a little apart, as if she were about to begin a set of calisthenics. Will remembers this, because it looked so odd, intentional, as if it might be another grief suppressant, equally ineffective, because her cheeks were wet; tears were running down her neck.

"It is, isn't it?" He picked up the photograph, careful to hold it by the edges, to keep the oil from his fingers from marring the image.

How had this happened? Was it Luke who'd given his grandfather this new vision, one both tender and exalted? Could he have shown him the view from on high, shown him what God or a god might see were he to look at humankind, creatures who greeted death with starched curtains and polished door knockers? McCaddam's Funeral Home, with its swept steps and braided mat, plumped cushions on the porch swing, a sign whose letters were painted with care. Will had paused on those steps the first time he entered, noting where faint ruled lines had ensured that whoever made the letters would keep them absolutely straight. Here was a house where Death, no matter how punctilious, wouldn't hesitate to spend a night, confident that pots were scoured and toilets scrubbed. Perhaps wearing white gloves so as to check along the picture moldings and the tops of door and window frames, just to see, as in the old TV commercial: Had everything been dusted?

Inside, across the silent room with the too-short casket, that much more obscene for being child-sized, Carol was sitting next to his mother, her head in his mother's lap, her eyes open, her face expressionless. His mother's hand moved over his wife's head, smoothly and steadily, like the pendulum of a big clock, a nearly frictionless arc marking the passage of time. His mother wasn't brisk with Carole as she was with him. It was easier to love his wife, perhaps. After all, Carole never baited her like he did.

Will has always found his mother reliable, industrious, and reticent, if not actually guarded. She doesn't seem to have much of a sense of humor, and her feelings, though spontaneous, are controlled; they never carry her away. He wonders sometimes if the mother he knows might not be a deliberate construction, a false front assembled to disguise the more unusual and complicated structure behind it, but then he has to ask himself if this idea might not issue from his desire for a less emotionally circumspect mother. A mother who is . . . who is what? Indulgent, he guesses.

At some point during that long afternoon, that endless day, Carole sat up and his mother stood to retrieve his father, who was, they all assumed, still in the old station wagon with the fake-wood side panels, the dog fence in place behind the front seat, even though it had been years since he'd had any occasion to pick up or deliver an animal. Will's father understood the pain of animals. The suffering of a dog was suffering for which he had an arsenal of responses. But what was it that could cure, or even assuage, human misery? Will imagined his father with one hand on the steering wheel, the other on the key, which he hadn't removed from the ignition. Possibly he hadn't moved since turning off the engine and was frozen to the car's vinyl seat, hidden by the reflection on the windshield, as motionless as one of his own perplexing still lives. But when Will looked out the window, he saw his father kneeling on the sidewalk with his head under the black cloth, peering through his big box camera at the funeral home.

"Hank!" his mother said, and she said the name again, more loudly, but Will's father didn't answer, and she left him there.

The funeral home was in fact a *home*, a white clapboard house built in the thirties, with round wood columns, copper rain gutters oxidized green, meticulously painted black trim and window frames, dormers on the roof, a stone chimney, a brass door knocker cast in the shape of a hand, fingers curled to rap the polished plate beneath them, starched white curtains hanging in freshly washed windows that reflected the nearby lake, itself lit by the bright sun, each pane shining silver—it almost hurt to look at them.

Will's father took his time under the black cloth, exposing one negative after another while, inside, Will completed arrangements for having Luke's body cremated.

"Didn't you want to come in, say good-bye?" Will asked before his parents drove away.

He leaned into the driver's-side window, and his father looked at him. He shook his head. "I'm sorry, Will," he said. "I thought I could, but I can't." His father got out of the car and hugged him, a long hug, longer than any in memory, Will keenly conscious of his father's body and the comfort it offered him. Flesh of his flesh. He remembers, after the accident, thinking the words over and over, applying them to his son and not, until that moment, to his father. After, when they'd released each other, they stood in the bright sun, silent and even shy, each man, Will is sure, unable to dismiss the feeling of the other's silent crying, how fearsome it was, to feel a man's back shake under your touch.

"This David character," Will's father is saying to him now, "he has a lot to say about each photograph, some of it the expectable claptrap, negative space and kinetic something or other, plus a few genuine comments here and there. Bends my ear for an hour. Very complimentary, but I found myself wanting to punch him."

"Yeah," Will says. "I kind of feel like I want to, too."

But what Will really feels is a grudging bond with the man, whoever he is. He expects people to be impressed by his father's work. Especially by the prints Charlotte bought, six among a series of thirty that will be published as a monograph in the coming year.

His father's camera had looked at McCaddam's straight on from the sidewalk, so the photograph presented only the front of the building with its painted door and clean windows, but, curiously, the effect was of seeing it from a distance, or a great height; it implied perspective. To look at the image was to understand that we are mortal, all of us, and that in the moments we know this, we're afraid, and that when it comes down to brass tacks, this fear doesn't inspire sonnets or arias or Impressionism so much as it does the determination to do very well the small habitual thing we do every day: keep house.

Brass tacks. If those weren't the weapons of a housewife, what were?

In the year after Luke's death, Will's father made a pilgrimage up and down and all over New York, Vermont, Connecticut, New Hampshire, even up as far as Augusta, Maine, taking photographs of funeral homes, small mom-and-pop places, each image composed so that the viewer saw the business as if he had hesitated on the sidewalk, paused to take a breath, gather resolve, say a prayer: whatever was required to prepare himself to walk the path and ring the bell. This was as far as Will's father ever got—*I thought I could but I can't*—and over and over, in one city after another, he recorded the same moment, a failure for which Will can't fault his father because he finds it quintessentially human: brave, but not enough to go inside; intelligent, but not enough to understand; awake, but not enough to be entirely conscious. Filled with love, but not enough to overcome fear. Made in the image of God, perhaps, but, if so, like a fifth-generation photocopy, or the fax of a fax of a fax, so that even the outline is approximate.

Daniel has asked Will if he is angry at his father for not going inside McCaddam's, and he's told him no. In fact, while looking at the photographs his father has made of funeral homes, Will has been overwhelmed not by anger but by love for him, and the feeling has arrived physically. Deep under his ribs, he's felt something he imagines like the crease made by folding a sheet of paper: a sensation, almost pain, that's shown him a place he might tear more easily.

Across the table, his father is buttering a slice of bread. "I'm standing there, my hands in my pockets, thinking I don't know what, probably that the mayor's not even five feet tall, and the guy says to me, 'Did you intend for them to be religious images?' He stands there, looking at me with his arms crossed, waiting for me to expound."

"What'd you say?" Will asks.

"Nothing. Smiled like an idiot." He shakes his head, opens the wine list.

"Did you?"

His father looks up. "Did I what?"

"Did you make them out of some religious impulse?"

He shakes his head. "That's not the way I think of them."

"Then how? How do you think of them?"

"I don't." His father shrugs. "I see them, that's all."

Will nods. "He still there?" he asks after a minute.

"Off and on. Went back to his place but seems to have left things behind, has to keep coming around to look for them."

"Does he work?"

"Dermatologist."

"Geez," Will says. "Everyone's a dermatologist."

"No, they aren't. What's that mean?"

"Nothing. I guess I was thinking of someone I ran into last summer, a woman who's become a prominent dermatologist."

"Who's that?"

"No one. A girl I was boffing twenty-five years ago."

"You know what you want?" his father asks him.

Will looks over the menu. "Free-range chicken."

"Glass of wine?"

He shakes his head. "Takes the edge off."

"Isn't that the point?" his father says.

"Yes, but I have a session at three, and even one glass makes me that much less, what, present, I guess." Will takes his glasses off and lays them on the table, rubs his eyes. "Even were I inclined to dull my edge, this wouldn't be the day to do it. I've got a couple of patients right now for whom I really have to be at the top of my game. Consistently at the top." He puts his glasses back on. "Well, one of them I just have to get rid of."

"What do you mean, 'get rid of'?"

"Refer to another therapist."

"Personality conflict?"

"No. She's out of control. I'm going to send her to a woman."

"How come?"

"Long story. Well, not that long. Begins treatment because she has a history of compulsive promiscuity. That's what she says, anyway. *Promiscuity* is my word, not hers. 'Collecting' is what she calls her pattern of staking out older men and enticing them into sex. It's about power more than sex, her ability to seduce."

Will's father frowns in concentration. "Hookups," he says. "Sex for sex's sake. No emotional entanglement."

"Right," Will says, "exactly." Every once in a while his father makes an observation meant to prove he's not out of touch, leaving Will feeling less impressed than protective of whatever inspires this earnestness, because this is the quality that's most palpable when his father produces what he believes to be evidence of his being hip, or, as he'd say, "in the know," and it's the same quality that insures he'll never be hip.

"She's very flirtatious," Will says of the girl. "Which, ordinarily, isn't an issue. A lot of patients flirt. Some can't convey affection or even respect without using a vocabulary of implicitly sexual words and gestures. But this is different. Deliberate. Conscious rather than unconscious. She spent an entire session giving me an unnecessarily and provocatively detailed account of how she came on to a professor she picked up at the place she waitresses. I'm talking explicit. There's nothing this girl doesn't say. No physical transaction she won't fully describe. Then, at the end of the session she, uh—well, she kissed me."

"Kissed?"

"Kissed."

"How'd she do that?"

"Smoothly. Very, very smoothly. When I thought about it later, it reminded me of the time I got mugged by that kid on the bike. Remember my telling you about that? Came up from behind on the sidewalk? Just glided in front of me, cut me off, and caught me in the angle he made with his bike and the wall. Expert, almost choreographed. Same thing with this girl. As she's leaving, she pretends to have trouble with the doorknob. Says she needs my help. I come over to where she's waiting, and before I even get to the allegedly problematic knob, she's doing it."

"Wow." His father whistles. "Doing it how?"

"Not chastely."

Will's father raises his eyebrows. "Sexual?" he asks.

"Definitely sexual."

"Mouth open?"

"And a lot of tongue."

His father smiles. "So what'd the doctor do?"

"Nothing. I didn't do a thing. She slipped out the door and left me standing there like some hormone-addled teenager." Will leans forward over the table, lowers his voice. "She put her hand on my fly, too, Dad, and I was clearly not, uh, unaffected."

To this, Will's father says nothing, and he doesn't smile. His expression, if he has one, is of judgment withheld.

"I see her Thursday," Will says. "I've called her already, left a message. Told her I was referring her to a couple of other therapists. Both women."

His father puts his knife and newly straightened fork to one side of his plate. Having been a veterinary surgeon, his handling of any small implement is dexterous, unusually graceful. "I guess you had better," his father says, and he says it again. "I guess you had."

Y ou know what's weird?"

"What?" Daniel asks.

"I'm dogged by the sense that I'm lying even when I'm telling the truth. Or especially when I'm telling the truth." Will shakes his head. "Not that I'm ever dishonest with you—I'm not. What I mean is, it's when I'm especially conscious of trying to tell the absolute truth that I feel most strongly that I'm lying."

Daniel frowns and shakes his head slowly, communicating Will's failure to make him understand.

"In here, I mean," Will says, "with you."

"Are you talking about omissions?"

"Omissions? Omissions of what?"

"I thought you were telling me—for a moment I thought you might be saying that there was more to the story of what happened between you and that patient. More than you'd reported."

"God no! Don't you think a French kiss and her goosing me is enough?"

"I'm sorry, Will. Please, go on."

Will stands. He paces in front of Daniel's desk, his hands in his pockets, agitating the coins and keys within. He stops in front of his chair and faces Daniel, but he doesn't sit. "In this room, talking to you, I am scrupulously honest. I know that. I'm as honest as I know how to be. But as soon as I've said something, or even sooner, while I'm still speaking, I'm flooded with the sense that I'm lying. I feel guilty. I reexamine what I've said. Succumb to doubts. It's as if everything I say breaks down under the pressure of my scrutiny. The whole idea of anything being completely true seems ridiculous."

"It is," Daniel says.

"I know. I know. Truth's a direction, not a destination. No capital *T*." Will makes a chopping gesture with one hand, lets it fall to his side. "That's not what I'm talking about. I'm not speaking philosophically or even analytically. I mean that I, literally, in the most pedestrian sense, feel as if I'm telling lies. Whoppers. And I'm not." He drops back into his chair. "Why?"

Daniel silently turns his unlit pipe in his hand. It's at least a minute before he speaks, and it feels to Will like ten. "I had a patient," he says, "who told me that each time as she prepared to come here, as she rode the train and walked from the subway stop to my office, she invented falsehoods she intended to tell me. Right up until the moment she was on the couch, silently she'd be embellishing intricate tales of abuse and perversion, of adulterous relationships with colleagues, of eating disorders she didn't have. Shoplifting. Setting fires. Pedophilia. You name it."

"And?" Will says when he doesn't continue.

"I wondered what you made of it."

"A defense. She overcame her reluctance to make herself vulnerable by imagining that she wouldn't reveal herself to you. Instead, she'd disguise her true neuroses with decoys, those she made up."

Daniel nods slowly, still frowning at the pipe in his hands. "That was my conclusion."

"But what does it have to do with me? With what I've told you?"

"Maybe nothing. But it seemed to me that her case offered us a hint."

"What is it?"

"There's no direct parallel. She rehearsed lies and told the truth. You intend to be truthful, and in fact you are truthful, but you feel that you're lying."

"So she fears being revealed, and I fear that no matter how hard I try, I'm not revealing myself?"

Daniel shrugs. He smiles at Will and lifts his hands over his desk, palms up, empty, holding no answers.

O n Little Squam Lake, in New Hampshire: a shingled summer cottage at the bottom of a track through the woods, a steep incline that made it impossible to walk toward the front door, especially if you were carrying something heavy, a suitcase or a bag of groceries. Gravity pulled you into a run, flung you at the house, which was long and low and filled with liquid, green light, sun reflected off water and filtered through trees in lush, midsummer leaf. They'd rented it for a month, sight unseen, through one of those minuscule ads in the back pages of *The New Yorker.*

A lake chart was tacked to the kitchen wall, where renters would be sure to see it. Originally, the chart had been black-and-white, but someone had amplified it with a red marker, highlighting certain rocks and shallows. With time, one wet season following on another, the ink had spread into pink aureoles, as if those places were charged with magic rather than danger. During the day, you didn't hear the lake tonguing the foundation. You heard outboard motors and the cries of swimmers; you heard neighbors laughing or arguing, the sounds of a distant tennis game, the percussive return of the ball broken by an occasional long pause when one of the players went off into the woods to retrieve it.

Will can picture the four of them eating dinner in that house, laughing, talking, helping themselves to more food, their faces flushed and shining, and he aches with sympathy for the family he sees, innocent of what's to come. The people at the table are like the cast of an expertly made movie—Will doesn't know them, not personally, not anymore; and it seems impossible to him that they are so carefree, that they don't feel something—anything—for how can destruction not announce itself, the way earthquakes and tornadoes are said to do with a peculiar, heavy stillness, a greening of the light?

But in that house the light was green already, and the family around the table saw nothing, not so much as a ripple on the surface of the lake. Did they miss it, a warning that only a more evolved species might perceive? A single high note, perhaps, out of the range of the human ear?

Outside, tied to the dock they shared with the neighboring cottage, was the Sunfish Will had rented in town. When the wind rose, the lake nudged it into one of the pilings. "Can't you stop that?" Carole said when he came to bed that night, the last night. Luke's last.

"Stop what?"

"The boat. Every time I fall asleep, it wakes me up." She spoke from under the pillow, where she'd hidden her head to muffle the keening of loons, the trickle and slap of the lake, the knocking of the boat. "Can't you tie it so it doesn't do that? I keep dreaming someone's come to the door. That I have to get up and answer the door."

"Maybe. I'll go out and see."

He stumbled on the steps leading down to the dock, mesmerized by moonlight on the lake, like countless sequins on the water's heaving black bosom. He retied the boat, pulled it snug so it wouldn't knock, and sat dangling his feet from the dock, listening for another of the loons' weird calls.

He was never a careless person. Particularly, he was never careless with the children, who always wore seat belts in the car, helmets when riding bikes, and life preservers on a boat. When he played baseball, Luke wore the chest guard he hated, but, as had been established by the misfortune of other families, a perfectly placed blow to the sternum could stop a child's heart. Luke was two when Will enrolled himself and Carole in a course called "Baby Life." Taught at a local hospital, it focused on infants and young children: what to do in case of a head injury, when to call Poison Control, how to recognize the onset of anaphylactic shock, and how to perform the Heimlich maneuver and CPR on small bodies. Health insurance; home insurance; trip insurance: maximum coverage never struck Will as too expensive. He paid to have his children's teeth sealed against cavities, checked their bodies for deer ticks every night after a day spent in the woods. Flu shots. Multivitamins. Antimicrobial soap. A water filter installed on the kitchen tap; fire alarms hardwired throughout the house; window guards on every window above the first floor. Regular maintenance on the car and the furnace.

A friend of Carole's had given her a joint as a little going-away present, and Will wasn't as enthusiastic about the gift as she'd expected. "Maybe we should just leave it at home," he said while they were packing.

"No," Carole said. "Come on."

"I don't know. Lake sports and dope—it seems like a bad combination."

"Will, it's not as if we're going to get stoned and go water-skiing."

To counteract any perception of himself as an uptight killjoy, Will was the one who suggested they smoke the joint. They'd been at the lake for a couple of weeks. The kids were in bed, and he and Carole were sitting outside on the dock. It was true what they said: marijuana was a lot stronger than it had been when he was in college.

Before they'd smoked even half the joint, they were lying on their backs reduced to monosyllables, holding hands and watching a sky spattered with stars they never saw in the city.

"It's . . ." one of them would say. Or, "I wonder . . ." But neither of them finished a thought, and the two of them laughed at each other, and themselves.

"Let's swim," Carole said after a silence so long that Will was lost in some genius theory that interpreted constellations as if they were messages rendered in a Braille-like language of luminous dots, sentences that shifted with the reader's vantage so that inhabitants of one galaxy received one message while other beings on other planets read something entirely different, allowing God an infinite combination of signifiers to manipulate, tailoring revelation to the particular needs of—

"Will? Let's go swimming."

"No."

"Please. Why not?"

He laughed. "Way, way too fucked up." A long pause.

"We could stand," she said.

"Stand?"

"Stand in the water. Instead of swim. We're not too fucked up to stand."

"Okay. But first can I tell you what I was thinking?"

"What?"

Will tried to articulate his theory of celestial communication but got no farther than drawing an analogy between stars and Braille dots before understanding that the revelation he'd experienced was itself a pattern of dots and therefore untranslatable into English. He stopped speaking.

"We could get naked," Carole said, enough time having passed that she'd forgotten whatever weird point Will had started to make.

"Yes. Let's."

So they stripped and dropped their clothes where they'd forget to collect them, and stood together in the shallows, bodies pressed tight, feet sinking into the cool, velvety ooze of the lake's bottom.

"We don't kiss enough," Will said when they pulled apart.

"Because we're in a hurry," Carole said. "We're always in a hurry."

"I'm not always in a hurry."

Carole laughed. "I am," she said.

"How come?"

"Greedy. I'm a glutton. An orgasm pig."

Will slipped a finger between her legs. "Because you can be. If men could have multiple orgasms . . ." He didn't finish the sentence.

"Then?"

"Death of civilization."

"Beginning, more like."

"Yeah?"

"Uh-huh. Because men would fornicate without stopping, and women would run things. We'd use you for stud, that's all."

"In that case," Will said, "let's go inside. I have to practice for the regime shift."

In the morning, Luke and Samantha brought their parents' clothes to the breakfast table. "Did you guys take your pants off outside?" Luke asked, frowning.

"Mom washed them in the lake," Will answered. "Like an Indian."

"Native American," Luke corrected.

"Right. Native American. Although I believe Native Americans refer to themselves as Indians."

"But so do black people sometimes call each other niggers."

"Excellent point." Will shook the arts section out of the paper and handed it to Carole.

"Anyway," Luke went on, "it's not true what you said about Mom washing clothes in the lake, because they're not wet, they're only damp from lying out in the dew." Will looked at him.

"Can't you stop being so smart for a minute? Eat some toast or something?"

It was later that day, about four o'clock, that Will woke from one of those disorienting daytime naps he never knows whether to consider a luxury or a mistake. "How about a sail?" he asked Luke when he came outside, figuring it might dispel the dull, hungover feeling that always overcame him after sleeping during daylight hours. Off the dock was a shed, and inside it old fishing rods, a tangle of mildewed tarps, a rusted shovel and rake, and a few life jackets, also mildewed. He chose the smallest for Luke; once he'd tightened the webbing belts it didn't seem overly large. His own was missing its plastic clasps, and so he tied the belts, using not one but two knots and making a show of the procedure as an example to Luke, a claustrophobic child who tended, surreptitiously, to squirm out of whatever he found confining. Luke rode miserably in a car, holding the seat belt's diagonal strap off his chest and away from his neck because if it touched him, it made him "sweaty," it made him "carsick," it made him "suffocate."

"Isn't it a little late for sailing?" Carole asked as they walked past her chaise on the way to the dock, and Will saw himself reflected in the mirrored lenses of her sunglasses. He didn't answer what was more comment than question, and she unscrewed the lid from the Coppertone bottle, reapplied it to her shins, and went back to what she was reading. When Will thinks of that scene, Carole in the chaise on the dock, he sees her with one of her lust murders. But this is wrong, anachronistic. They are a habit she acquired after Luke's death.

The Sunfish was not even fourteen feet long, white fiberglass with a wood daggerboard, a mainsail—no stay—striped red and yellow and blue. On the weekends the lake was crowded with others like it, a popularity granted by the boat's size and lightness, the simplicity of only one sail, and a kick-up rudder that made for easy landings on a beach. It seemed more toy than real boat, an invitation to the inexperienced, and the people who sailed Sunfish often had mishaps. They collided and capsized and lay their bright sails down on the dark water surrounded by woods, water that looked black no matter what the hour. From the dock Will had watched a number of accidents, all greeted with hilarity. Often the sailors were laughing so hard, hanging on to the hull, that it took them some time to right their boats.

It was one of those perfectly clear midsummer afternoons, the kind that require people without sunglasses to duck their heads—squinting wasn't enough. Even late in the afternoon the silver face of his watch was invisible under the crystal's hot stare. What—who—could stand up to the sun's relentless scrutiny? Only the water; the rocks and the hammock-sized spiderwebs; the trees on the shore, each leaf shining dark and impenetrable, mysterious; mushrooms glowing orange in the shadows; the heads of mallard ducks that glinted from the lake like giant cabochons. As for himself: soft, smudged, and apologetic, excluded from the light's benediction.

Why does he describe it like that? Was that how it was? He's been reading a book that attempts to explain the process of memory. Written by an expert on the nature of consciousness and the neurochemical impact of torment versus pleasure, the text summarizes the results of clinical trials suggesting that each time the mind revisits an experience, retrieving a scene from where it's stored, that scene is contaminated by the new context. For example, if, having attended a party that Carole missed, Will subsequently told her all that had transpired, who had said what and to whom, the next time he remembered the party it might seem to him that his wife had been there. He might be so sure that Carole had joined in conversations he'd shared with her only after the fact that he'd argue the point, willing to bet on his word over hers.

This adhesive property, the tendency of memory to incorporate what it encounters—like a stream of water carrying along silt, pebbles, lost lures, a message in a bottle, all that it passes over and through—applies to emotion, as well. A happy, sunny moment can darken if exposed to grief. A smell, like that of Coppertone, generally evoking languid contentment, can become its own opposite, summoning anxiety and dread with notes as clear and loud as Pavlov's bell.

They got in the boat, and once more Will checked Luke's jacket. They waved and called good-bye to Carole, who was still trying to read, and to Samantha, standing by her mother's chair with a mud patty in her hands. "No, honey," he heard Carole say, "not on the chair. Put it in your bucket." Trying to come up with something, anything, that might occupy a five-year-old while she skimmed another paragraph, she asked Sam to fetch a plastic cup of water and pour it on her feet. "Mom's toes are so hot and thirsty. She needs you to water them."

They crossed the lake, laughing because it was so much fun and so effortless. Will had the tiller and Luke sat, leaning when his father told him to lean, closing his eyes to give himself more completely to the acceleration. It felt as if they were riding a few inches above the water, on air, and trusting his ability to recall the lake chart, the position of those pink-ringed rocks, Will continued on around the little island in the middle of Squam, beyond the part of the lake he'd sailed before. Despite the sun, it was cold on the water, and Will was glad he'd nagged Luke until he put on a sweater. Even so, the boy's lips were blue. It was time to go back. Will said, "Come about," and reminded him to get out of the way of the boom. Luke had had three sailing lessons—Carole enrolled both children in a beginner's class when they arrived in town, and he knew the basics—

but before they could change direction the prow struck one of those submarine rocks outlined in red on the lake chart in the kitchen. Scale, scale, Will thought. Had he never checked the scale? The lake must be larger than he'd known, much larger, the rocks farther from the shoreline.

As they capsized, there was a moment when Will and Luke touched. A part of his son glanced across Will's face, his thigh, perhaps, because his torso and arms were covered, and Will has the distinct memory of bare skin warm and smooth against his mouth, like a violent kiss, an indelible instant to which Will has returned again and again—how many times, he wonders, were he to add up all the waking and dreaming moments in a year? Say an average of ten per day, times 365 days, times three. 10,950. And yet ten seems to him a fair, even conservative, estimate. The rate having decreased from fifty or maybe even a hundred times a day in the first weeks and months to now, when occasionally a day passes without his revisiting the accident. Progress, he thinks, when he notes such a day, the note being itself a reference, but secondary.

"Not direct," he reports to Daniel. "And this is good. I know it's good, it's right, it's what Luke would want. But"—he stops until he's able to speak again. "It's . . . it's as though I've abandoned him."

"Will," Daniel says. "Will. Can you not counsel your own best self as you would a patient? Can you not be grateful for whatever resilience you possess?"

They surfaced on opposite sides of the Sunfish—at least Will thought they did. Even without his glasses—he'd lost them when they capsized; he wasn't wearing the Croakies Carole had bought him, the elastic strap that might have kept them on—he could see

Luke's orange life jacket in the water just beyond the boat, and he swam for it, afraid Luke had been knocked out, because he couldn't see him kicking and he didn't answer when Will shouted his name.

As he swam he reviewed the basics of CPR for children. Check for breathing, check for pulse—it could take him as long as five minutes to get him to the shore, then, if—God forbid—if there wasn't a pulse, if he didn't breathe, please God don't let that happen. But if, oh God, if it did, then onto his back on a flat surface, lift his chin, tilt his head, open his mouth. Check for an obstruction in the airway—no more than a minute's grace by then; he would make it enough, there wasn't a choice. Pinch the nose closed and breathe into the mouth, lips sealed around lips, and look to see that the chest rises with each breath. Then find the right spot: two fingers' width above the xiphoid process, and with the heel of his hand on that part of the sternum—never press on the xiphoid process itself, a rib could tear away from the notch of cartilage, it could puncture a lung—he'd push down, gently and firmly, straight down, no more than an inch. Then release. Press and release. Press and release. Five compressions, five seconds apart, and another breath, a slow breath, just enough to see the chest rise.

But when he got to the life jacket, it was empty. Unbuckled. As was his habit, Luke must have undone it while his father was occupied with sailing the boat. Too clearly, Will could see his son, unconscious, sliding from the jacket's embrace, down below the surface, dragged by sweater and shoes.

"Luke!" He called the name over and over, and when he paused to breathe, he heard children, the antiphon of a distant game of Marco Polo. Marco? Marco? Then someone, far away, answering Polo.

It used to be, when Will thought about the accident, that he brought his hand to his mouth, not a gesture of shock or even grief but an attempt to conjure the sensation of flesh glancing off his lips. At times he did this over and over, not purposefully—he was never really conscious of the act and, on occasion, performed it in public— on the subway, sometimes, or while listening to someone on the other end of the phone. Once, at a dinner party, Carole pulled him aside to tell him to stop. It disturbed people, she said, and not without reason. "I know what you're doing, but they don't," she whispered.

There was a dog on the shore, and the dog was barking. A man came out of a house and called to the dog, but the dog wouldn't come. The man yelled, *Nine-one-one, nine-one-one,* a message for him, Will assumed, a question. *Yes! yes!* he yelled back, and the man disappeared; presumably, he'd gone inside to dial.

It was more than an hour before anyone called Carole. Later, she told him she'd seen the rescue boat cross from one side of the lake to the other, and when the phone rang she was watching from the dock. She was wondering what had happened, and to whom.

Will buzzes in his three o'clock—that is, he buzzes in someone he thinks is his three o'clock but, as announced by her distinctive, staccato ascension of the uncarpeted stairs, it's the girl. It's been three weeks since he terminated treatment with her—since he told her what she has not accepted. Instead she's hounded him with messages and voice mails, some polite and beseeching, a few bordering on abusive. She's even called his home number, spoken with Carole.

"You have to leave," he tells her now. "I'm expecting a patient."

"I have to talk to you."

Will inhales deeply, lets the breath out through his nose. "My—we don't have anything to talk about. We are no longer engaged in—"

"No," she says. "You don't understand. I need to talk to you. Please." The look on her face is one of what appears to be genuine desperation.

"Have you contacted either of the people to whom I referred you?" he asks her.

"No. No, I—"

The buzzer buzzes, and Will pushes a button by the light switch to release the lock downstairs. "My three o'clock," he says. "You have to leave now."

"I'll wait," she says.

His patient starts up the stairs; the girl starts down; as they pass each other, the patient averts her face in the usual manner of an encounter at the analyst's office: deferential, blind. As Will closes the door behind her, he sees that the girl is sitting on the landing downstairs, rummaging in her backpack.

When he looks out his door at 3:50, she's reading.

"What can I say to help you understand that we cannot continue to work together?" he says as soon as his patient has left the building.

"Please," she says, coming up the stairs. "Give me another chance. I don't know why I pulled that shit. I know I behaved badly, but I promise nothing like that will ever happen again." Will watches her face as she speaks. Either she's sincere, or she's an actress with genuine talent.

"It's best—best for you—to begin over again, with someone else."

"I don't want to! I can't. I swear I can't. Please!" Will doesn't answer. If only she'd stop saying "please" like that. Mitch could always get him to do anything if he just said "please" enough times. Will's impulse—his determination—was always to even things up between the two of them.

"Please forgive me," the girl says, striking at this vulnerability with the accuracy of a mind reader. "We can start over."

"Our professional relationship has been compromised. Compromised in a way that would lessen my effectiveness in treating you."

"But why can't what happened be part of what we talk about? Wouldn't that be, like, useful? Useful in figuring out what makes me do these things?" Will doesn't answer her, and she throws herself onto the couch. She's wearing a pair of trousers that are, he guesses, a kind of commentary, or protest. Made of camouflage material in which the army greens and browns have been replaced with bright

pinks and purples, their legs are absurdly wide, each one sewn from
enough fabric to upholster a chair. "I don't get why you're making
such a big deal about this," she says. "You act like I stabbed you or
something."

Sitting cross-legged, the girl takes off her pullover the way a little boy might, by grabbing the scruff of its neck and dragging it over
her head, making her hair crackle with static. Underneath is one of
those sleeveless undershirts commonly known as wife-beaters. Her
bra, visible through the sheer fabric, looks like the top of a bikini; it's
striped blue and white. She reclines, arms behind her head.

"Please do not lie on my couch."

"Because I'm not your patient?"

"Yes." Will turns his back on her, and on the little surge of panic
he feels, dismissing it as claustrophobia. Across from his office, someone turns on the light in the dance studio. A few students enter and
begin stretching. Will twists the Lucite wand that adjusts the blind;
he turns around to tell her once and for all to go, good-bye, good
luck, but what he sees stuns him into silence.

"Put on your clothes," he says as soon as he's recovered his voice.
"Put them on now."

"No."

"Yes," he says. "Or you'll have to leave without them."

"What are you going to do? Drag me out into the street? That
doesn't seem like such a great idea, actually. I mean, all I have to do is
start kicking and screaming, right?"

Will opens his mouth, then closes it. If she screams, if she accuses
him of assaulting her, then what? He has no witness to prove otherwise. She takes a compact from her backpack and consults the mirror
within, considering her reflection. Paralyzed, he watches her. She's
still young enough to be caught instantly by her own reflection,
caught and consumed. She stares into her own face, licking her finger

and rubbing at the makeup smudged under one eye, and Will—as is his tendency when threatened—responds by hyperanalyzing the situation, sure that in the moment she's forgotten him.

Wouldn't that be the appeal of an affair with a much younger woman? All those times she didn't understand or even notice you, and the attendant freedom from having to work constantly at interpreting pregnant silences and meaningful glances, all the weary, oft-traversed terrain of marital responsibility. And it's not just Will. It's the same with every patient, every marriage: an unlimited number of dialectics leading to the same disagreement. To each couple its own insoluble, often inarticulable conflict. If you discounted lust—which would, of course, be a mistake—the key motivation for infidelity might be the chance to bed a woman who didn't engage reflexively in the fight you'd fought so often before, the Rome of every conjugal union, the one to which all quarrels lead.

And what's his own? The psychic equivalent of an earthquake or tidal wave, Luke's death revised the landscape of his marriage, shoved aside the mountains he and Carole had made of molehills, filled in the old quicksands and quagmires and rabbit holes. And, yet, how long did it take, really, before he and Carole began to redraw their respective maps, excavating paths they used to travel? No matter how a fight begins, still it always arrives at a point that reminds Will of one of those Starship *Enterprise* doors that slide quickly and silently shut, separating one of the *Star Trek* crew from whoever is on the other side.

What is it with him? Why is he subject to these damningly juvenile references, consistently failing to produce the Proustian allusions such situations demand? Or forget Proust, he'd take Updike, Chandler, Norman Mailer. He would, except that his wife does happen to remind him of Dr. Spock: evolved, intelligent, a being of one mind, never two (let alone more), not quite, it would appear sometimes, human. And yet, those redemptive glimpses of emotion, of her poise breaking down every once in a while into irrationality. As for Will, prey as he is to lust, he's stuck being Captain Kirk, whose gold uniform always made him look that much more like a man losing a battle with his appetites. That insatiable, wolfish squint. With Carole it's only so far and no farther. Will is scripted as the one who knocks; she as the one who may not answer. He leans forward, she leans back.

"What is it with you?" Carole says if he tries to articulate this dynamic. "You invent problems that don't exist. You're a conflict junkie."

"No, I'm not."

"Yes, you are. You absolutely are. It must be recreational for you. Or you can't stop working—you come home but you're still at work. Your head's still at work. Righting wrongs. Except in our case there isn't one. There's only what you imagine as a problem."

On and on they go. They might never stop but for exhaustion, and sometimes it strikes Will that this might be the glue of marriage, not just his but everyone's: both partners continue to show up for battle, helpless to resist it. Perhaps even eager for the comfort of it, the familiarity: this is our fight we're fighting; this is who we are; this conflict defines us; it makes us different from the rest.

If self-knowledge is the goal of psychotherapy, identity must be its most intractable enemy. When Will fails a patient, when he can't move a person toward a more livable life, it's often because that patient refuses to relinquish his or her neuroses, even costly and dangerous ones. How can she, if whatever it is—anorexia, OCD, agoraphobia, pyromania—is part of what that patient relies on to recognize herself; if the illness is what gives the individual a means of picking her small self out of the terrifying, endless mass of indiscriminate humanity?

Will looks at the girl looking at herself. She may not be drop-dead beautiful, but her body comes close, very close. She snaps her compact closed and tosses it onto the pile of her discarded clothes. "What's the matter, Dr. Moreland?" she says, taking a step toward him. "Pussy got your tongue?" She's close enough now to put her hand on his crotch. "See?" she says. "I told you you liked me." Deftly, she unbuckles his belt, unbuttons and unzips his fly, and puts her hand against his cock, feeling how hard he is through his shorts before pushing and pulling his trousers down, underwear along with them.

Will stares at her breasts, at what strikes him as their almost impertinent defiance of gravity, the delicate color of her small, flattish nipples. Carole, by contrast, has big, ruddy nipples, sexy but in a very different way. She's nursed two children for a total of more than four years and in doing so reformed her breasts into flesh that is deferential, not pert but self-sacrificing, at once modest and unselfconscious. They're mammalian, he supposes; their attraction rests in the fulfillment of nature rather than in the conceit of beauty for a beholder. Although, in the end, isn't it just that the girl is young, Carole not so young, a simple animal fact that he has convoluted into a thesis?

Her legs look even longer unclothed, and her pubic hair has been barbered into a narrow strip. "Brazilian," she says, seeing him look there.

"Brazilian?" he repeats. He hears his own voice as if it's been brought to him long-distance, in the days before fiber-optic cable, delayed as if it were an echo.

"Yeah. A Brazilian wax. You know? As in J sisters?"

"Jay sisters?" Maybe he really can't talk anymore, only parrot one or two words.

"Yeah. J as in the letter *J*. I thought everyone in this city knew about the J sisters. Where the bikini wax was, like, invented? At least for Norteamericanas." She lifts an eyebrow at him.

"Skip Brazil," she says when he still hasn't replied or moved so much as an inch from where he's standing. "Think of it as your landing strip." She sits and pats the couch next to her. "Why don't you take a step closer because . . . well, your cock's big, but no one's is that big." She takes him in her hand, guiding him forward. "Cold hands, warm mouth," she says, and then he's on his back on the narrow, black leather couch not even seeing the ceiling, not even seeing, eyes open and blind because of what she's doing. Between his legs, with her teeth, gently—gently enough—she's nibbling along the shaft of his cock, her tongue hot and slippery and all over the glans, the root of it in a tightening ring of thumb and forefinger and—"You just have to . . . you have to stop," he forces himself to say, "just—stop. Please. Don't move your mouth. I . . ." But instead, she picks up speed, tightens her grip, and he comes fast, feeling it up to his neck, those last strokes or licks or sucks or whatever it is that she did, every atom of him concentrated into one accelerating charge. "Oh God, oh Jesus, oh—" and Christ, she doesn't break stride, doesn't even flinch. She's a swallower, heaven help him. Different, not better, just different from Carole. His wife's less predatory, but that's just a—

"Okay, now we fuck." Will picks his head up to look at her, back at work lest he get soft. She's keeping the blood in his cock with some twenty-first-century tantric vacuum trick. Not a little-girl pout, after all, he—

"Check," he pants. "Check—"

"Check what?" She sounds irritated by the interruption.

"Door."

She stands to let him up from the couch. "I think we better get down on the rug, anyway," she says after he's ascertained that the door is, in fact, locked. She points at the couch. "Too narrow," she says.

As soon as he lowers himself to the floor she takes his cock in one hand and plants the other in the middle of his chest and pushes until he's flat on his back. Less than a minute in her feverish mouth and he's hard again, as hard as before. She straddles him and starts moving, back arched so that her pelvis is tilted into the shaft of his cock and going at it hard enough to make him ache. "Do I have the right tempo?" she asks, clearly uninterested in his response to a question that's just knee-jerk sexual etiquette, no more personal than saying bless you to a sneezing stranger. He watches her face, her eyes open and glassy, preoccupied by what she's doing to herself with her fingers.

She comes again and then once more, each time arching her back to pump him until it hurts. He searches her eyes, finds them empty. Not that he'd expected affection, or any other emotion, just some indication of pleasure. But she looks businesslike.

"Your turn on top," she says, "but only if you promise not to come. Not yet. I might want to go back to this. And I don't want to skip all fours." She lies on her back and slowly guides him into her. She's unbelievably wet and tight and impossibly, almost unnaturally, slippery.

"Astroglide," she says, reading his expression.

He stops moving. "What?"

"I used some—a lot, actually—while your attention was, let's say, elsewhere."

"A lot of what?"

"Astroglide?" She lifts the last syllable into a question: You're so last season / last year / last century that you've never heard of Astroglide?

"What's that?"

"Some super-poly something. Poly-propyl-glycerin-glyco-blah-blah-whatever. Lubricant, but different from that old K-Y junk. This stuff's for real. Better than spit. A triumph of science over nature."

What happens when she's through with him? Will she move on, according to habit? That's what he's counting on, he realizes, that's what he's decided will happen. Having collected him, she'll lose him, lose interest, refocus on the next in her series of old guys. Maybe she'll leave afterward, and tell no one, and he'll get away with it, this transgression that's been forced upon him. Hasn't it? Already he's trying to figure out just how culpable he is in this. Whether he communicated his lust to her unconsciously but still intentionally. Whether the fact that he's as turned on as he is makes him guilty, no matter who initiated the sex. Whether his fear of being exposed and accused of attempted rape makes him dishonorable. Well, of course it does. She reaches over her head to where a little bottle with a white cap is lying on her camouflage pants, almost invisible.

"Check this out," she says. Before he can protest she has a finger in his asshole, all the way in. "Hey, relax will you? This'll be good. I know how to make this feel good."

Will closes his eyes. The only other finger that's ever been up there is the internist's, a quick rubber-glove (and, yes, K-Y) check of his prostate, neither man looking at each other and neither, he's quite sure, with an erection. But with her space-age product she's doing some kind of inside-out hand job—finger job, he guesses he'd have to call it—and it's . . . it is good. It's really, really good.

"Oh no," she says, "no no," just as he's wondering shamefully (meaning he's ashamed but he's still thinking what he's thinking) how suspicious Carole would be were he to introduce her to a little bottle of—

Out goes the finger, and she pulls away on the back stroke, rolls right out from under him. "Getting a little too close to the finale."

Will doesn't answer, jerked back from the precipice so suddenly that he's dizzy with teased lust; but it doesn't matter, she goes on talking regardless of his regression into a state of mute passivity.

"Here's the deal," she says. "First you go down on me. I want to get off at least three times. Then I'm still bottom, you're top, but this time it's from the back, hands and knees, and I want it in the ass with plenty of this." She holds up the bottle. "Don't worry. I'm clean. I always make sure. After that, when I tell you, we do vaginal but still on all fours and you fuck me, and you go deep—you're in as far as you can possibly get, until I come, which might take a little while, or it could be fast. We'll just have to see. The good news is then you're rewarded for all your hard work. You don't have to hold back any longer."

It's accurate to say that a lot of him feels good while somewhere on the periphery of himself he's aware of a slight, shivery sort of nausea, like the distant approach of a migraine or fever, that first warning of infection. "My God," he hears himself say to Daniel, "do you know what I've done?"

She tastes like no other woman he's encountered. Of course, he hasn't had his tongue between anyone's legs besides Carole's for seventeen years, and it's not as if he was some junior Casanova before, but something about this girl, maybe it's the Astroglide, reminds him of a low-calorie sweetener, sucralose or aspartame, a slightly puckery, syrupy savor like those old fluoride treatments he'd get at the dentist's office when he was a kid, anticavity gel leaking from the mold into his mouth, a gaggy trickle going down the back of his throat.

Her first orgasm is demure compared with the bucking and howling he expected; the second, after an intermission of less than a minute, a carbon copy of the first. The third he has to work for, resorting to a fail-safe, tongue-punishing technique that leaves his mouth ringing with exertion. She curls up so abruptly that it's a challenge to hang on to her, to keep his tongue in the spot he's found, the right spot, the one that makes her writhe and howl, a freaky, unfeminine noise, the kind of noise, frankly, he would have thought a woman couldn't make, but so sexy: throaty and wet, a low growl that rises octave by octave into a wail. As long as it takes for her to arrive at this climax, and as long as it is that she manages to ride it, there's no denouement: one minute she's curled up, spine lifted from the floor and her face twisted in a knot of concentration; the next she pops up and flips right over, pushing the Astro stuff into his hand before she settles into position on her hands and knees.

"Slather it all over," she says. "Enough so you're, you know, really slick, and put some on me, too. You don't have to put your finger in or anything. I mean you don't if you're squeamish. If you're not, it's okay by me."

Will squirts the clear, colorless stuff on himself, a line of mustard on a hot dog, more than enough, it turns out. He uses his shirttail to wipe some away, otherwise he'll never achieve any friction at all. He holds his breath and pushes in. The girl gasps, very softly, a whispered gasp, if there is such a thing, and he pauses, a bit too long, evidently, because she twitches in obvious irritation.

"Hey," she says. "How about, you know? Moving? It is supposed to be a form of, like, sex."

Will pulls back and pushes in, feeling the rush of blood summoned by the heat of her. She's tight, tighter than anything he's ever felt before, and beyond that close grip, the rest of him is in a hot, soft place, encountering no resistance, none at all. Hands on her hips, he's got the two of them in a slow back-and-forth, guiding her along the shaft of his cock as much as thrusting himself in, afraid to hurt her.

She's sweating; tiny glittery beads form on her shoulders and

spine, and she shivers; he feels the tremor under his hands. "Am I—
I'm not hurting you, am I?" he asks, but all the response he gets is a
huffing uh-uh. Or is it *uh-huh*?

"Keep moving," she says, and they go on until, as before, she
takes the opportunity to pull away on his back stroke, sliding off him
and onto her stomach.

"Are you clean?" she asks after a minute, sitting on her heels, her
back to him, breathing hard enough that he sees her ribs rise and fall.
"Just look all over yourself, will you? On the underside, too. Because
you have to be, like, totally clean." She walks forward on her hands,
back in position.

"All right," he says. "I'm . . . I am."

"Go on, then. Use more glide if you want."

After so many and so deliberate a sequence of preludes, intercourse itself seems an afterthought if not, by definition, an anticli-
max. As with all that preceded it, Will has no sense of any choice, and
when she says "Deeper!" he thrusts deeper. Ditto faster, ditto slower.

He's stupid with sex, or maybe the right word is *stuporous*. When
she comes, moaning, the noise startles him, as if he's forgotten what
they've been doing. His own orgasm, produced dutifully, is silent,
second-class, undeserving of sound effects.

They both lie on the carpeted floor, saying nothing, she on her
stomach, he on his back. He closes his eyes and is instantly asleep.

7:07 by the digital clock on the desk. Will sits up.
"I'm leaving," he says. He stands to gather his clothes, and the abrupt
ascension makes his head reel so that he has to sit back down on the
couch. When he looks at her, she's sitting up, her left cheek bearing
the impress of the ringed fingers she laid it on. She tilts her head to
one side, scrubs at her eyes with her knuckles.

"I keep expecting you to guess who I am," she says. "I don't know why. For some reason it seems so obvious. Like it should be obvious to you."

Will is bending to retrieve a sock from under the couch. Something is about to happen, he thinks to himself, remembering that before they began, he'd had the sense, for a second he did, that he was failing to save himself, protect himself, to say nothing of his wife, his family, from getting shanghaied into a fateful—perhaps he means *fated*—voyage.

Something that will change everything is about to happen, Will realizes. But no thought follows this one, which disappears, sinks without leaving even a ripple on the smooth, reflective surface of his consciousness. He pulls on the left sock, then the right, and sits up, a hand on either knee. He makes a dizzy survey of the content of his own head, everything bent and inverted like the picture in one of those convex mirrors placed in a hairpin turn. But that kind of warning works only reflexively; allow yourself to engage with what's in the shining orb, try to think your way toward correcting the reflection's backwardness and distortion, and it's too late: you've already crashed.

The girl stares back at Will, whose thoughts tumble forward, pulled by their own momentum and the logic, or illogic, of undirected association. *Free* he'd call it, talking to a patient, as in free association, an exercise at which he's always been particularly bad because of his hyperactive intellectualizing. But for the moment something—adultery?—has incapacitated the rational part of his brain and, as if he's lost his footing on a hill, he slides from one image to another, from the round mirror in the road to the one his mother used to set on the holiday table. Meant to represent a frozen pond, on its shiny surface she arranged a set of lead figurines, tiny people dressed in furs who skated, danced, and trimmed a tiny tree. One rode behind another on a bobsled no longer than a matchstick. Each year their father made a wreath of holly to disguise the mirror's edge. "Poisonous," he'd say. "Remember the berries are poisonous." Invariably, their mother would add, then, that lead was poisonous, also.

"Who are you?" Will says at last. Again that distance and delay in his voice, as if he'd taken an international trunk call from himself. His head feels like a filled balloon, at once empty and under pressure.

"Jennifer."

"Jennifer?"

The girls nods and gives him a mild, almost social smile, as if they've only just been introduced. "You know. Elizabeth's daughter?" She reaches up and pulls a strand of hair from her head, holds it out to him. "You wanted one of these?" She gets up from the floor, still naked, and takes a step toward where he sits on the couch, the single strand pinched between her thumb and forefinger. "Here," she says. "A little present from me to you." Will doesn't move. The single hair hangs in space, glinting, a tiny filament blowing to one side, pushed by an air current too small to feel.

"Don't you want it?" After a minute she drops her hand to her side. "The thing is," she says, "even if you do have the DNA analyzed to compare mine with your own, and even if it does match, you still won't know."

"I won't know." His words are neither question nor assent, just an echo of hers.

She shakes her head, continues as if this were ordinary small talk, words exchanged in a waiting room or between bites of a sandwich. "No. Because twenty-four years ago—twenty-five, I mean—my mother was sleeping around. But that's not the point. I mean, she's not the point, her sexual mores aren't. The point is that when you were having sex with her, she was having sex with four men. You. Paul—that's my dad. A guy called Tim DeAngelo." She counts them off on her fingers, leaving the last one up. "And Mitchell Moreland."

"Mitchell? My . . . my brother Mitch?"

She nods, expressionless. "Your twin brother." Her voice, too, is without affect, flat. As if what she says is so unremarkable that it summons no inflection. "Whose genetic material is the same as yours."

She stands and rummages through her pile of clothing until she finds her underpants. Styled like boys' briefs, they're red with a fly piped in bright blue. On the butt is a silk-screened picture of a waitress with a tray. Underneath, a caption reads "Patsy's Oyster Bar." She pulls on her socks, then her black sweater and voluminous pants, leaves her bra lying next to her boots. Will watches her dress, saying nothing. He has a hot feeling in his head, behind his eyes. Not a headache but a . . . a what? He doesn't know.

"The way I figure it, if you don't have the hair tested, the odds of my being your daughter, biologically, are one in four. If you do have it tested, you either find out, first, that we're not related at all or, second, that I'm maybe your daughter, maybe your niece. And if it's the second, since both the potential fathers have the same DNA, nobody will ever know whose I really am." She sits on the floor to pull on her boots, crams her bra into her backpack. From the outer pocket she takes an envelope and hands it to him. "Just the way you wanted it. A hair taped to an index card." She swings the backpack over her right shoulder. "Bye," she says.

He's still staring at the envelope, sealed and addressed in green ink to #39, when a pair of feet come drumming up the stairs and someone knocks at the door.

"Who is it!" He stands at the door listening carefully. What else could she possibly want?

"Hey!" she says, loudly, almost yelling. "I forgot my coat." She pushes past him to the closet, jerks the sleeve of her long suede coat so that it comes off the hanger into her hands. She drops her backpack to put the thing on, and again he finds himself staring at the grease stains around its pockets, remembers—it seems a year ago—having interpreted her slovenliness in a sexual light. She fastens a button as she walks out. The metal hangers are still chiming together as the door sighs shut behind her.

An hour later, Will is lying, fully dressed, on his couch, rubbing one thumb on the smooth black leather that matches that of his emblematic Eames chair. He's in shock, or something like it, a feeling that reminds him of coming home from the dentist's and touching the part of his face that hasn't awakened from the Novocain. The way the information from his fingertips argues against that from his brain, insisting that the warm skin and stubble of beard belong to someone else. He tries to scroll through all the surprising revelations that have been uttered in this room, crises created and/or endured by the people who have lain on this same couch. Surely some must have been as bad as this. But he can't remember them. He can't think of anything, can't address one issue—the possibility of incest—because others keep interrupting. The betrayal by his brother, by Elizabeth. His own betrayal of Carole, of himself. Even of the girl, a girl who was a patient and whom he failed to protect from herself. Elizabeth, too, in a way. He should have suspected. Known. Why didn't he?

He sits up, elbows on knees, head in hands. Carole must be tucking Sam into bed about now. He called her and said he had a patient emergency and would be home late. He's given himself until midnight to pull himself together. Looking forward to that hour when one day turns into the next, when today will be yesterday. So unlike himself, the time miser—to want to hasten the clock.

What has he allowed to happen? It's—if it's true—it's the kind of scene familiar to audiences of Greek tragedies, a transgression both fated and unintended, proceeding from the hero's tragic flaw. But what is Will's? Aren't tragic flaws supposed to be a bit more grand than lust? After all, lust belongs to man's baser, more animal nature, it doesn't grasp for what can belong only to the gods. And was it lust that got him into this mess? Maybe it's whatever Elizabeth identified as his attempt to stanch grief with the fantasy of having fathered another child. What did she call that? Aside from a pathetic illusion? If only, please God, it could be. How he wants Elizabeth to be right.

He's just had sex with a girl who may be his daughter. She may not be, but if she is, according to the ancients, he's knocked the cosmos out of kilter. A blight on harvests. A blight on herds. A blight on women in childbirth. Plague and bloodshed. Athens wrecked. Jocasta in her blood-soaked bed. Right about now, in the wake of discovery, Will is supposed to be gouging his eyes out, or falling on his sword. What he's done—what he may have done—reduces adultery, only this morning a significant sin, almost to marital misdemeanor.

Unless Jennifer is lying, unless Elizabeth has lied to Jennifer, there's another betrayal: Mitch's betrayal of him, with Elizabeth. A hateful, perverse theft, to cuckold your own brother. Of course, if it's true, then Will has been cuckolded by Elizabeth, as well, but that seems a lesser insult. What Mitch has done is . . . It's just . . . it's . . . What is it? Will doesn't have a word for what he feels.

That it happened twenty-five years ago seems to make no difference. He's only just found out about it, so for him it's happening now, inspiring brutal fantasies of smashing in his brother's head, cutting off his perfidious balls. Anger so intense it summons the restless, coiled energy that demands violence, the feel of something— anything—yielding under his hands, even as it's short-circuited by something else: shame. Mitch, the brother he fought to protect, the person whose anguish he felt more keenly than his own—how can he think of hurting Mitch, killing him?

As if trapped in some awful carnival contraption, a Tilt-A-Whirl or whatever it is that jolts back and forth and up and down, Will lurches from horror to anger to shame and then back, whipped along a sickening emotional arc, unsustainable. In between scenes of violent dismemberment, his own and his brother's, his eyes for Mitch's balls, he keeps returning to the toast Mitch made at his wedding, the reference—suddenly less cryptic—to first girlfriends, and the bitterness in his brother's voice.

But that's nothing. Mitch's hostility that once seemed so intense, even threatening, it feels like nothing compared with Will's anger. Especially at the person who got him into this mess: himself. Why does he feel, though, that he doesn't know what's going on, exactly? Can it be paranoia that insists there's some worse something lurking beneath what's already a disaster?

mmediately, his own house is made strange to him. At the insertion of his key a new music tumbles from the front-door lock. Hinges keen, floorboards sigh under the weight of his feet. As he walks in, hours after midnight, Will is reminded of house hunting with Carole, afternoons long past, the two of them following real estate agents through one house after another, rooms that seemed as if they'd been evacuated by the arrival of catastrophe rather than for a prospective buyer. And, who knew, perhaps they had—not an earthquake, war, or epidemic, but the smaller, private cataclysm of financial ruin, divorce, a death in the family.

Lingering behind his wife and the agent, Will was so distracted by the evidence of other lives—titles of books on shelves, photographs hanging on walls, a series of framed paintings made by a child, Joshua, age eight, eleven, twelve—that he had trouble concentrating on the relevant features of whatever house they were considering. Kitchens, bathrooms, bay windows, walk-in closets, laundry rooms, skylights, coffin turns, pocket doors: he missed all of these as he hung behind to look at what had been pinned to the bulletin board by the door: memos, receipts, invitations, a snapshot of a child—Joshua?—wearing a fireman's hat, a list of names under the heading Thank You Notes, the first few crossed off.

Now, coming home—God, how did it get to be 3:47?—it's the same with his own house. *Who are the people who live here?* Will finds himself wondering as he walks through the living room. *Whose chair? Whose collection of inkwells gathering dust? Whose subscription to* The Atlantic?

A single plate rests in the drainer by the sink, and he picks it up, thinking of the long-ago couple who bought the set of blue and white china from Macy's Cellar, spending whole hours on a choice that made so little difference: What color? What pattern? The owners of the dish in his hands are people he no longer knows. In fact, it's hard to picture them.

I should eat something, he thinks, not at all hungry, but his head aches and he's dizzy; it's been fourteen hours since he had lunch. He gets out a loaf of bread and tries to find the jar of peanut butter, stands staring into the open pantry door, his hand on the knob, asking himself questions the real owner wouldn't ask.

Where would they keep the peanut butter? he wonders. Not we. They.

ronic," Will says to Daniel. "Don't you think? Carole grows up in a house where all these languages are spoken, inspiring her to devote most of her waking life to helping children learn to communicate effectively, and yet she herself turns out to be so cryptic and unforthcoming. I find her very resistant to revealing her inner life. There's a secretive aspect to her silences—whenever I ask her what she's thinking, she says, 'Nothing.'

"And then there's yoga, her downed dogs and one-legged roosters or whatever she calls them—I just can't help feeling suspicious of yoga. There's something so smug and self-satisfied about it. All these punitive-looking postures maintained for unnaturally long periods of time. Doesn't that imply—or require—a dedication to restraint, to being self-contained to a fault? The whole point of yoga, for Carole anyway, is to practice a kind of refusal to let down her guard. At least that's what I think it is."

Daniel, who is examining the end of his tie—a lustrous, pearly gray silk with small polka dots in different jewel-like colors—looks up at Will. "Have you always found her so opaque?"

Will takes off his glasses, replaces them on his nose, takes them off again. He's caught himself doing this lately, when he's with Daniel. Why? he wonders. Is he acting out some ambivalence about seeing clearly? "I don't know," he says. "I've asked myself if Carole seems more intent on maintaining—what?—not silence, exactly. I've wondered if she's more reserved since Luke's death, but it's impossible to say, for the standard reason—projection. Any answer I give is my answer. Reflects my loneliness rather than her intent to evade me. I know that."

Daniel nods, says nothing, folds his hands on his desk, looks at him expectantly. "What are we talking about, Will?"

"That patient?" Will says, surprised to hear the words. "The one who kissed me?"

"What about her?"

"I had sex with her."

Daniel's expression remains as it was: attentive, calm. "Before or after you terminated treatment?" he asks.

"After."

"Tell me what happened." Daniel betrays no more interest in Will's revelation than he would if Will were telling him what he'd had for lunch the previous day. "Huh," is all he says when Will has disclosed the whole mess, including Jennifer's announcement of his possible paternity. And then he says it again, "Huh." After a silence, he asks, "Have you told Carole?"

"No."

"Why not?"

"Well, for the obvious reasons. Cowardice. Avoidance of conflict. And I wanted to talk to you first. But also because, I don't know, I keep going over all the pieces, trying to figure out, I don't know what. It's all so weird. It feels . . . old."

"Old?"

"Old like it happened before. Like déjà vu. Arriving in a city where I know I've never been, and yet I could swear I had. Also, I don't know how to predict how Carole will react. If I knew what to expect, it might seem less impossible to tell her. But the more I think about it, the less sure I am where Carole is these days. I mean, she could flip, of course, and how would I know what that would be like? We've never had any real knock-down-drag-outs. Maybe we should have. What if she's weirdly understanding? That could happen. I mean, it's not as if I knew this girl was . . . well. And I've waited years now for Carole to lose it over Luke, and she never has. Shouldn't she scream at me or, or keen or . . . shouldn't she do something? It seems like it can't be over, Luke's death won't ever be over, until Carole reacts, really reacts. But she hasn't. So maybe she wouldn't react to something like this, either."

"What has your response been to her grieving so quietly about Luke?"

"My reaction to her nonreaction?"

"To her apparent nonreaction. You told me she cried a lot in the early months."

"Yes. Silently."

"Does that make the tears invalid?"

"It stresses me out! As if my head were this emotional seismograph—an affect-o-graph. Turned up way too high, sensitive to every minuscule mood vibration, pens scribbling all the time, reams and reams of fluctuations to interpret and parse and, and—I don't know what. All in the service of predicting when it's going to happen. When the fault lines split open and swallow up everything— marriage, child, careers, house, car. Annihilate us."

"Annihilate."

"Yes. Because I have to assume it's coming, the big one. It's delayed, that's all. It's only a matter of time before she blows. Because the longer it takes to arrive, the more forcefully she's repressed it, the more she's felt she had to repress. Thus the more intense and destructive it's going to be."

"Maybe you're wrong. Maybe she isn't going to 'blow.'"

"Maybe."

Daniel sticks his index finger into the bowl of his pipe, twists it around with a thoughtful look on his face. "Is it possible you let this happen to provoke Carole to anger? To get the dramatic response you crave? Like lancing an abscess?"

"But I didn't *do* anything. I mean, I told you. She took her clothes off, said she'd scream rape if I . . . maybe I should have . . ."

"Should have what?"

"I don't know. If I'd called the police or even just charged past her, out the door, she'd have framed me."

"All right. Say you were passive and compliant to avoid further persecution. Then why use words like *hidden* and *sinister*?"

"I wasn't . . . it wasn't a reference to myself so much as to . . . to this sense I have that I'm missing what's going on. Really going on."

"What do you mean?"

"I don't know what I mean." Will puts his face in his hands. "Lately I feel like I'm thinking so hard I'm doing damage to my brain. The actual gray matter. Like redlining a car engine. And to no purpose. Getting nowhere. Spinning wheels."

"All right, Will. As far as I understand it, what's happened is that you didn't effectively prevent a young woman, recently your patient, from manipulating you into sexual intercourse. You were not the aggressor, but you didn't stop it, either. And while you're anxious in the wake of betraying Carole—anxious about the possibility of incest and about sexual contact with a woman so recently in your professional care, angry with your brother, angry with your wife, you're also troubled by your own behavior. Worried that there are motives you don't perceive." He stops, looks at Will, who says nothing. "Is that a fair statement?" he asks. Will nods. "And yet today you began by talking about what you find is Carole's tendency to be withholding. But, in fact, it's you who are keeping a secret from her."

"I know. I know." Will shakes his head. "Embarrassing to be so obvious a case."

"Will?" Daniel interrupts a lengthening silence. "Where are you?"

"I was thinking about our different—I won't say conflicting—orientations. My insistence on parsing and interpreting and assigning meaning to everything, and Carole's tendency to just, I don't know. Live instead of think, maybe. Like she's discovered the trick of being rather than becoming."

"Becoming?" Daniel says.

"Yes. My whole life, my work life and my personal life, is devoted to this . . . this conceit of becoming. To helping people become better adjusted, free of neuroses and compulsions on which they squander their time and energy. Conscious, if they can't be happy.

"And consciousness—becoming more and more fully conscious—is what I want for myself. I accuse Carole of campaigning to evolve, but that's unfair. I'm just seeing myself. Just because she corrects impaired children's development doesn't mean she's bent on her own evolution. In fact, she never seems to struggle to attain her calm collectedness. She's not really any different from the young woman she was when we met."

"Why do you call it a conceit?"

"Call what a conceit?"

"Becoming. The idea of becoming."

"I don't know. I mean, obviously, I believe in becoming. But maybe the god I serve is false. Maybe I'm deluded."

"Maybe we all make our own gods, each as valid as the next person's."

"Uh-uh," Will says, "I'm not going there with you."

Daniel smiles at him. "Just because I'm an atheist?" he says.

He nods. "Did I ever tell you about our first date?"

"So that's why you're a speech pathologist," Will said to Carole. She'd just finished telling him about her father's death. She stared at him.

"Why?" she said, gray eyes wide in anticipation.

"Because." Will frowned. "Well, here you were in college, studying communications, and you had this, this articulate and gifted father, who has a stroke, a series of strokes and, having been a polyglot, a man who commanded ten, eleven languages, he loses his ability to speak. Loses it one language at a time, and dies unable to say a thing. Unable to say two words to his daughter—Happy birthday. Happy birthday, Carole. This accomplished and generous man, a translator and a scholar who helped so many other people understand one another, this father you adored, he died. And immediately you change your major, you go from communications—media—to speech therapy, so you can become someone, ultimately, who helps children who can't speak, who guides them at the very important beginning of their lives. These people, very young people, who can't make themselves understood, who come to you and falter in the same way your father did at the end of his life. They open their mouths and nothing comes out. Or the wrong thing comes out, a sound they didn't mean to make. And you've made it your purpose to change that, to help them—and thus yourself—toward a different outcome." Will stopped here, feeling quite satisfied with this interpretation, reductive though it might have been. The pretty woman across the table would understand him to be a sensitive and aware sort of male, the very kind, he hoped, who would appeal to her. Convince her, just possibly, to sleep with him. Maybe even that night, after dinner, dessert, another glass of wine.

Carole tilted her head to one side. "I never thought of it that way," she said.

"You didn't?"

She shook her head.

"But what other way is there to think of it?" Will regarded her with puzzlement. Here was a woman who worked side by side with social workers and school psychologists and family therapists and all the other energetic zealots who populated the landscape of secular optimism—and she made no connection between her father's being silenced and her own missionary pursuit of fluency? How was that possible?

"I don't know." Carole made a face, eyebrows drawn together, as if straining to understand what Will thought was so obvious. "I took this phonetics class, and I learned this system of . . . well, what phonetics is, is the discipline that breaks language down into phonemes, which are the smallest units of sound. Each has its own symbol, so a phonetic spelling of a word doesn't look like English. Anyway, I found it very clean and straightforward. It's transcribed in what's called IPA, for international phonetic alphabet, and I learned it easily, almost without effort. It was fun, that's all." She shrugged self-consciously at this admission. Worrying, perhaps, that he might judge her as shallow.

"So," she continued, "I began transcribing everything, all the notes for my other classes, in IPA. No one could borrow them—they didn't understand them. It was a foreign language, after all, a code, a set of signifiers. But it was easy, nothing like learning German, which I'd found so impossible. IPA was, I don't know, irresistible I guess. And I didn't resist it. I'd almost completed the requirements for a communications major when I switched to speech pathology, so I had to stay another year. Well, a year plus one semester." Carole put down her fork and picked up her napkin. She held it in front of her mouth, not dabbing but covering her lips, as if she were hiding them from him.

"Dessert?" he asked. "Another glass of wine?" Or maybe he offered her—he hopes he didn't, but maybe he asked did she want Armagnac or Remy or something he thought might imply sophistication.

She shook her head, still holding the napkin. He picked up the check and they walked together to her apartment, where he stood with her on the street for what seemed a long time, waiting for her to ask him upstairs. He doesn't know why, but it wasn't uncomfortable. He remembers that when he looked down, so as to take a break from looking at her face, he saw that her feet were aligned, precisely together, and her knees were, too. She held the strap of her handbag with both hands, one fist next to the other, both right in front of her crotch. And she looked right at him, smiling slightly, a friendly look that didn't seem expectant. Self-contained, Will guesses it was.

"Are you thinking about what I said at dinner?" he asked her.

"Said about what?"

"I don't know. Your father. The speech thing."

"No." She shook her head.

"What then?"

"Nothing."

He took a deep breath and held it, puffed out his cheeks, let it go in a gust. "So, uh—"

"Do you want to come up?" she asked.

"Of course."

She nodded, still staring at him in that disconcerting, almost detached way she had. "Are you prepared?"

"Prepared?" he said, confused.

She looked away and then back, conveying exasperation, but not in a hostile way. "Did you bring a condom with you?" Will flushed, not something he did often, but he felt as he had when he was chosen to act out an exemplary scenario for his junior-high health class. He'd never slept with a girl who wasn't on the pill or didn't have an IUD or a diaphragm. This was before safe sex, after all. What could it mean, her not routinely using contraceptives? Impossible that she was still a virgin.

"Do you want me to go with you to buy them?" Carole asked. She took his hand and walked him west along the block. "I'll stay here," she said when they went into the drugstore, and she began to look through a display of greeting cards. She pulled one out to read the message inside. He still remembers the picture on the front. It was Linus, drawn by Charles Schulz, and he was in midair, upside down, Lucy having pulled his blanket out from under him.

As a child, Will used to follow *Peanuts* with attention rather than pleasure, as if it might tell him something he needed to know. He cut out the little black-and-white daily strips, which always seemed more serious and instructive than the colored Sunday ones, and saved them in a binder, organizing them by topic and (as if unconsciously anticipating the reference manual of his as yet unknown career, the *DSM*) cataloging emotion as if it were disease. He called one section "The Effect of Unrequited Love," and there were also "Anger and Betrayal" and the thickest section of all, "Angst." He was twelve, a seventh-grader whose reading comprehension tested at college level.

"I wish I still had that binder," Will says to Daniel. "I'd like to look through it, assess its assessments. Even then I was trying to figure out what the fuck was going on. Figure out my brother. *Peanuts* isn't a very funny strip when you think about it."

And they were never really children, those awkward, tormented characters, hunched over Bible verses or Beethoven scores, as alienated by talent as by failure, pining for unavailable valentines, losing their kites, losing their softball games, quoting the Book of Luke on the birth of Christ, suffering gender dysmorphia and slavish devotion (Peppermint Patty and her weird little sidekick who called her Sir), dragging along their tattered transitional objects, waiting with Beckett for the Great and Nonexistent Pumpkin-Godot, and, in the end, seeking dismissive counsel at Lucy's five-cent psychiatry booth.

"So," Daniel says to Will, glancing at his watch—an abbreviated gesture, not to see the time but as a cue: ten minutes before the hour.

"So," Will repeats.

"Now what?"

"I guess I contact Elizabeth. Check the story out. Be sure it's all true." Will stands, hands in his pockets. "Then I'll talk to Carole. I'll call you. I'll keep you posted."

"Please." Daniel walks him to the door. "Next week?"

"Unless you think I've got my multifaceted crisis all wrapped up."

Daniel puts his hand on Will's shoulder, a gesture Will notes for its infrequency. Rarity. In this room, they do not touch beyond the occasional handshake. "Take care," Daniel says, squeezing the shoulder.

B ut she was. In New York City, in 1987, Carole was a twenty-four-year-old, post-sexual-revolution virgin.

"Really?" Will said, and then he said something ridiculous. "Are you sure?"

"Am I sure?" Carole laughed. "Yes."

Why? he wanted to ask, but he couldn't think of a polite way to put the question. In any case, what he meant was, *Why me?* What about him invited or allowed this . . . this what? Awakening? Rite of passage? But he wasn't going to ask that question either, lest her answer was to change her mind.

"I mean, I'm not completely without experience. I've . . . well, I've . . . I just haven't done that."

Will nodded. "The first time for me," he said, "I was fifteen."

"Okay."

"Okay?"

Carole looked away and then back. "I mean, I don't mind, if that's what you're asking. Does it matter?"

"No. No, it doesn't matter. And you, your . . . it's nice. For me, I mean. But . . ."

"But what?"

Will shook his head. "Nothing." He'd been going to say that he felt a burden of responsibility, but that wasn't the right thing to say either. "I just want to know if you're sure, that's all. Sure you want to do this."

"Yes, I am." Carole unbuttoned her shirt and shrugged out of its sleeves, stepped out of her shoes and skirt. She reached around her back with both hands to unclasp her bra. It was black; he remembers this because he'd expected it to be white, because of stereotype: didn't virgins wear white underclothes? But her panties were black, too, sexy against her white skin. Not only does he remember being aroused, he can almost feel the barely contained, wet-dreamy quality of that erection, intensified by the slightest stimulus, physical or imagined. She pushed the black panties down and sat on the end of her bed, knees together, and watched as Will untied his shoelaces, leaning over in her rocking chair so that it tipped all the way forward.

"Maybe you don't want the overhead light?" he suggested when he looked up. "Maybe a candle or something?"

"Okay." Carole stood. "I don't have candles. But I could turn off the overhead and leave the bathroom one on with the door ajar. That way, only a little would come in."

"All right." Will left his clothes on the chair and lay on her bed. Feeling self-conscious, he put the condom on her bedside table. Carole stood at the end of the bed for a moment, then she lay down next to him.

"Can we kiss for a while first?" she asked, breaking the silence. He nodded and pulled her on top of him, and then one smooth thigh was on either side of his cock.

"I'm going to be . . . I'm going to do the best I can," he said, pulling back from her mouth, and again she laughed. "I don't mean to be funny. I . . . I know this is the second time I've made you laugh. But, well, I was being sincere."

"It just sounded funny, that's all. Like taking the GRE or M-CAT's or something."

"I'd like . . . If it's all right with you, I'd like to touch you first."

"Touch me?"

"With my mouth." He put his hand between her legs. "Touch you here." She nodded and reached for the condom where he'd left it on the table by the bed. "What are you doing?" he asked her.

Carole sat up. "The books, um. I read a book that said I should . . . I mean that the girl, the woman, she should make putting the condom on part of foreplay. You know, so it's, uh, erotic."

"*The Joy of Sex*?" Will asked. "Was that the one?" Now it was she who flushed. "That's all right," he said. "I don't . . . I'll do it after, when I'm ready."

"I don't mind doing it."

"No, I . . . It's just that they're not sexy. Condoms aren't. So I'd rather do it. But not until after I do this." Carole lay back down, and he settled himself between her legs, nudging them farther apart with his shoulders. "Bend your knees," he said, and when she didn't move he took her, one ankle at a time, and arranged her on the mattress.

"Sorry," he said, after they'd made love and had rolled apart. "I didn't last as long as I wanted to." Carole pulled the blanket up, covering both of them. "I was, uh, I guess I was excited."

"More than usual?"

"Well, your being a virgin. I . . . I guess the idea of it, of your having never been with anyone before, it . . . I lost my, my restraint."

"That's okay."

"Was it—did it feel all right?"

"Yes." She rolled up against him, her cheek on his chest. "The thing is," she said, "what you did with your tongue felt so good that the rest was a little anticlimactic."

"No pun intended?"

"Pun very much intended."

"Why me?" Will asked after a silence, but the question came out wrong. He'd meant to sound grateful, not perplexed, and he worried that to her ears the question might have sounded worse than perplexed, even petulant.

"Why you what?" she asked.

"Why am I the first?"

"Oh," Carole said. "Because."

"Because why?"

"Because I'm going to marry you."

Will didn't reply. He was still trying to figure out her meaning— irony? romantic fantasy?—when she kissed his cheek. "You'll see," she said, and she turned over and went to sleep.

E lizabeth has agreed to meet him at Philadelphia's Thirtieth Street Station, a point midway between his home in New York and Baltimore, where she lives. They are to meet at 11:30, but Will's train arrives at 11:12, so he waits for her in one of the station's big pewlike benches, watching as clots of passengers emerge from the platform stairways. A few people move briskly toward one or another exit; others set down luggage and packages to consult the readouts on their cell phones, make calls, locate connecting trains on the departure board. Or they just stand, passive and expectant as children, awaiting the arrival of friend or kin, someone to collect and bear them away.

He hasn't told Carole where he was going and doesn't expect to be caught in his subterfuge. It's Thursday, so Samantha stays after school for a swim class that isn't over until 4:45. He plans to return on the 1:40, arriving at Penn Station by 3:00, so even a major subway snafu, like a stalled train or a sick passenger or a police chase, any of the menu of expectable daily disasters (assuming terrorists are lying low, plotting rather than acting) that could slow him down won't stop him from getting back home to pick Samantha up in time.

So far, Will isn't enjoying the discovery of how easy it is to exit his life without explanation, like slipping unnoticed through a secret portal, leaving one world, waiting to arrive in another. The ridiculous transporter from *Star Trek* pops into his mind, that shimmering column of a crew member in the moment when he's neither aboard the *Enterprise* nor reassembled on an unexplored planet but in the limbo of molecular disarray, a trembling, staticky silhouette. He tries to shove aside the thought of himself back home that evening, glancing across the room at his wife, trying to decide what to say as he searches Carole's face unobtrusively. On top of feeling sick about what happened with the girl, Jennifer, although he hasn't quite gotten to the point at which he can think of her by that name—a guilty, nervous nausea that intensifies when he's near his wife—he'll be that much more disturbed having disappeared successfully for these few hours. Assuming he is successful in his deceit.

11:35. Maybe her train has been delayed—a mechanical failure, or a human one. The word *stickup* pops into Will's head animated by Daffy Duck sputtering in cartoon fear, flecks of spittle flying everywhere. Why is it that the more agitated he gets, the more childish are the images that assault him, all of them dating back to afternoons spent with his brother, the two of them on the living room floor under the television's blue gaze?

Maybe she isn't going to show. But how could she not? Will's e-mail described a young woman with a pair of stainless steel studs on either side of the bridge of her nose, fingernails bitten to the quick, and a citation from Cicero's "First Oration Against Catiline" tattooed on her chest. Not even New York City could contain two such young women.

Almost six months have elapsed since the college reunion, months during which Will has changed from the man he used to recognize as himself. After fifteen years of negligible marital sins, those of omission, mostly—instances of laziness or lack of consideration inspiring the familiar wifely complaints—he's become not only an adulterer but possibly an incestuous father, a man whom almost every culture throughout all time would recognize as a criminal breaker of taboo. His chronic fear of seducing a patient has been obliterated by a set of new terrors resulting from having been seduced by a patient. For the first time in memory, Will can't get it up. The previous evening, after lying next to him in the dark for a few minutes, Carole sat up in bed and switched the light back on.

"So, uh, Will?" she said.

"Yes?" He was lying on his back, one arm across his face to keep the light out of his eyes.

"What's up?"

"I don't know," he lied. "I'm not feeling great, I guess."

"You mean you're sick?"

"No, not sick exactly. Sort of."

"Because—tell me if I'm wrong—but I think we've made out when you had the flu, I mean the real flu, that Coxsackie thing you caught from Sam, several sinus infections, strep throat, the back thing after the cab accident, innumerable colds, fevers, upset stomachs, et cetera. I can't remember your ever being sick enough to forgo sex." Will didn't answer. "Is there anything going on?" she asked. "Anything we should maybe talk about?"

"No," Will said, "not now. I'm just . . . I don't feel well. Can we turn off the light?" She did, and they lay there, awake but not talking for what seemed a long time. Both of them must have noted that it was Carole who pressed for dialogue while Will resisted—not a first, but very unusual.

And here's another distressing development: lately Will has caught himself immersed in sadistic fantasies of fratricide in which he goes after his brother with a blowtorch, or, in the more elaborately plotted scenario, drives a Humvee, one of those automotive paeans to testosterone, through the desert with Mitch chained to its massive bumper. Will forces his brother to walk barefoot as fast as Will chooses through a desert terrain, over blistering sand and rocks and cactus spines—the inverse of the environment of his expertise, cold water. Soon lamed, Mitch falters and begs, completely at his mercy.

Will slumps on the bench, rests his head on the wood back, exhausted by himself. Looking up, he sees that birds are flying inside the station. Its central hall is so large, the ceiling so high, that they appear content to swoop back and forth, gliding by the vast windows without succumbing to panic and diving against the glass panes. Directly over his head a shiny silver Mylar balloon is trapped in a ceiling coffer. Will dislikes these balloons and their forced, tinselly enthusiasm, the way they imply the inadequacy of regular balloons. And they never burst. Samantha got one on her last birthday, and the thing has remained in the house for months, floating at eye level, wrinkled and flaccid but still ascendant, somehow needling in its longevity, the way it persists in celebrating an occasion that even Sam has forgotten.

11:41, according to the oppressively large clock on the station wall, the slack middle of a weekday, without the bustle and press of commuters, and yet Will would have picked her out just as quickly from a crowd. She rises from platform 3 into the waiting area, her bright head gliding upward, carried along the unnaturally smooth trajectory of the escalator. When she steps off, she's standing in a long pale bar of sunlight that falls from one of the monumental windows. Without looking around, she turns herself in his direction, as if she knew by instinct which bench he would choose, and approaches with her characteristic walk, efficient and unhurried, her feet, in their low heels, striking the floor soundlessly. Her hands are shoved in the pockets of her belted black trench coat, which makes the color of her hair appear even more flamelike.

He stands, and she stops walking. Obviously she's decided against contact even as minimal as a handshake. Two yards—the length of a body—remain between them. "Elizabeth," he says.

"William."

"Why don't we sit over there?" He gestures toward the food court.

"Fine," she says, and she sets off in that direction.

He follows her through the concessions. "Do you want anything?" she asks. "Because I never had breakfast," she goes on, as if to justify the distasteful necessity of sharing a meal with him, "and by the time I get back to the unit I won't have had a chance to eat." Without waiting for him to answer, she takes two croissant sandwiches squashed under Saran Wrap and slaps them on a tray.

"What was it you said you practiced?" he asks, straining for a neutral prelude to what will be a necessarily unpleasant dialogue. "What kind of dermatology?"

"Burns."

"Burns. As in fires?"

"Or chemical. There's also the occasional idiot who pulls off the trick of a third-degree sunburn. I direct the acute-care facility at Johns Hopkins." Her voice conveys either surprise that Will can have forgotten an appointment of this stature, or her more general—and justifiable—irritation with him for having created a crisis that has interrupted both their lives and demanded the inconvenience of this meeting.

"Sorry," he says, "of course. I'm preoccupied. Lately, I mean." How clearly he can picture Elizabeth presiding over a room filled with those state-of-the-art tank beds, each holding a body suspended in some advanced regeneration gel. Suddenly, he remembers that the previous night (in anticipation of this meeting, no doubt) he dreamed of austere white-coated Elizabeth as she ministered to a body on a bed of unguent, a body so burned that it had no skin. And yet there was no blood, either, no unsightly, blistered bits or charred wounds. It was flesh as decorative as that of a transparent man in an encyclopedia.

"Well?" Elizabeth says. She shoves a waxed paper cup under a nozzle that pours Diet Dr Pepper over a few lumps of ice. This is his, evidently, because she moves on to a selection of tea bags, picking through them until she finds one she deems acceptable. She unwraps it with care, leaving the fragile paper envelope intact, drops it into a Styrofoam cup, and pushes a red button to discharge a stream of hot water onto the bag. Then she marches, with him in tow, to the cashier. "Your treat." She enunciates the word *treat* so sharply that it sounds as unpleasant and cold as, say, sleet.

The only unoccupied table is a large one with a big, striped umbrella planted in its center. "God, I hate that," Elizabeth says. "It's just too stupid. As if to fool you into thinking you're dining on some patio on the Riviera." She points at the chair opposite hers, an imperious gesture, employer to underling or professor to failing student. Three plastic saltshakers are lying on the table among a scattering of crystals, and she rights them in the center, brushes the spilled salt off with a paper napkin. Having spent only ten minutes in her caustic company, Will is already debilitated.

"So," he says, "I'd just like . . . I know time is short, but I'd like to quickly sum up my encounters with your daughter."

"Jennifer."

"Jennifer."

After saying the name they both look at each other in silence. "So," he begins after a swallow of Diet Dr Pepper. "Last month a young woman who calls herself Andrea, and who claims she's been referred to me by another of my patients, begins treatment for a specific problem. She describes a compulsion to seduce older men and characterizes her pursuit of these objects as driven by a rigid set of criteria. They must be no younger than forty-five. They have to be professionals, gainfully employed. Glasses are a plus; baldness, obesity, and hearing aids unacceptable. There's more, but you get the picture.

"As she tells it, it's clear that her physical satisfaction is secondary to the brief reassurance, or abatement of anxiety, that sex with these partners affords her. She draws an analogy between her sexual trophies and a collection of paperweights to which she was attached as an adolescent." Will pauses to underscore the paperweight allusion; Elizabeth regards him without affect, as if his face belongs not to a human being but to a clock or a speedometer, a tin plate under a veneer of paint. As they watch each other, Will feels a profound weariness, so leaden it's as if his substance, the stuff of which he's made, has changed without warning, his molecular weight doubled or squared so that gravity now presses him that much harder into his plastic chair. It's the moment when the twinkling silhouette disappears from the *Enterprise*, the transported body of whoever it was reassembled on a planet with an alien, possibly injurious atmosphere.

Elizabeth is still tilted forward in her seat. What's he doing here anyway? It's not too late, he can stand, apologize for inconveniencing this woman who has become, after all these years, a stranger. He can go home. He can, except that somehow he can't.

"Well," she says, "we don't have all day, William. I don't, anyway."

"So far there have been, the young woman estimates, thirty-eight of these seductions. A better word would be *transactions*, because the intercourse she describes is without emotional content. She has no interest in her partner's feelings; the sex is dispassionate; the partner fits a profile, no more, no less; this is the extent of his worth." Will watches Elizabeth sip her tea.

"I'm listening," she says, looking down at the unfinished sandwich on her plate. The part in her hair is very straight and pale, and Will thinks of the girl's bitten fingernails, the shiny pink flesh that rises around them, hot and swollen. "Angry," his mother would say of the bitten nails, as in "an angry cut."

In spite of his intent to banish them from his consciousness, the unfortunate tips of Jennifer's fingers have become an erotic snag, a penetrating detail that insinuates itself into his thoughts, pulling the girl's whole body along after them. Even so tangential a catalyst as the controlled part in her mother's hair is enough to summon them, the clean line of the part demanding the answer of their raw vehemence. Under the table, the red-tipped fingers find his fly; they close around his cock, even as his awareness of having potentially bedded a girl who might be his own child makes him feel literally sick. Will stops unwrapping his sandwich, unbuttons the collar of his shirt.

"So," Will goes on, "the young woman tells me she's tried approaches other than psychoanalysis to cure this problem. She's seen counselors at school, dismisses them as incompetent; ditto for cognitive therapy, the Skinnerite behavior-mod specialist, the Menninger disciple, the yoga instructor, the acupuncturist, and the chiropractor, who tried to remove whatever obstruction had diverted the flow of her sexual energy, making her desire old men.

"Anyway, as I said in the e-mail, the young woman, 'Andrea,' knows details of your past that only you can have provided, and she has 'Quo usque tandem' et cetera tattooed on her chest. Clearly she is, unbeknownst to me, your child, with whom you've shared my impulsive suggestion of DNA testing." Will, whose mouth is dry, takes another swallow of the Diet Dr Pepper, which tastes more vile than he could have imagined, like watered-down, carbonated prune juice. Elizabeth continues to regard him without expression.

"Well?" she says, when he doesn't say anything. "Will you please get to the point? We do know all this. We have established this much."

"Here's the point. While I assume that she bears no relationship to me—why would I think otherwise?—she's checking me out. She has a definite agenda. She arrives on time for her second session, and we address the problem she described the previous week. This entails a detailed account of her most recent 'date' with an older man, a narrative that strikes every possible erotic note and one that's obviously an attempt to put the moves on me."

"On you!" Elizabeth slaps the table with her open hand. "My God, William, have you completely lost it?"

"Let me finish. So after a 'blow-by-blow'—her words, not mine—description of how she seduced a professor at the place where she waits tables, she gets up to leave and hesitates at the door to my office. Asks me for help with the knob because, she claims, she has carpal tunnel syndrome and can't turn it. This being the very same knob she turned the previous week, but what she really wants has nothing to do with the knob; she—"

Elizabeth surges up from her green metal chair, her thigh hitting the tabletop so that the umbrella sways, tea and Dr Pepper slosh over the lips of their respective cups. "She does! Jennifer does have CTS, and as you'd know if you were a real doctor, it is not a constant thing, it goes into remission for a time and then it's—"

"Fine," Will says. "Fine. Jennifer has carpal tunnel. But it didn't prevent her from accompanying her open-mouth, big-tongued kiss with some very dexterous, very nimble manipulation of my genitals. Despite her crippled hands."

"She did not!" Elizabeth cries. "That did not happen!"

"Yes," Will says. "It did. But that's not all, Elizabeth."

"You're telling me that my daughter put her hand down your pants?"

"Not exactly. She fondled me through the fabric of my trousers while she French-kissed me. And that's still not the end."

Elizabeth sets her lips in a tight line.

"I discontinue treatment and refer her to a colleague. I assure her that I will not share any of our conversations or her unusual behavior with that colleague. She'll have a fresh start, a clean slate, whatever she wants to call it. But that's not what she wants. She has no interest in starting over, no interest in analysis or any other kind of psychotherapy. Her agenda is decidedly outside of the therapeutic envelope. She calls me; she leaves messages with my service. When I don't return her calls, she tracks me down at my home number. I hang up, or, when Carole answers, I refuse to take the call, explaining—honestly, or so I think—that I'm under siege from a patient with whom I've discontinued treatment. I even tell Carole why it was I discontinued treatment, and we talk about the occupational hazards of working with unbalanced individuals.

"Anyway, when she can't reach me by phone, she comes to my office one afternoon and, thinking she's my three o'clock, who happens to be late, I buzz her in. I manage to get her out of my office when the patient does arrive, but she doesn't leave the building. Instead, she sits on the stairs, she comes back up when the session is over. She has to see me, she's sorry, needs my help, doesn't want to start over with a different therapist. Please, please. And why am I making such a big deal out of a kiss if, as I've told her, she's no longer my patient? After all, outside the context of any professional involvement, a kiss is no big deal. By now, I've turned my back on her for a minute so I can collect my thoughts, figure out how to get rid of this person without physically throwing her out of the building. But whatever I've planned to say goes right out of my head. That's how shocked I am to find that while I wasn't watching her she's taken her clothes off. All of them. She refuses to dress or to leave. She threatens to cause a scene—'kick and scream' is how she put it—if I don't play the game her way."

Elizabeth's mouth, which has been open for some time, begins to speak in an unnaturally calm and measured tone, the voice of someone who works a 911 line, who gives the same directions countless times each day, who is prepared to listen and respond to heart attacks and drug overdoses, babies who can't be woken, criminals with guns, fires in the attic, and more. "There's a phenomenon," she says, "I'd think you'd be familiar with it, William. It's called erotomania. Erotomaniacs suffer the delusion that other people are sexually fixated on them. Maybe after the accident, after your son drowned, maybe you got a little unglued and—"

"Of course I came unglued! Not a little, a lot! And, yes, Elizabeth, I do know what erotomania is. How is it that all these years later, as other people our age arrive at a more nuanced and humane maturity, you remain so condescending? Do you actually believe you've got it all figured out? That the rest of us are just struggling to catch up? I'm not talking about erotomania, and I'm not talking about me. I'm talking about a young woman who is endangering herself and others with her amoral and pathologically narciss—"

"Oh, spare me! I'm not one of the suckers you can fool with your psychojargon. As you've said, Jennifer is not your patient. You have no idea who she is."

"Do you? Do you have any idea who she is? Maybe the rest of this story will be illuminating. Maybe not. Maybe it will come as no surprise." He folds his arms, waiting for her to ask him to continue.

"Well," Elizabeth says. "Don't stop at the cliff-hanger. What happened?"

"She steps up, unbuckles my belt, unzips my fly, and we have sex."

"Oh fuck," Elizabeth says, and she closes her eyes. Her face, no longer animated by her eyes, looks exhausted. He sees lines he hadn't noticed before, around her mouth and on her forehead. "Why! Why didn't you stop her?"

"Well, first of all, don't forget, I think she's Andrea whoever, a young woman who is no longer my patient. Second, I'm . . . she . . . I was worried about protecting my career, my family. I didn't have any faith that I could resist her effectively. Without her framing me. I was—"

"You were a schmuck!"

"And you know what's the worst part of this mess? I don't know what I should be worrying about most. Potential incest? Adultery? An STD? Or the idea of you and my brother?"

"Your brother?" Elizabeth looks at him sharply. "What does your brother have to do with this?"

"Jennifer said you were sexually involved with both me and Mitch at the same time. And two other men. Four potential fathers." Elizabeth stares at Will, not saying anything. "After Jennifer offered me a strand of her hair," he goes on, "she explained that it might not be so bad. I hadn't necessarily done it with my daughter; she could just as easily be my niece. And that's because"—Will's voice gets louder—"you were fucking my brother!"

"Don't yell," Elizabeth says.

"Were you or were you not fucking Mitch?"

"Don't yell."

"Were you?"

"Yes."

"Yes!"

"I told you, yes."

"I cannot, I can not—well, I can—but no, I cannot believe that my brother, that, that you . . . why?"

"You know, William, I can't help but suspect that you're making a big deal out of this in order to draw attention away from the fact that you had sex with my daughter."

"She assaulted me."

"According to you."

"She was the aggressor, and I didn't know her real identity because she lied."

"Okay, so you were screwing a patient twenty-five years younger than you. Ex-patient. Let's not claim moral high ground. Anyway, we're talking twenty-five years ago. When we were kids. Is it such a big fucking deal if when we were kids I slept with your brother?"

"Why?" Will asks. "Tell me why. Why were you screwing Mitch and me at the same time?"

"Oh, Christ. Can we get back to the real topic? And it's not like it started out that way. For a long while it was just you."

"And then?"

"And then it wasn't. But we're not talking about the past. We're talking about—"

"It was and then it wasn't? What is that supposed to mean?"

She shrugs. "I don't know. I guess he came on to me."

"Mitch came on to you? When did he?"

"Actually, it was more complicated than that." Elizabeth frowns, pinches her lower lip. "He sort of led me to believe it was you, that he was you, and by the time I knew he wasn't, it was too late."

"How the hell did he do that?"

Elizabeth raises her hands, wiggles her fingers theatrically. "Under cover of darkness," she says. "You're twins, remember? Identical. Built the same, sound the same. You guys were so square you even had the same haircuts." She takes a sip of her tea, now cold, and makes a face.

"Go on," Will says.

"He came over, this was sometime senior year—I was living off-campus in that house on Maplewood—and he slipped in that back door—you know which one, you used it yourself. So he made his way to my room and got into bed with me. I thought that was pretty ballsy. I liked it—it was sexy. You seemed suddenly sexier, or you seemed sexy in a way you'd never been before. Of course at first that's who I thought it was—you. After, when he revealed himself, I was irked."

"*Irked? You were* irked?"

"Yes, pissed off. I guess because I was a little freaked out. But then, after a minute or two, it didn't seem so bad."

"A minute or two! That's how long it took you to adjust?"

Elizabeth leans forward. "About as long as it took for Jennifer to go from being a person to whom you owed professional respect to just another piece of ass."

Will ignores this. *Sexy in a way you'd never been before.* Mitch, who he thought was celibate. "So was that . . . was it . . . was that the only time?"

"No."

"No?"

"No."

"How many?"

"I don't know."

"You lost count?"

"I never tried to count. Jesus, why are men so petty and small-minded? Do you think I made hatch marks on my bedpost? I'm a woman, I don't have to do that. I'm not living in constant fear of sexual inadequacy. I don't worry that my penis isn't big enough or that I won't be able to get it up or—"

"Okay, okay. For how long?"

"I don't know. He came back. I didn't stop him. I don't remember for how long."

"Yes, you do."

"You're right, I do."

"Why?" Will says. "Why did you let it go on?"

"It was, I don't know, interesting."

"It was *interesting*?"

"Yes, interesting. Sophisticated. Cool. It seemed hip and liberated. Counterculture. All those things we wanted to be. It seemed free."

"Who? Who wanted to be cool and counterculture?"

"All of us." She raises her eyebrows at him. "I did. Didn't you?"

"What's free about deceiving someone? A person who loved you?"

"I don't know, William. You were always . . . you made everything so claustrophobic. You were always all over me, and I don't mean physically. I felt like I couldn't get any air when I was with you." She stops, frowning in concentration, and he sees the same frown as her daughter's. Why, why hadn't he put things together? "In retrospect," she says, "I think it must have seemed like a way to escape you without doing anything terribly wrong. You and Mitch being twins made it seem like it wasn't cheating, exactly, or it wasn't such serious cheat—"

"Are you kidding! It's worse that he's my brother!"

"Now, maybe. To you, maybe. But to me, back then, the fact that he was so nearly you mitigated that aspect of it. I know that sounds like a rationalization, but it is how it felt. And it's not as if you and I were engaged or something. I never said I wasn't sleeping with anyone else. Besides, I didn't think you'd get hurt. I didn't think anyone would find out. And no one did, William. This all started because you were so weird and fixated at the reunion. I mean, it's been twenty-five years. Have you forgotten that we were young? We were, you know, kids. Careless."

"I wasn't. I was never careless with you."

"Well, I guess I just must have been less *evolved*."

"Less evolved! The person you're describing is someone with the moral intelligence of a bait worm!"

"Jesus, William. Will you just lighten up?"

"Who was better?" he asks.

"Better?"

"Who was better in bed?"

"You must be joking."

"Not at all. Who was the better lover?"

"Both of you were what, twenty? No one is a *lover* at twenty." Elizabeth uses the index and middle finger of each hand to make quotation marks in the air when she says the word *lover*.

"Fine. Who lasted longer? Who was more considerate, more deft, more creative? Who made you feel good? Who went down on you? Who made you come?"

"I'm not going to answer any of this."

Will reaches across the table and grabs Elizabeth's wrist, aware that he's out of control, but it's like noticing your car's brakes have failed when you're already going down a hill: he can't stop. "Yes, you are," he says. "You are."

She twists out of his grasp, stands up. "I'm leaving. I've had enough."

"So have I. But it's not over yet."

"Yes it is." She ties the belt of her trench coat and shoves her hands in her pockets. "If you contact me—if you e-mail me again, or call me, or Jennifer—I'll report you to the police. I'll tell them you sexually assaulted my daughter. If Jennifer is half as calculating as the person you've described, then maybe she didn't use a condom because she wanted her underpants to collect some, what shall we call it? Proof of your trespass?" Elizabeth looks at Will and, when he doesn't answer, continues. "Any number of strategies might present themselves to an amoral, ambitious, sexually experienced girl like Jennifer. I hope she didn't perform fellatio on you. Only too easy to have hidden a Ziploc bag somewhere. A quick spit and, zip, she'd—"

"There was nothing like that," Will says.

"Oh, I don't know, William. And neither do you. Under such circumstances you must have been distracted. 'Thinking with the little head' would, I believe, be the appropriate expression. Consider this. You're a forty-seven-year-old man. She's a girl of twenty-four. Who do you think anyone would believe?" Without waiting for an answer, Elizabeth turns and starts walking away, toward the platforms.

How long before it occurs to Will that if Mitch slept with Elizabeth, he might have slept with other girls—other of his girlfriends?

On the crowded train home from Philadelphia, Will has a backward-facing seat and blames this for contributing to his sense of disorientation. He stares silently out the window, watching the string of fenced yards unspool backward into the distance, as if they were moving and he sitting still. Squalid little houses, some of them, sagging laundry lines and broken toys spread across the withered grass. Something that looks like half a house slides past, rooms missing walls, naked and flimsy under the pale afternoon sun. As for Will, a big chunk of his own foundation, the block of certainties upon which he'd piled all sorts of other assumptions he'd made about his life, has officially been removed. Is this melodramatic? Yes. Still, he wonders if the chunk was a keystone, and how much of the rest of him will go down with it. Isn't this how patients describe breakdowns? First that vertiginous sense of losing one's footing, then the teetering, finally the plummet. How bad would it be? How far?

Will reviews his list of worries, something he pictures like a pull-down menu on a computer screen, growing ever longer. Now it includes the possibility that Jennifer has saved his semen, that his brother betrayed him with other people, that even as he struggles to direct his patients to deeper levels of self-awareness, he doesn't know essential aspects of his own life.

Incest. He has a patient whose background includes her father's molesting her; having seen her for fifteen years, he's still surprised by the malarial quality of the damage, the way it won't fade, arrives without warning and dismantles her. "I'm no better than a dog on a chain," she said. "I can only get so far before it yanks me back. I'm forty fucking years old, and it is never ever going to go away." But Jennifer isn't a child; he didn't force himself on her; he didn't know. And it might not be true. Please, let it not be true.

And now what? What's he supposed to do now? He doesn't understand Elizabeth's casual attitude toward sleeping with twin brothers, her lying to him and, presumably, to the man she married. And what to make of her suggestion that he and Mitch were not entirely distinct from each other, not enough anyway to be considered separate individuals? Didn't that have to be bullshit, a tidy lie to ease her conscience? And yet, hasn't Will himself feared their over-identification? Still, his deepest sexual transgression—with the girl, possibly breaking taboo—was unknowing. While Mitch's, also in defiance of taboo, was conscious, deliberate.

Will remembers his own lust at twenty, twenty-one. His brother's would have to have been the same, wouldn't it? Same biology, same wiring. And Mitch had always been too self-conscious about his disfigurement to even talk to a girl. Too proud to allow anyone the tiniest sliver of compassion for him, because he could never feel sympathy as distinct from pity.

He should just let the whole thing go, shouldn't he? If he can't do this out of generosity toward Mitch, if he can't summon forgiveness, then perhaps he can out of a sense of self-preservation. Let go before it develops into exactly the kind of obsessive pursuit he's heard patients describe as the prelude to a crisis. Because Will has enough crises. Infidelity. Impotence. Incest!

Every time he approaches the idea of Jennifer, whatever analytical ability he possesses disappears. Thoughts don't proceed in logical argument; they ricochet around inside his skull, cracking into one another like pinballs and destroying every coherent mental construction in their path. Images of Carole and Samantha jumble with parts of Jennifer he wishes he'd never seen, paranoid scenarios of sex police knocking at his door, incarceration in dank jails filled with rapists and pederasts, his old, respectable colleagues replaced by new ones: criminals, perverts. Perps.

He takes out his cell phone and dials Daniel's number, gets his voice mail, and leaves a message.

What does it mean to be caught in two simultaneous snares of obsessive thought, both concerning sexual transgression? Thoughts of Mitch with one woman competing with thoughts of himself with that same woman's daughter, a daughter who isn't much older than her mother had been when her mother was involved with Mitch and Will. Were these a patient's parallel obsessions, Will would have to agree with Elizabeth's initial, knee-jerk diagnosis: the whole construct must represent an unconscious strategy for avoiding an even more unacceptable and unbelievable something. But what? Luke's death? It's been three years.

Of course, that argument does tend to collapse in the face of his fury over Mitch and Elizabeth having been involved twenty-five years ago. And, if his patients are at all representative of the human condition, the past isn't past until it's lived. Not lived through, *lived*. Felt.

Fuck it, Will thinks. Fuck me. Fuck you, William Moreland. And fuck you, too, Mitchell Moreland. You have made a big fat fucking mess, so fuck you. He hits redial, gets Daniel's voice mail again, and hangs up. Then he reconsiders and hits redial to leave a second message. "I have to talk to you," he says. "I have to talk to you tonight."

How is a person to ignore information that changes everything? It's not as if he's made any of this up. And it's no small deceit that Elizabeth described—Mitch's entering her house after dark, pretending to be Will, and penetrating Elizabeth's room, her bed, her body, a trespass followed by the confession that he wasn't who she assumed—no, not a confession. Confession implies shame, and the scene Will imagines doesn't include his brother's feeling ashamed. When had Mitch ever betrayed any form of regret? Mitch was angry, angry enough to have always spoken in a soft voice and moved with silent grace. If he hadn't been conscious of his rage, some part of him knew he was carrying explosive cargo and carried it very carefully. So carefully that even his twin—or especially his twin: his obligingly, willfully blind twin—hadn't felt it.

Will had been nearing the midpoint of his training analysis before he could attempt to address his brother's peculiarly thoughtful and deliberate passage through the years, leading up to college, acts of what seemed to be impulsive, helpless generosity accomplished with a nearly visible tremor of determination. Mitch hadn't lied when he said he couldn't resist carrying an old woman's groceries to her car or mowing the neighbor's lawn while that neighbor recuperated from surgery. When he first began to question his brother's motives, Will misunderstood these as acts of hypocrisy, but in truth they'd been far more insidious. They were opportunities for Mitch to cloak his misanthropy, to disguise his hatred for the unmarked faces all around him. Hide it from himself before anyone else. Because, like anyone dedicated to a performance, Mitch was his own first audience, the one person above all others whom he had to convince.

In the dark, in Elizabeth's bedroom, having just fucked her, Will's brother wouldn't have confessed his identity; he'd have announced it—crowed, in effect. He would have loved how it felt to steal Elizabeth. Loved the discovery enough to do it again, and again.

If in fact this was a discovery.

If Elizabeth was the first of Will's girlfriends that Mitch seduced.

Will closes his eyes. His head aches and he succumbs to a flight of hypochondria, hurrying through the relatively benign and less interesting causes of cranial miseries—eye strain, sinus infection, food allergy—to arrive at potentially fatal diagnoses, like critically high blood pressure, which would explain why he always feels his collar tightening during the course of a day. Then there's the even more affecting brain tumor, which he accessorizes with tableaux of his confinement in a hospital bed, Samantha playing with the buttons and making his pitifully bandaged head and wasted legs go up and then down. Stoic and pale, Carole resists going over all the papers and insurance documents he wants her to review before his death, insisting that he can make himself better, if only he will try to believe in the possibility of recovery, and swallow ayurvedic potions.

Will gets out a pad of paper and begins a list of some of the girls he's dated. The ones Mitch could maybe have crossed paths with.

April Pedly

Marna Yardham

Esther (Newton?)

Christine Johnson

Elizabeth Fuller

Julie Applegate

Lisa Christianson

Jean McMinnamin (sp.?)

So, start with April, the girl with whom he lost his virginity. April had been at camp with them, not the camp from which Will had been expelled, but the one he and Mitch attended the following summer, when they were fifteen. Pale and lanky—languid—her limbs a little too pliable, she'd seemed lacking in vitality, a doll whose batteries were drained. But Will had found her blue eyes extraordinary. Bloodshot and red-rimmed from allergies, they suggested not hay fever so much as a consuming, destructive passion. In the context of her enervation, they seemed to indicate a secret love marked by epic, unrequited weeping in her bunk on the girls' side of the camp.

Penetrating the divide between the boys' and girls' sides hadn't presented a problem. The junior counselors, who lived in the cabins with the campers, never even tried to prevent the consummation of nighttime pilgrimages through the little copse of struggling maples and birch trees that separated the two clusters of cabins—too much of a hassle, not to mention a loss of sleep, and for what? Under the trees the ground was lush with poison ivy, and if that didn't dampen lust, what could? Of course, any kid who wanted to advertise himself as an initiate into the mysteries of sex didn't wear socks or long pants because he considered a poison ivy rash to be a badge of honor. Anyone with raw and oozing shins claimed, in effect, to have gotten his rocks off. Now that Will thinks about it, there must have been more than a few boys who went only as far as the copse, exposed their unprotected legs to the oily green leaves, and then headed back, seeking to enlarge their reputations rather than their experience.

Will made at least five nocturnal visits to the girls' side, summoning the wan and ectomorphic April from her cabin. She slept lightly, wheezing by a window whose flimsy screen could be removed with little effort. After they'd done it—not so much a memorable initiation as his confused fumbling toward what must have been a painful disappointment for April, a few stabbing thrusts and then he pulled back enough to come on rather than in her—Will hurried back to his bunk. The next morning he showed off the broken skin above his sock lines, barely waiting past breakfast to prop his red legs up on benches and fence rails, scratching exhibitionistically, silently bragging that he was no longer a virgin.

Will never told Mitch about visiting April—he never spoke with his brother about any of his romantic quests, even the failed ones, because he didn't want to hurt him or underscore his isolation, his imprisonment behind his face. But Mitch knew—of course he did, because everyone knew who was getting any and how often. It would have been a simple thing for Mitch to lie awake until he was sure that Will was asleep in the bed above his, that Will wasn't going through the copse that night. Then, in the shadows, only too easy to slip out and over to the girls' side, legs well protected, pants tucked into socks. Who slept in which cabin was practically announced by the camp post office, where mail was sorted into boxes labeled with the names of the cabins. Perhaps April, Will's first, was also Mitch's first, and camp the setting in which he acquired the cover of night as his M.O.

Given the pressure of the moment—the hurrying, the excitement, the lust—it would have been easy to mistake Mitch for Will. As long as Mitch chose a night when the moon was new or the sky overcast, as long as he kept within the shadows, April, like Elizabeth, would have had no reason to suspect the boy who came to her might be anyone other than Will. In retrospect, she didn't seem a very perceptive girl, not the sharpest blade in the drawer. But that's not fair. Probably it was just that April, like the rest of them, was self-involved to the point that she paid little attention to anyone but herself. At fifteen, the prospect of getting laid was more than enough to eclipse every competing thought, and even older lovers are blind to a lover's true identity. The bed trick was one of the oldest in the book—all the way back to Genesis. Abraham, Leah, Rachel.

So, April, then. Will uncaps his pen, staring at the little houses that flash by his window, each a white square, identical except for the odd detail, racing past like single frames of a film. Will and Mitch sharing the same girl. Almost like fucking each other, Will thinks, allowing the thought for only a second. Funny how you could hold one of the houses in your vision, follow it for a beat or two, so long as you picked only one from out of the stream. One second was enough to note two or three details: the empty plastic pool, the red tricycle next to the round, red barbecue. For an instant he could see all this, and then it was gone. And, for a finger snap of consciousness, Will understands that, driving into the red-eyed, pale-lipped April, Mitch had chosen the wet center of a girl as the place for the brothers' brief reunion. What better than this primal consummation for two who were once one, two who would always remain a single idea for a person?

The epiphany—if that's what it is—lasts no longer than the image of the one little house among many; it arrives, departs, and is replaced by another. And maybe it's more a conceit than a truth, a projection of Will's, not Mitch's but Will's, desire for the return of his absent twin, the version of himself defaced. The birthmark had robbed Will's brother of a face, left him faceless, humiliated, having suffered a literal loss of face. Well, whatever the thought is, Will has no time to explore it before it's gone, returned to his unconscious, out of reach, but not before a few synapses have fired in its wake, a sequence that summons a wave of tiny contractions, minute *erector pili* muscles, one per follicle, each lifting a single hair on the back of his neck, together raising his hackles; Will shudders. It's the deep sort of shudder imaginatively linked to a stranger walking over one's future grave. He shifts in his seat, makes a check mark next to the name April Pedly, indicating that he's thought through a scenario and concluded that betrayal was plausible, if not proven.

Marna Yardham he can't quite remember, or, to be more truthful, he remembers a few parts of her so well, so pungently, that they obliterate others. Marna was his tenth-grade girlfriend; she lived off Majors Road, one of those girls who kept a horse, sexually precocious with her own species while romantically fixated on another. Will used to visit her at the stables and watch as she braided Pilot's mane with ribbons, clamped a big foot between her thighs to pick the bottom of its hoof clean. She washed, curried, and kissed Pilot, fed him a carrot with her own mouth, lips puckered around the wider end of the root, waiting for his big teeth to eat their way nearly to her face before she let the last bite go.

Esther—forget Esther, he can't even be sure he's remembered her last name correctly. He can't remember the color of her hair. All he knows is she had a car too small for sex, a blue Toyota Corolla, and that that hadn't stopped them.

Christine Johnson: dark hair, round face, long legs. Earnest to a fault, no sense of humor, especially with regard to herself. Christine had intended to Make a Difference. She was going to be the next Madame Curie or Mary Wollstonecraft, transcend injustices imposed by the patriarchy, redeem womankind. They dated Will's freshman year of college, which would have been Mitch's freshman year as well. Poor Christine. At the reunion he'd heard she married a religious fanatic and was living in a commune, raising six children, each named for a Hindu deity—Parvati, Rudra, Siva—he can't remember the other three.

At home Will's parents had debated the advantages and disadvantages of Will and Mitch attending the same university. Mitch, present for these after-dinner talks—he wasn't given a choice—said nothing, and neither did their mother, while Will and their father crept toward the conclusion that perhaps the right institution could provide an interim period of adjustment for the two brothers. Cornell was a big school, large enough that each twin could find his own separate path, and yet students lived within walking distance of one another. Mitch could draw comfort from Will's relative proximity.

Or, were this his brother's purpose, figure out a way to secretly share Will's sexual partners.

Will looks at the little paper with the list of girls, then folds and shoves it into his breast pocket. He'll Google all the names at home, later. Or he can use Cornell's online alumni directory. As a graduate of the university, he'd been given a code that allowed him to access its database. A resource he discovered at the reunion, the fateful reunion.

W ell?" Daniel says as Will sits down.
"I haven't told her."

"No?"

"I feel like I'm . . . I just have to get a few things straight before I talk to Carole. Straight in my head."

"How will you do that?"

"I've contacted one of them, a woman named Lisa Christianson. E-mailed her. She said she'd see me."

"See you."

"Yes. Talk to me. I mean, I didn't tell her what it was I wanted to talk about. I . . . well, I led her to believe that I was going to be in the area. In Albany. Said I'd like to stop in."

"What will you do?" Daniel says.

"Ask her, I guess. I'll ask her."

"Then what?"

"I don't know. I'm not sure. If she says no, that it never happened, then I guess I might try someone else. And if that woman says no, I'll drop it. I'll tell Carole what happened with the girl. Ask her forgiveness. I mean, what are the choices?"

"And if she says yes?"

"Lisa Christianson?"

Daniel nods. "What if she confirms your suspicions?" he asks.

"I don't know. I have no idea. I mean, I already feel like I don't know anything anymore. Or anyone. Or myself. I ran into a friend yesterday, John York. We talked for a while; then he asked me to return his boxed set of Charles Mingus. Said he wouldn't ask if it weren't a rare recording that's no longer available. But I never borrowed any CD's from him. The only time I see the guy is on the racquetball court." Will shakes his head. "It wasn't that he accused me, but I could tell he didn't believe me when I said I didn't have it. That he thought I'd borrowed the recording and forgotten about it. Or that I was lying intentionally. And even though I was sure I didn't have his CD's, that he hadn't ever loaned me any recordings at all, when I got home I went through all our music, twice, looking for something I've never seen before."

Daniel is silent. Then, "Another instance of confusion or ambiguity over what's true, what's a lie," he says.

"I know. I know. But I don't get the significance. I mean, was I being paranoid? Maybe I was. Maybe he didn't think I was lying. Maybe my feelings about that transaction have nothing to do with John at all, but with something else, something present under or behind every essentially meaningless event, with the power to show through what's happening on the surface. Like, like a black bra showing through a white blouse." Will shakes his head. "I'll have to . . . if Lisa says yes, I'll have to go through the past. Factor in this, this . . . factor in whatever she tells me. Correct my misapprehension of everything."

"That's a striking image you used."

"What? The black bra?"

"Yes."

"Sexual," Will says, nodding. "It just popped out."

"So I assumed."

"You know, I can't . . . ever since Jennifer, I can't get it up. I don't know if it's the possibility of her being related to me, or if it's that . . . well, it wasn't my plan, but I did cheat on my wife." Will slumps down in the seat, pinches the skin over his Adam's apple. "Or if it's because of Mitch." He closes his eyes, stops speaking.

"If your ability to perform sexually has been dismantled by what you've learned about your brother?"

Will nods. "You know," he says after a silence, "I'm not going to get anywhere in here, with you, until I've straightened out this, this thing about Mitch. Until I know if it was just Elizabeth or . . ." He stands up. "I'm sorry. I think I'd like to leave, come back to talk after I've seen Lisa."

Daniel pushes his chair back from his desk and stands. "You know, Will, I think it's been a mistake not to use the couch over the last few months."

"A mistake?" Will looks at him. "Don't you mean a dodge?"

Daniel nods. "Yes," he says, "that is what I mean."

He drives their blue minivan north without stopping for anything but gas, coffee, and a Little Debbie cinnamon roll, the pastry stuck to the clear wrapper with white sugar glaze. After a couple of bites, he drops the rest into the garbage can next to the pumps. The bonsai nursery Lisa Christianson runs with her husband is a little less than 200 miles northwest of New York City. To get there, Will follows the MapQuest directions he got off the Internet, pulling off I-87 onto a poorly paved road through short, forested hills, where evergreens give way to pockets of deciduous trees, naked now, their branches bare. A light snow is falling.

The greenhouses, eight of them, are in a small valley, each one vast and filled with steaming life. So much condensation runs down the inside surface of the glass panes that the plants within look blurred, like an Impressionist painting.

Will pulls the minivan off the narrow access road and parks where he won't block anyone's way. When he gets out, a small pack of lap dogs comes tearing out from behind one of the glass structures, barking and jumping at him. The most aggressive is a Yorkshire terrier that seems as if it may actually bite him or at least take hold of his pant leg, and despite the foolish aspect of retreating from so small a foe, he's just getting back into his car when a woman in a khaki barn coat emerges from one of the far greenhouses. She calls the dogs off with a whistle, the kind requiring two fingers under the tongue, a trick that many times he'd tried and failed to teach Luke. The woman in the khaki coat approaches.

"Hello," Will says. She looks different than he expected.

"Hello," the woman says. She stands with her hands shoved in her coat pockets. Either she's changed in some way he can't identify, or he can't remember her twenty-one-year-old self well enough to make a match with the woman standing before him, and this disturbs Will; it makes him feel as if he can't be sure he's arrived at the right place after all. He has to fight his desire to ask all the questions that were already answered during their e-mail correspondence. Is she the Lisa Christianson who double-majored in economics and art history? Whose sister had lupus? Who slept with him for a couple of months the summer between junior and senior year?

"I have some work I have to finish," she says. "Maybe we could visit while I . . . I guess what I'm saying is I'd be more relaxed if we could talk while I work."

"Of course," Will says, and he follows her back to the greenhouse.

"I have a couple gross of trees to prune and train, and others to pack for trucking. Sean's over at his brother's, and both our workers are out with some flu thing."

The little trees, each planted in a glazed, black ceramic dish, are grouped along a huge trestle table, its surface pitted and stained. To one side are shelves filled with unassembled cartons and stacks of Styrofoam inserts sized to fit inside the cartons.

"We move a lot of plants during the holidays," she says, and Will reaches out to touch the dark, shiny green leaves on a tiny, gnarled tree. "That's a Fukien tea tree. Subtropical. All the ones inside are subtropical. The evergreens and deciduous—maples mostly, but we do some birch and crab apple—they stay outside through the winter."

"Do you sell them to florists?" Will asks. "Or to, I don't know, garden centers?"

"More and more, we sell them online and ship them via UPS. The rest go to retailers closer to the city."

"It must be—I imagine you have to harden yourself to the idea that a lot of the trees that thrived under your care die after you sell them," he says. Lisa looks at Will as if he's said something strange.

"So," she says, turning toward a table whose surface holds an array of small clippers and spools of wire. "You didn't come here to talk about horticulture, did you?"

"No. I came because"—*I'm going through a midlife crisis*, he almost says, a tempting if radical abridgment of the truth. But if he wants her to be forthcoming with him, then he has to be honest himself. "I need to talk to you about something. For the past fifteen years or so I've been estranged from my brother. I think you may have known that I had—have—a—"

"Mitch," she says, nodding. "Except that now he's the renowned Mitchell Moreland."

"Right."

"Estranged?" She tilts her head to one side in a questioning gesture. "How come?"

"I'm not sure," he says. "I don't have . . . what I'm going to ask you—your answer, I mean—I hope it may illuminate something." As if he were a teenager again and trying to get up the nerve to ask a girl on a date, Will feels his heart accelerate, that funny, dizzy headache he associates with standing up too quickly.

Lisa Christianson shifts her attention away from him to the tiny spruce in front of her. She turns it around and around on the table, considering its shape before taking off one branch, and then, after another revolution, a second. She bends one of the remaining limbs, wires it, and bends it further, until it assumes the asymmetry she wants. She looks up at Will. "What do you want to know?" she asks. The tone of her voice strikes him as wary, or is this his imagination?

"This is awkward, but I'm wondering . . . did Mitch . . ." Will stops, silently rehearses his question and then blurts it out. "Were you ever sexually involved with my brother?"

Lisa sets the little clippers on the plank table. Rather than looking at him, she addresses a spot over his left shoulder. "I guess I thought you knew that," she says.

Will closes his eyes briefly, feeling the adrenaline wash through his body from somewhere in his chest, all the purely physical responses it provokes, pulse climbing, arms tingling.

"Do you . . . I drank a lot of coffee on the road," he says. "I should have asked to use the men's room before we began talking."

"There's a, well, it's not a men's room. More like a porta-potty." She points through the wet glass to a green blot. "Back over by that last greenhouse." She looks at him again, as if she's trying to figure something out.

The porta-potty must be for the hired hands, he guesses, breathing through his mouth to avoid the smell of disinfectant with its undertow of human waste. He stands for a moment before going out the green plastic door, trying to collect his thoughts.

"Are you all right?" Lisa says when he returns, not very promptly. "I, um, I do have enough time for us to go inside for a bit. Have a cup of tea or something."

"I'm fine," Will says, manufacturing an expression to go with the words.

"Well." She stands up. "I think I'd like to go in."

He follows her into the house, which conforms to his idea of a dwelling occupied by a pair of bonsai experts. Sleek, modern furniture, blank white walls—not one picture—a long, narrow table holding six bonsai in red dishes.

"No kids?" he says, not so much a question as an observation prompted by the absence of stains and clutter, the temerity of owning a pair of white sofas.

"Nope." She slips out of her yellow rubber work clogs. "Tea?"

"Water's fine."

"So I take it you didn't have any arrangement with your brother, any of those weird twin things, where you conspire to have some fun with a girl who's good-natured enough not to take it too hard when she discovers herself in flagrante with the other brother, rather than the one she thought she was with?"

Will shakes his head slowly. "No," he says. She sits on the sofa across from the one he's chosen, puts her hands together and clamps them between her knees, studies his face.

"Do you not feel well?" she asks him.

"I've felt better."

"Yeah, I guess you would have." She bites her lower lip. "I'm . . . I'm sorry. But—"

"You're not at fault."

"Couldn't I get you something? Seltzer maybe? I think we have ginger ale."

"All right. Yes." Will closes his eyes, unable to determine if he feels suddenly sick, really sick, or if he's felt this way for weeks now and his ability to deny it has been disabled without warning. When he opens them, she's standing in front of him, glass in one hand, coaster in the other. "Thank you," he says. "Perhaps I'll just wash my hands?"

She points at a hallway. "Second door," she says.

At least it's just bile, he thinks. And no carpet. Thank God, no carpet. He's turned the bathtub taps on in an attempt to mask the sounds of his vomiting, doesn't even know if the tears coming out of his eyes are a response to all the stomach acid he's forced up into his sinuses or if he's really crying. It requires a focused, almost impossible act of will to stop retching, and then, sitting back on his heels, he's subject to convulsive aftershocks, like the residual heaves of sobbing.

He leans on the side of the tub and turns off both taps, looks around himself.

He's on hands and knees, hunting for splatters and wiping them up with toilet paper, when he hears just what he's been praying he wouldn't hear, a hesitant knock on the door.

"Yes?" he says, surprised by the normal tone of his voice.

"I just . . . nothing."

"I'll be out in a moment."

He washes his hands, his face, rinses his mouth, checks his shirt, his trousers. He feels awful but he looks all right. Back in the living room he sits carefully in the spot he'd chosen before. The couch is upholstered in a suedelike fabric, very soft.

"Look," Lisa says after a silence. "Am I supposed to, what, pretend that you weren't just violently ill?" Will returns her stare.

"If you wouldn't mind," he says.

She tilts her head up, her face toward the ceiling. Hands folded in her lap, she remains in this posture for what seems to Will a long time. Her shoulders rise and fall with a deep breath she takes through her nose, a relaxation technique maybe. He wonders if this might be a gesture of dismissal, if she's going to remain like that, her face averted until he gets up to leave, when she looks back at him. "Okay," she says, "so." She claps her hands together, and the sound they make

is a crisp snap, like that of a wet towel. "Do you want to know anything more?"

"More?" he says stupidly.

"Yes. I assume that after driving all this way you might want more
than . . . than, well, just more, that's all."

He nods. "How many times?" he asks.

"How many times did he . . . did we—"

"Yes."

"I don't know." She lifts and drops one hand. "How long were
you and I involved? July, then August? So, two months times a couple, maybe three, times a week. What does that come out to?
Twenty? Twenty-five?"

"And after the first time, after that you knew? He revealed himself the first time?"

"Yes. You—no, not you, it was his idea, but I thought it was yours,
or what I mean is, I thought he was you. He said for us to meet in my
dad's milking parlor at one. One in the morning. So I go there to
wait, and he—but I think it's you, right? I don't know it's your
brother—he sneaks up behind me and says, 'Close your eyes.' Then
he blindfolds me and says he's going to take me to a special place.
Have I ever been skinny dipping? he wants to know. We end up at the
quarry, where he asks, have I ever done it in the water? Have I ever
had sex in the water? 'Making love' was probably how he put it. And
of course I hadn't. I was, what? A kid. A girl with an overbite from
upstate New York."

"I knew there was something," Will says. "I was trying to figure
out what was different about you."

"Yeah." She touches her mouth, a reflexive gesture. In it, all the
polish she's acquired evaporates. "I got them fixed when I could afford it. My folks never did have that kind of money. They just, you

know, we were dairy farmers. They didn't have money to spend on stuff like braces. But as soon as Sean and I were in the black, I got them. Anyway." She sits up straight, once again someone other than a dairy farmer's daughter.

"So Mitch took you blindfolded to the quarry for submarine sex?"

She smiles, self-conscious. "I know it's silly. When I think back, I do see that it was dumb. But then I *was* dumb. What did I know? I was a kid. Undiscerning. Nervous. Easily impressed. I'm sure I must have thought it was going to be romantic. When we got there, it was so dark, pitch-black, that even without the blindfold I couldn't see a thing, practically. I still didn't know it wasn't you.

"Anyway, well, I don't know if you've ever tried, but it's not that easy having . . . doing it in water, even under the best of circumstances. And do you remember the quarry? All that slime underfoot? It was hard to keep your footing. As for the sex itself, it's not like everything glides into place. The water, somehow water just does not help. It wasn't how I imagined it would be. We couldn't even . . . in the end, we had to get out before he could even, you know, get inside me.

"He had this blanket thing spread on the ground and, this is going to make me sound, I don't know, dumb or superficial or something, but I was getting eaten alive by bugs. I counted, honestly, over a hundred mosquito bites the next day. So by the time I figured out it was him instead of you, I think I barely reacted. I was just begging him to hurry up so we could put on our clothes and get out of there.

"And it wasn't until I was back home that I thought about how strange it was, the whole night. On the drive back I just sat there like a lump. I don't remember thinking a single thing. I wanted to go home, that's all. And the next morning, gosh, my parents and my sister were mystified by the welts all over my arms and my back, everywhere. They asked all these questions. Did I take the screen off my bedroom window? Did I sleep without pajamas?" She pauses. "I didn't say anything in the e-mails, but Margie died."

"She did? I'm so sorry. When did she?" Will tries to picture Lisa's pale sister, who stayed inside all the time because the sun aggravated her lupus and gave her rashes.

"The fall of 'ninety-nine. Just before Thanksgiving."

"I'm, I'm very sorry. How old was she?"

"Thirty-eight. It pretty much destroyed my folks."

"I'm so sorry," Will says again.

"Yeah. Thanks. Me, too. Anyway"—she shakes her head as if to clear it—"later, after the bites stopped itching so much, I told myself I had to talk to you, or to Mitch. Sort of sort it all out. I mean, I just didn't know what to think. Or even how to feel."

Will slouches down in order to rest his head on the low sofa back. Without raising his head he asks her what she thinks about it now.

She snorts. "Well, obviously, it didn't have much to do with me. Whatever it was, was between you two. I was just the chump."

"By why didn't you ever talk to me?" He tilts his head to see her face. "How could it have gone on for six or eight or however many weeks without my knowing about it?"

"Because when I went to your house to talk to you, your brother was there, and he made me promise never to bring it up. He told me it was this thing the two of you had, you and him, and the deal was that talking about it, even mentioning it, wasn't allowed. He said that if it ever came up, everything would be over between us—all three of us. Not a bad idea, right? But the thing is, I was scared. Scared of Mitch. He seemed—not that he was ever violent or abusive, he wasn't—but I could tell he had that capacity. He never yelled at me or punched walls or anything direct like that. He just had this . . . this . . . I don't know. This concealed rage. Except every once in a while I'd catch a glimpse of it. He'd overreact or something, you know?"

"Yes," Will says. "I do. I do know."

"Over and over, I almost said something to you, but then . . . I just couldn't. I thought maybe you knew. And I was afraid you might be angry, too. And remember how I had plans for that August? I was going to go down to Virginia, where my mom's sister lived. But then Uncle Rob had a fall, broke his leg, and I ended up staying home. So it wasn't over when I told myself it would be, but then there was only a few weeks left before school, and I, I just went through the motions, you know?"

"Did you go on dates together? Movies? Out to dinner?"

"No, that was only with you. With Mitch it was always just sex. Sex at night. Late." She shakes her head, frowning. "Weird, I know. Like I had this boyfriend who was split into two halves, one who took me out for ice cream or whatever and one I had sex with."

"But," Will can't help saying, "but we had sex, too."

"Of course, of course. I didn't mean we didn't. Just that—"

"Just that it wasn't sexy sex. Sort of comfortable and safe, like a back rub or an old armchair."

"No. That's not what I meant."

"My brother, the demon lover."

"Will." She says it with two syllables. Wi-ill. "Come on, you can't not know it was all about his face. Anyway, I wouldn't have been so passive if I'd been older. But it's hard for girls—you can't know. As a man, you don't realize that there are a lot of things girls feel they have no choice about."

"No," says Will. "I do get that." He closes his eyes, and for a while neither of them speaks. It's so quiet in her house that he can hear the faint buzz of an appliance in another room, a clothes dryer, maybe.

"Hey," she says. "I'm alone here today. Like I said, Sean's gone to pick up some stuff, and I have no help." She brings her hands together in another little clap, an awkward, hearty gesture. "So I have to get back to work. But you can . . . I think it would be a good idea for you to take a nap or even just a rest before you get back on the road."

"Yes," Will says. "I should do that."

"You stay there." Lisa stands up. "I'll get you a blanket."

After parking the van, its sides streaked with mud, Will sits for a few minutes in the driver's seat.

Inside the empty house, he stops to use the bathroom and then heads upstairs to Luke's room, undisturbed for more than three years now. Not untouched, because once a month or so, Elena, who cleans the rest of the house, comes in to dust and vacuum. Hired after Luke died, she's never asked about the child who does and does not occupy the room. Either she refuses to trespass where she might cause pain, or her nascent English cannot accommodate the questions she would ask in her own language.

Will sits on his son's narrow bed. Characters from *The Adventures of Tintin*—Snowy, Captain Haddock, and Tintin himself—pursue one another across the bedding that Carole discovered by chance in a SoHo boutique. Will found he couldn't object to the price tag, not really; he loved Luke's discovery of the 1930s comic by Hergé, his reading and rereading and then reading once again English translations of all the old adventures, sitting up in bed, literally bundled within the romp of imagined intrigue, asking endless questions about Soviet spies and Shanghai gangsters.

In the bookcase are other favorites of Luke's, *A Wrinkle in Time* by Madeleine L'Engle, *The Chronicles of Narnia*, and *The Lord of the Rings*. Religious stories, all of them, David and Goliath tales of good battling a vast and seemingly uncontrollable evil, of love prevailing only at the eleventh hour (the fifty-ninth minute, fifty-ninth second), the moment of absurd, laughable—necessary—hope.

Tintin sheets, fantasy novels, and the mythic athlete-hero: Luke's bedroom is papered with posters of Derek Jeter, Jason Giambi, Alfonso Soriano, Yankees mostly, out of geographic loyalty, but there are stars from other teams as well. Suzuki, A-Rod, Bonds, Sosa. Of course, now A-Rod was a Yankee, Soriano gone, Will can't remember where, because he can't watch baseball, can't listen to it on the radio or follow the box scores, not anymore. Not yet. Luke had been so earnest and credulous in his love; his adulation of Sammy Sosa, for example, blinded him to the man's obvious deceit.

"Lukey," Will remembers saying, gently, "there were maybe thirty or forty bats to choose from, and Sosa took the one corked bat. It's just not likely for that to have been an accident."

"It was just a mistake," Luke said, not even defensive.

Over the desk was a huge black-and-white poster of Muhammad Ali, with the caption "Impossible is nothing," the fighter in his beautiful prime, white satin trunks luminous against his velvet skin. "That's how Jesus looks," Luke had told Will, prompting a spasm of guilt that he and Carole had never managed to get it together to send their kids to Sunday school or provide them any religious instruction whatsoever.

One entire wall of Luke's bedroom is consecrated to Mitch, the uncle he never met, the one he discovered in a magazine article, a man with the same last name as himself and his father, a man bearing his father's familiar face, except for the livid splash of purple, which, in two dimensions at least, presented itself as the distinctive feature of a superhero, a demiurge endowed with powers that, like any other immortal's, marked his face and body. Spiderman was masked by webbing, the Hulk prone to shirt-tearing episodes of swelling green muscles, and Mitchell Moreland had an arresting yin-yang face.

"I don't get why you guys don't even talk to each other," Luke complained to Will, unable to reconcile himself to the injustice of having an uncle who was a bona fide sports star and never getting to see him, not even on a holiday, not even once a year. The more Luke pressed for rapprochement, the more terse and defensive Will had become, unable to manufacture a seemingly casual that's-just-the-way-it-worked-out response.

With a child's unerring ability to identify, aim for, and repeatedly strike his parents' weak spots, Luke became a clamorous Mitchell Moreland fan, loudly celebrating Mitch's exploits and media conquests, making a show of tearing pages from magazines, sending away for not one but three pairs of swim goggles endorsed by Mitch's signature and acquired with proofs of purchase torn from boxes of a cereal no one could stomach but which Carole bought under the duress of an aisle 5 (breakfast foods) tantrum. Carole sidestepped public conflict even more determinedly than the domestic variety, and having threatened a supermarket tantrum, Luke hadn't even had to work all that hard for the five or ten or however many box tops torn from the inedible vitamin-rich whatevers.

In the year before he drowned—irony, irony, yes, Will does recognize irony—Luke discovered that he could use the cable guide to hunt for mentions of Mitch on ESPN or ESPN2 and he found the rerun of an interview that included tape of swims Mitch made between 1990 and 2000, a sports documentary that aired once during school hours and again at 2 A.M., necessitating a video recording, which, as they didn't get ESPN, Will had dutifully petitioned a friend to make, resisting the temptation to say the show had been canceled. For faithfully fulfilling this promise, he was repaid by Luke's replaying it over and over and over, not so much for its entertainment value (there was so little), Will suspects, as for its ability to dissolve his parents' composure.

Every so often Will visits Luke's room and lies on the Tintin quilt, staring at the Wall of Mitch, as he's come to think of it, a sort of private Wailing Wall whose cracks he wants to find, chinks into which he can thrust little folded prayers, or, more likely, questions. Questions like, *What the fuck happened? Tell me why. Tell me how.*

Or: What's the meaning of having a brother who swims with the unnatural ease and grace of a fish and a son who in an instant slipped from the safety of a little boat—a boat his father failed to balance—and drowned? How can Will accommodate the coincidence of his identical twin, a disfigured copy of himself, vanishing onto the page and into the broadcast, multiplied into a legion of virtual incarnations who swim into the death of human, familial attachment, and a son who failed to swim and sank to a terribly nonmetaphoric death?

Is irony the only vantage from which to observe these irreconcilable facts? Irony isn't what Will wants, nor what he's come to understand he needs. It isn't transition. It isn't a way from here to there. It grants no solace, no transcendence. It's cheap. It's a last resort. It's a word to apply to the limits of human comprehension, a word that makes the inadequacy sound like sophistication.

"He's so cool. It's just not fair that I never get to meet him or anything." That Will couldn't explain his estrangement from Mitch made Luke regard his father with suspicion. It must be that Will had blundered somehow, insulted and alienated Mitch. Or maybe, Luke never said but implied, it was because a star like Mitch might not have had time for a brother who was a shrink. Some of Luke's friends—"Who?" Will demanded. "Who?" "Parker, that's who."—said that psychoanalysts were just plain psycho and that they were also homo and freakazoid. And if Will was a psycho-homo-freakazoid, then why would his cool brother want anything to do with him?

"Look," Will said to Luke, "you're right. Mitch is cool. He's famous and cool, and a lot of people admire him. But that wasn't always true. Because of the way he looked, the way his face was marked, he had a hard time as a kid. He was shy. He didn't have friends. He spent a lot of time alone. And when he was older, when he was a teenager and then a young man, he spent all his time swimming, hours and hours of swimming by himself, which was not only a way for him to stop feeling bad about his face but helped him make himself into a great athlete. And now that so many people admire and respect him and don't care about how he looks, or maybe they even think his face is cool because it's his—now that all those things are true, maybe Mitch just doesn't want to be with the people he was with when his life was hard and he was unhappy. Maybe Mom-Mom and Granddad and I remind him of a painful time, when he was young and living at home, and when kids at school either didn't talk to him or they teased him, and when he was so self-conscious that he was afraid of girls, afraid they'd never see him behind the birthmark on his face. It could be that now he's started over, now that he has a new life, he prefers not to be with us because that would force him to remember the old one." Will stopped, realizing that, faced with Luke's grave, assessing stare, he'd begun to repeat himself. "Do you understand what I'm saying?" he asked.

"Yes," Luke said. "But I don't think you're right."

"Why?"

"Because."

"Because why?"

"Because that kind of person who would just go away and never talk to his mother or father or brother—that would be a coward."

"He would be a coward."

"That's what I said."

"No, you said *that* instead of *he*."

"Okay, okay, so *he* would be a coward, and a person who goes to the Bermuda Triangle and swims in water with sharks where whole airplanes have disappeared can't be a coward because, you know, a great white shark could easily kill him. It would take—it would be like you killing a little bug or something."

"But, Lukey, there are different kinds of bravery. I agree absolutely that Mitch is brave—very brave—but I think it's a kind of bravery that he had to invent to help himself feel better about the early part of his life. Did you know, a lot of people who were unhappy as children turn into adults who achieve great things? Like Abraham Lincoln. Or President Clinton. Mike Tyson. Well, maybe Mike Tyson's not such a good example. No, actually, I take that back. He is. Because Tyson's way out of the misfortunes of his youth was his talent as a boxer, but even though he developed that ability, made it bigger and more pow- erful, he remained a complicated man; he couldn't really do what he wanted to do, which was escape his past. That's what all these people wanted to do—to get away from the unhappiness they'd lived through as children. And what they accomplished helped, it made them feel better, but it didn't erase what came before. And if that's true about Mitch, then his not talking to me or your grandparents wouldn't be cowardly, it would just be choosing to leave us behind."

Luke shook his head. "But it would still make him a jerk. And I know he's not a jerk."

"Why?"

"Because only jerks run away and hurt people's feelings like that. Like the way Mom says me and Sam have to not chase balls into the street or stick paper clips in electric sockets or get into a stranger's car, because if anything happened—"

"Well, yes, but Mitch is a man, not a little boy, and he hasn't run away or been kidnapped. He's just stopped calling or visiting."

"But why? Why did he?"

"I don't know for sure. I told you what my guess is."

"I think you're wrong. I think it's something else."

"Don't you imagine that as I grew up with Mitch, who is my own twin brother, I might know him better than you? That I might be able to guess his reasons a little more closely? Because actually you've never met him. So probably I do know him better."

Luke shook his head. "No."

"Why?"

"I just don't think you do, that's all."

A month after Luke drowned, Will's mother came to stay with them, and—just to keep busy, she said, just to be useful—cleaned their house. She began with the ground floor and worked her way up, at last arriving at the top-floor bedroom where Luke had slept and where she stopped and stared, her momentum destroyed so that Will had his chance to save the room from being dismantled.

"William!" she called down the stairs. "Will-yam!" She was waiting on the landing. "Have you seen this!"

"Well, yeah, Mom, obviously."

"I must never have come up here. You and Carole and the kids were always with us on the holidays, and I can't remember the last time your dad and I visited you in the city. So I must never have seen all this. And I have to tell you, William, if I had seen it, I would not have approved."

"No," Will said. "I don't imagine you would."

"But apparently you didn't consider this"—she waved her hand at

the wall—"a, a, an unhealthy fixation. At least not enough of a problem to make him take it down."

"Mom," Will said. "It has nothing to do with my approving or
disapproving. Carole and I agreed not to interfere because we found
that even the slightest suggestion that we weren't pleased by Luke's
interest in Mitch only intensified it. You know how kids are, Mom,
they have this radar for psychic wounds."

"Well," she said. And she walked quickly across the room and had
already torn down two posters by the time Will caught up with her.

"Hey!" he said. "You can't do that!"

Will's mother tried to pull her wrist out of his grasp. "Let go!"
she said.

"No! Don't touch it! Don't touch any of it. And give me those."
Will took the posters from her hand and smoothed out the creases.
"Christ, Mom, it's been, what, a month? Leave it. Leave it."

"William. You of all people, with your jealous private parts and
unconscious hostilities and whatnot. You should have been the first
to put a stop to it."

"Well, it's a little late, Mom, wouldn't you say?"

"For Luke, yes. But there's Samantha to consider. You can't leave
the room as it is, with all this, this . . ." She closed her eyes, waiting
for the right word. "Memorabilia," she said.

"I am, actually. I'm leaving it just as it is."

"Why!"

"Because."

"Because why!"

"Because I haven't finished looking at it." Will leaned against the
doorjamb, his arms crossed.

"Well, I'm talking to Carole about this. I think it's plain wrong.
There's no point in morbid staring. You select a few special things
and put them away, along with his schoolwork and report cards and

all those condolence cards you got. You can take everything out and look over it when you're ready. The rest you take down and give away. Or, if it's not something another child can use, you throw it away. And you have this room repainted. You change the furniture around, maybe get a nice little table or a reading chair, and then you have a guest room."

"We already have a place for guests."

"So then you have a study."

"Each of us has an office."

"Well, get a billiards table or a, a, a big fish tank or something, for heaven's sake, but don't leave it like this because it's not good for any-one."

At dinner she enlisted Carole's support, and both women argued for not only stripping but renovating Luke's bedroom and then giv-ing it to Will. "Look at all the options!" his mother said in her most chipper "Heaven Help You" voice. A mini-gymnasium with a tread-mill and a set of free weights. A library for all those psychoanalytical texts he had moldering in the basement. A music room with a piano. A video and DVD haven with a gazillion-dollar, high-resolution, holographic, plasma screen monstrosity.

"I just cannot sanction your sitting up there in the shadows and dwelling on all that, that tragedy, or taking naps on that sad little bed." Will's mother began crying. Carole picked up her glass and let it hang in the air, neither taking a drink nor putting it back down on the table.

"Lukey's bed isn't sad," Samantha said to her grandmother. "It's nice and it's funny and it has pictures of Snowy, and Snowy is cuter even than a bug dog."

"Pug," Will said. "Pug dog. And you're right, sweetie, it isn't sad."

"Well." His mother wiped her eyes and polished the lenses of her glasses. "Well, hell's bells," she said.

Elena came in, she dusted, and every so often she ran the sheets through the wash, but Will would not let the room be changed. He took the occasional nap on the bed, not getting in but lying on top of the comforter. He noticed Sam was coming in, too, gradually removing all the Legos and the board games and those few construction sets she found worth carrying back to her room. Will found a note she'd left on her brother's desk: *Dear Lueky, if you want yore legos thier in my room. Love, Sam. P.S. monoply is ther too.* When he tried to pick it up he found that she'd taped it to the desk's surface.

Upstate, his mother ran out of improvements to impose on her own house (those she did make barely noticed by his father) and, after forcefully reorganizing her friends' pantries, reimmersed herself in her cleaning business. Since then, she's never referred to Luke's room, she rarely speaks of Luke himself, and she's developed a tic that attends anyone else's mentioning her grandson, a sort of helpless salute: her right arm flies up as if to block her eyes from an intense, sudden glare and then falls back to her side.

Will picks at the corner of a glossy fold-out from *Swim* magazine and peels it carefully away from the wall until the last corner lifts off. Where the photograph covered the blue paint is a clean rectangle, unmarked by the little-boy grime of the life that had unfolded in Luke's room. He steps back, all the way to the door, and considers the one blank spot. Then he folds the poster along the creases of the two original folds that allowed it to fit within the borders of a magazine.

The metal trash can in the corner, the one decorated with Yankee insignia, is empty, clean, and after a moment he balls up the poster and drops it in and listens to the sound it makes when it strikes the can's metal bottom, a low note that lingers in the silence.

The waiter is on his hands and knees, using a napkin to gather shards of the broken glass. "I am so sorry," he says.

"It's all right. Really." Will stands from the table. "It's only water."

"I hope it's not a bad omen," Will's father says wryly, a joke, although not the kind he makes ordinarily.

"Oh no," the maître d' says, having rushed over. "No no no. We will make it into a good one." He sends the waiter away, returns with two glasses on a tray. "An auspicious Pinot Noir," he says, his expression indicating that the wine is at least expensive, if not lucky. "*Very* auspicious. With our apologies."

Will sits back down. "Nice restaurant," he says. "Too nice." He gestures at the extravagantly appointed room beyond the table. "Is this an occasion of some sort?"

"No occasion. Figured it might be fun." Will's father takes a sip and puts his glass down. "Truth is, I'm going back upstate. Wanted us to go out on a bang." He fiddles with the knot in his tie, adjusting it around the unfamiliar confines of a snugly buttoned collar. "An occasion for expensive indigestion."

"Upstate? As in back upstate to Mom?"

"Yup."

"Wow," Will says. "Why? I mean, don't get me wrong, when it comes to my parents I'm just as conventional as the next guy. I want you and Mom together, in the same old town, same old house, et cetera. Did something happen with Lottie?"

"No." His father smiles, and the smile looks genuine, if a little foolish. "Nothing like a disagreement, if that's what you mean. Turns out this is a thing she does."

"What is?"

"Acquires works by some new face, then acquires the face. Moves on."

"You were just one in a series?"

"Something like."

"Was that . . . are you—"

"I'm fine." Will's father swats the air in a dismissive gesture.

"Yeah?"

"Yup." He nods. "I want to get back to work full-time. I get antsy when I'm down here. City's crammed with stuff I don't want to take pictures of."

"Huh." Will looks at his father. "So that's it? Back to Mom? Return to status quo? No questions asked?"

"Unless you know something I don't know."

"What could I know? It's not like I discuss you or any of this with her. I just thought, well, that she might be a little ticked off or something."

"Why? She wasn't before."

"You keep saying that. I keep finding it hard to believe."

"Well, Will." His father turns his palms up. "It's true." He picks up the menu in its black leather folder. "Know what you're having?" he asks.

"Hanger steak."

"I'll do the same." His father closes the folder, places it on the edge of the table.

"I thought you were trying to get off red meat."

"Gave up. I was sick of arguing with the doctor. Went on Tricor. Lipitor? I can't remember which. The thing is, once you're taking one of these damn cholesterol pills, then you feel like it's home free, anything goes." He smiles. "I had eggs for breakfast," he says. "Eggs Benedict."

"Does it work that way, really?"

"No, of course it doesn't. Anyhow, your mother will put the kibosh on all that. So, what's eating you?"

"What's what?"

"I said, what's eating you." Will's father leans forward over the table. "Something's on your mind. What is it?"

"That obvious, huh?"

His father shrugs. "You're doing that thing you do." He points at Will's left hand, thumb and finger pinching the skin over his Adam's apple. Will gives his hand a shake as if it might dislodge the habit. He takes a deep breath.

"Well, Dad, here it is." He stops, takes a swallow of water. "I got in touch with a couple of women who I used to know. Date, I mean. And I found out that they . . . they were with Mitch at the same time as they were with me."

His father doesn't say anything. Then he says, "What's brought this up? And why would you do that? Look people up?"

"Why?"

"No, not why. How? What I mean is, how'd all this get started?"

"The reunion. The Cornell thing I went to last summer."

His father takes a sip of wine, puts the glass back down on the table, turns it slowly as if considering some aspect of its manufacture.

"So," he says, "these girls, these women, they were dating you and your brother at the same time?"

"Not dating, Dad. Fucking." He says the word again, one he's never heard his father use. "Fucking. Mitch and Elizabeth—that's who I saw at the reunion—they were fucking at the same time that she and I were fucking."

"Now, why would she do that?"

"Well, obviously, that's a very compelling question to which I wanted the answer. Mitch tricked her at first, and then she said it felt liberated and counterculture."

"I don't mean the sex part. I mean, why's she bringing it up now? Why talk at all about this, this . . . why discuss what's twenty-five years in the past?"

"Why ask that?" Will says. "Why is that your first response?" He returns his father's mild expression with a frown. "I started it. I started the whole thing by asking her—Elizabeth—something I probably shouldn't have."

"What was that?"

The waiter comes to them and silently sets their plates before them. "*Très chaud,*" he says. "Please to be careful. Hot hot hot." Will waits for him to leave and then turns back to his father.

"Remember last time we had lunch? When I told you about a patient whose treatment I was about to terminate? A young woman who made a pass at me? Kissed me?"

His father removes his knife from the meat in front of him and lays it on the side of his plate. "Yes," he says, and he doesn't lift the bite on the end of the fork but lays that implement down as well. He looks at Will. "What does that have to do with the, the Elizabeth woman?"

"They're connected."

"The girl and the woman?" Will nods. "Well, that qualifies as ominous," says his father. "As in a genuinely bad omen."

"Except she wasn't an omen, in that omens predict. She was more like a . . . a . . ." Will surprises himself by starting to cry, not audibly, but tears fall from his eyes; he can't speak.

"A what?" his father asks, after giving him time to stop.

"A wish," Will says. "Not an omen, a wish."

His father picks up his fork and turns it in his fingers, looking at the cold morsel of steak. He puts it in his mouth, chews slowly in the manner of a person savoring what he eats. "I don't understand," he says after swallowing.

"No." Will shakes his head. "I haven't said anything understandable." He draws a deep breath. "In June, at the reunion, I got a class book that included letters from anyone in the class of 'seventy-nine who bothered to send one in. I went through them all, reading the ones written by people I remembered, a few friends. I came across Elizabeth's and read it closely—normal, right? she'd been my girlfriend—and in it I find references to a child born seven or eight months after we split up." Will stops. He looks at his father, who has cut his steak into precise squares and is eating them, one after another, no potato, no sip of wine, no salad, nothing between bites of meat.

"I'm listening to you," he says. "I'm paying attention."

Will drinks from both his water and wineglass. "So, are you beginning to understand?"

"Keep talking."

"I make the obvious conclusion. And, while I didn't admit this to myself in the moment—I wasn't aware of it—when I don't see Elizabeth the first night of the reunion I'm surprised by how disappointed I am. But the next evening, during this big reception, I do see her. We catch up on twenty years or so—pleasant, chatty, a little flirtatious. That tipsy, floaty kind of banter that can slide into a situation where you find yourself saying these, these things, and then later you wonder how it could have happened, how you could have been so, so— well, so the way you were.

"It's only a matter of time before I've told her about Luke. You know what's coming next. I ask if she was pregnant when she left me. And I ask if she might be willing to give me a sample of her child's— it's a girl—her daughter's hair." Will sees his father's expression. "I know, I know," he says. "Stupid. I hear myself tell you the story, and I know I've opened up what should have remained closed. But, honestly, Dad, while I was talking to her, at the reunion, it seemed like a natural enough desire. To know. It even seemed rational. Not risky or out-there."

"You wanted the hair for DNA testing?" his father asks.

Will nods.

"She give it to you?"

"No. She was pissed off. I should have backed down then, but I didn't. For some reason I just couldn't let go of the idea, couldn't give it up, and we part. Not amicably. We—I—well, the conversation deteriorated into something of a scene, raised voices, et cetera."

"Christ, Will, do not tell me—do not"—Will's father puts his hand up in a *Halt!* gesture—"do not connect the two stories into one big mess." He flags down a busboy and points to his empty wineglass.

Will slides his glass across the table. "Here, finish mine."

"You haven't eaten your meal," his father says.

"I can't eat and talk at once. So, for a month, two months, nothing. I do end up apologizing, via e-mail—no reply, and I'm increasingly relieved. I'm even—I have that little burst of excited happiness, like when a car just misses running you over—I know I've narrowly escaped screwing up my life."

"Enter the French-kissing patient."

"Enter the French-kissing patient. With whom I terminate treatment, and who stalks me, calls my office, my home, until, one day, she buzzes and, thinking it's a different patient, I let her in. Then she . . . well, she manipulates me into a sexual encounter."

"How the goddamn hell does she do that!"

"Shhh! Stop yelling."

"Don't tell me to be quiet! In your office! Your office! You had sex with her in your office!"

"Dad—"

"I want to know how the goddamn hell a twenty-year-old child can manipulate a forty-seven-year-old goddamn psychoanalyst into having sex with her in his goddamn office!"

"Twenty-four. And you know why I didn't throw her out right away? I'll tell you. Because she started saying 'please,' and 'give me another chance,' and it never occurred to me that she wasn't being sincere. The only thing I thought of, actually, was how when we were kids Mitch could always wear me down if he begged me long enough.

"Right after this, after the sex, she tells me who she is—Elizabeth's daughter, Jennifer. But that's not all she says. She says Elizabeth wasn't involved with me alone. She was also having sex with my brother and with two other guys. And since Mitch and I are twins, we'll never know, because the DNA could only show that it's one of us, not which one.

"I meet with Elizabeth, who confirms what her daughter said and is irate. Basically accuses me of being a rapist, a liar, and a nutcase. After talking with Elizabeth, it occurs to me that Mitch, who, incidentally, slept with Elizabeth not once but many times—slept with Elizabeth almost the entire time she was sleeping with me, tricked her into it at first, pretending to be me—Mitch could have had sex with other girlfriends of mine." Will shakes his head. "I don't know why, but I always thought of him as a—well, almost as a eunuch or something. He never seemed like he had a sex drive at all. I mean, when we were kids, there was the usual stuff. I knew he whacked off. He knew I did. We shared a bedroom. But by the time he was fifteen, sixteen, somewhere in there, he—it just seemed like he turned it off. Or funneled it all into swimming—that's what I assumed. The way an athlete—a real athlete who works out all day—is said to dampen physical desire, expend that energy another way. For a while I even thought he might be gay—"

"He wasn't gay," his father says. "And he wasn't a eunuch, either."

"I guess not." Will leans back to look at his father. "What do you know about it?" he says, but his father doesn't answer.

"Go on," he prompts Will.

"The first time with Elizabeth, at first she didn't know it wasn't me, because it was dark and there was no way to tell the difference between us in the dark. After all, she expected it to be me—it's not like she's going to, say, quiz him for answers only I'd be able to give. So the first time he tricks her." Will watches his father drink the last of a third glass of wine. "Aren't you at all drunk?" he asks.

"I wish I were." He stands. "However, I'll take the opportunity to use the men's room."

Will watches his father make his way through the tables, trying to decide if he expects the man he sees—white-haired, favoring his left hip—to help him pull himself together. Yes, he decides, he does. There may be no reason beyond habit, ancient filial hope, but this is enough. His father returns, sits in the opposite chair, crosses his arms. "All right," he says. "Let's get to the end of this."

"Okay. So. I use the Internet to search for whoever I can find from a list of all the girlfriends I remember—camp, college." Will looks at his father, who nods, makes a rolling gesture with one hand that says, Go on.

"I find a woman, Lisa Christianson, who lived not too far from us. I saw her the summer between junior and senior years, when both Mitch and I were home. That was the summer he got permission to use the high school gym, the pool and everything, and I was working for that landscape guy."

"The dairy Christiansons?"

"The same. She's upstate now, running a bonsai nursery with her husband. I e-mail to tell her I'd like to drop by. I drive up, go to Lisa's place, we talk, and guess what? I'm right. I can't believe it—well, I can, it's the reason I went up there—but I'm right, Mitch did have sex with her. Same idea. Tricked her the first time. Sometimes they even had sex on the same night I'd taken her to a movie or dinner. I drop her off at home, at eleven, conscientious because her dad was old-fashioned about those things. Two hours later—two hours after I've played the role of gentleman and fool—Mitch's screwing her.

"Again, the first time is undercover, in the dark, he has some blindfold trick and reveals himself only after they've had sex. Lisa doesn't think it's cool or liberated or whatever, and she's scared of Mitch. I don't know what he did to frighten her, but she doesn't disobey his directive to keep quiet. She goes on meeting him at night and follows his order not to tell me."

Will's father nods. "Then what?"

"Then what!"

"I mean, where are you now? Have you contacted anyone else?"

"No. I don't need to." Will shakes his head. "I don't know, Dad. What am I supposed to do with this?"

His father puts his hand across the table, takes Will's, gives it a squeeze.

"You know," Will says, taking his hand back, "I knew Lisa would tell me that it had happened with her, too. I did. I knew it. And yet I was shocked. Shocked sick. Literally." Will looks at his father, and the two of them watch each other without speaking until Will can't stand it anymore.

"I have a question, Dad," he says. "I've been thinking about it, thinking about asking you this question ever since I got back from talking to Lisa. No, before that. It occurred to me on the way home from seeing Elizabeth in Philadelphia, but I managed to, I don't know, put it aside." His father raises his eyebrows.

"Why did Mitch disappear after the rehearsal dinner? Why was it then that he broke off contact with us?"

Will's father leans back in his chair. He tips his head up, toward the ceiling, which, Will sees as he follows his father's eyes, is painted to look like the urban sky—not a celestial vision of *putti* and clouds, but buildings reaching upward, a slice of atmosphere between the expertly foreshortened façades of skyscrapers. After a minute, his father looks back at him.

"I told him to," he says.

"Why, Dad? Why?" Will shakes his head, eyes closed. "Oh shit," he says.

"She didn't know what to do. She came to me, knocked on our door at the hotel."

"What am I supposed to do with this!" Will says, loudly enough that the few remaining diners turn toward him, then look away.

"Look, I did what seemed like a . . . a . . . what seemed proportionate. Is that a word? The only thing I could think of that had a severity in proportion to the, the . . ." He holds his hands up, empty, and they look at each other. "I'm sorry, Will. I did what seemed . . . I did what I did. I hoped we'd all move on."

"Well," Will says. "I guess I know the punch line. I want the whole story. I want what came before." He pushes his plate away. "So," he says, "go ahead."

Will's father laces his fingers together and looks down at his hands. He makes a noise like a whistle, but lower. "You remember your bachelor party?"

"Not especially well. I was, I believe, getting plastered in the time-honored way."

"You remember your brother leaving at some point?"

"Maybe. I think he said he was going back to the hotel, that he was still in training, had to get a decent night's sleep."

His father nods. "Right. That would have been around ten-thirty, eleven."

Will shrugs. "We're talking fifteen years ago. All I know is that the party went on for a while without him."

"Call it ten-thirty. Carole and her bridesmaids, all the women from the rehearsal dinner, women friends from out of town, they were at—what was the name of that place?"

"I don't remember."

"Well, whatever the name was."

"It was a male strip club. Not Chippendale's, but the same idea. Her sister set the whole thing up. Carole was anxious about it, embarrassed. Thought it was vulgar. And it was, objectively speaking. Guys, handsome young guys dancing in G-strings. She was worried you and Mom would think it was white trash or something."

Will's father waves his hand. "We had no idea what it was. Anyway, at eleven, there's a surprise guest at the girls' party. Looks familiar, height, hands, knees, his face is hidden. Now Mitch's always been in top physical condition, but he carries some fat for insulation, and in a smoky, dark nightclub . . . Also, it's just before your wedding, when you were, what, thirty-two? Still working out, running in the morning." Will nods. "So, Mitch, wearing a G-thing and a—I don't know—whatever getup those guys had instead of clothes. He's gotten himself dressed in the club outfit, what there was of it. A G-thing and a bow tie, and he's wearing one of those gorilla masks."

"A gorilla mask?"

"Yeah, like King Kong. Black rubber with hair—fur—stuck in, big ape face, the kind of mask that covers your whole head. The only significant aspect is that it disguises the one physical thing that would distinguish him from you."

"Yes, I get that. Go on."

"He comes up behind Carole, speaking with a voice that sounds just like yours, says something to the effect that her little bachelorette party is nearly over and he has a special treat for her. Lots of giggling and shenanigans. The women're all drunk, too, remember. Making off-color jokes about deflowering, which really is a joke since, as we all know, today everyone lives together before they marry—if they marry—and the white dress is only an old-fashioned reference. But, anyway, there's some kind of playacting or teasing—your wife—your fiancée at that moment—she was too hysterical to tell us the exact subterfuge, but whatever it was, she ends up leaving the party to be with you. To be with a man dressed as a stripper who she thinks is you.

"She does find it strange that you insist on wearing the mask while making love, but she's tired and overstimulated and, like I said, drunk, and she figures that you, too, are tired, overstimulated, and drunk, and if she doesn't think it's funny, maybe you do." He shakes his head.

"Where is this happening?"

"In your room, yours and Carole's, at the hotel—Carole has the key. You—I mean Mitch, but she thinks it's you—you say you've left yours behind, you're wearing someone else's clothes over the G-thing—"

"String! G-string!"

"Okay. String. String. Somehow you've gotten separated from

your clothes and had to borrow another guy's to drive back to the hotel. She's changed out of her party dress into a—well, I don't know. Mitch's wearing the King Kong thing, has sex with Carole—consensual, because, remember, she thinks it's you—and, as with Elizabeth and the other one, I guess, doesn't reveal himself until after it's over. Carole has no idea—why would she? It's unthinkable, so she doesn't think it. Until—"

"Until he pulls off his mask."

"At which point she starts screaming. It's late enough and she screams loud enough and long enough that other hotel guests alert the management. Someone calls the front desk to say there's a robbery or a rape or God knows what in room whichever. The front desk calls the room. Mitch picks up and hangs up the receiver without answering the person on the other end. Pulls on his trousers, and by the time the hotel has someone knocking on the door, he's back in his own room, lights out, all quiet. After all, the story was he was tired or what have you, he came back to the hotel to go to bed.

"Carole answers the door, pulls herself together enough to tell security or whoever they sent up that everything is all right, she saw what she thought was a man in her room but it turned out to be nothing, a coat hanging in the shadows, you know how that can happen. Why didn't she answer the phone? security wants to know. She doesn't know. It's late, she's nervous. She's sorry she's disturbed the other guests, but she's getting married the next day, it's just nerves. Is she sure there wasn't any man? Yes. Does she want a new room? No, no, everything is fine, she's sorry for causing any trouble.

"Hotel whoever leaves. She takes a shower, tries to calm down in the shower. The only thing she can think to do is to tell us, your mother and me. Her mother's not there yet, remember, and if she tells you, if she tells her sister, if she calls the police—if she does any of these, it'll end up ruining the wedding and hurting you. So she gets dressed, and she comes to our room. Figures we know Mitch. Assumes we do, anyhow.

"It's past midnight, both the parties are still going—yours and hers—only old folks like us are in their rooms, them and Mitch. She knocks at the door, wakes us up. Your mother opens the door, sees Carole crying and thinks the two of you have had a spat, or that Carole has cold feet or you do, or she's sick or you're sick, or it's late and you haven't come back from the party or—she doesn't know what to think. Asks Carole in, sits her down. For a long time, seemed like an hour but it couldn't have been that long, your wife is crying. She's curled up in a chair, feet on the cushion, hugging her knees, and, well, we're mystified, we have no idea what the heck is going on.

"Finally, after coaxing and coaxing and frankly begging, finally she says, 'Mitchell.'

"'Mitchell what?' we ask. Something's happened to Mitch? Mitch's sick? Mitch has had an accident? A fight—a physical fight—with you? What is it? We don't understand. We want to help but we don't understand.

"Carole is still, at this point, hysterical. Not hysterics as in loud, but she's shaking her head, crying, and not telling us a thing. At which point your mother decides to give her a pill, one of those old Miltown things, probably too stale to have an effect—after all, they've been in her handbag since 1972 or whenever it was she had that Bell's palsy and the doctor thought it was nerves. Carole takes the pill, and your mother has her lie down, puts a cold washrag over her eyes, tells her if she doesn't stop crying, her face will be swollen, and she wants to look pretty on her wedding day, of course she does, she wants to be beautiful, and finally—never underestimate the placebo effect, or the power of female vanity. Pride's maybe a better word. Don't get me wrong, I'm not saying Carole's vain. Anyway, she stops crying, she's calm enough to speak.

"'Will's brother came to the club dressed as a . . . as an entertainer,' she says. 'He was wearing a mask that covered his face and he said he was Will.' She's calm now. Absolutely calm. Considering the Carole of five minutes before, her composure is almost as disturbing as her hysterics, but, well, at least we're making progress. Your mother asks questions, Carole answers them.

"'Mitch pretended he was Will?' your mother says.

"'Yes,' Carole says. 'He said he was coming to take me back to the hotel and that then we were going to make love.'

"Hearing this, your mother puts her hand over her mouth and that's the end for her, she doesn't say another thing. So I start asking the questions. Carole's lying on the bed, and the washrag is still over her eyes. She speaks very deliberately, calmly. Your mother's a zombie, and me, well, somehow I've fallen into some goddamn Ingmar Bergman movie, one of those subtitled things where you don't really want to figure out what's going on.

"'He didn't have a key to our room,' she tells me, 'because he wasn't Will. But I didn't know he wasn't Will.'

"Bit by bit she tells us the story I just told you, and then we all sit there. Not one of us says a thing.

"'It's one-thirty,' I say, when that's the time. 'Everyone's coming back to the hotel soon. Will's going to be back soon—maybe he's on his way now. I think you should go to your room. I'll deal with Mitch.'

"'How?' She wants to know, and your mother wants to hear the answer, too. And, put on the spot, without having had a plan the minute before, I say that—assuming Carole doesn't want to press charges—and I ask her again, this is the fourth time, at least the fourth time, 'Are you sure you don't want to press charges?' Because she would have been—the fact that Mitch was about to become her brother-in-law didn't alter the fact that he'd sexually, uh, what, assaulted her. Well, not assaulted exactly, but a woman can't consent to be with someone who she doesn't know who he is." Will's father frowns. "That might've come out wrong, but you know what I mean.

"Anyway, Carole's sure she doesn't want to press charges. She wants to get married in nine hours, ten hours, however long it is until eleven that morning. As if ever since your mother told her to lie down and not cry and spoil her looks, she's decided that the thing to do is to go on with the show. She's adamant that you don't find out what happened—not now, not that night. It's not her fault, clearly, but she acts as if it is. She seems ashamed and—"

"How could you have allowed this to happen! How could you—my own father—conspire to deceive me? It's, it's—you contributed to what he did! You added to his betrayal!"

"I don't know. I guess I made a mistake, that's how. You know I'm—for Chrissakes, Will, it's always been a joke in this family about how bad I am in these situations. You know—Hank Moreland became a veterinarian so he'd never have to make conversation with a patient. Would never have to answer a difficult question. Not exactly serendipitous then, that a mess of this proportion would fall into my hands, but it did. And I made a mistake. I see that, I saw it long ago. But I wanted to do anything that would get Carole calmed down and just, I don't know, patch it up, have the wedding go on as planned. It was her marriage, hers and yours. I figured she knew best."

"You betrayed me."

"I apologize." They stare at each other.

"All right," Will says. "I accept your apology. What choice do I have?"

"Well, there's two," Will's father says. "You can accept it. Or you can refuse it." He takes a mouthful of water and swishes it around in his mouth before swallowing it. "Dry tongue. That's the trouble with red wine."

Will drinks from his glass of water. "I accept," he says. "I'm just angry, that's all."

His father nods. "Well, all right. I accept that. Your anger. Do you want me to go on with—"

"Yeah, let's get to the end."

"I tell Carole if she can stand for your brother to be at the service and the reception, then what I propose is, I'll tell Mitch that I know what's happened, that Carole's told your mother and me, and that he'll have to leave directly after the wedding. He's—he has to leave. If he doesn't comply, then he'll face rape charges. I suggest that she, since she's not reporting the rape, not being examined by a doctor or giving a sample of—a swab to determine whose sperm—maybe she can keep, I don't know, underpants or a nightgown or whatever might have Mitch's, uh, seminal fluid on it.

"There's nothing like that, she says, and anyway, what good is it if he's your twin? Obvious, right, but I'm so rattled I'm not thinking straight. She agrees to the plan, and I escort her to her room, check to make sure it's empty, safe, and then leave her there. I tell her to keep the chain thing on until you get back—I'll be talking with Mitch.

"Mitch answers his door. Pretends to have been asleep. He must know why I'm there, but he pretends he's confused, doesn't understand what I'm talking about. He's innocent, Carole's crazy. She was probably having sex with you and the both of you were drunk or something. 'Search me,' he says. 'Search the room. There's no mask or anything here.' 'Of course there isn't,' I say. 'What does that prove? Besides, Will is still at the stag thing, there's a roomful of family and friends who've been with him all night, and they know he didn't leave to spirit Carole back to the hotel for a, a romantic interlude.'

"So then he admits what he's done. He's without remorse." Will's father shakes his head, turns up his empty palms. "Carole's ashamed. He's not. How to square that? My own son—he seemed like no one I knew. He wouldn't speak of the motivation—the hatefulness—behind the act. He seemed like a, a sociopath, a person you read about, not anyone you know, certainly not someone you're related to. A person without the ability to imagine, let alone care about, another human being's feelings. Or to . . . to realize that other people's feelings are as important as his. Not that he's showing any emotion, he's not. I'm confused by him, the whole thing. Way out of my depth, whatever's happening inside that head.

"I tell him the conditions under which he can avoid being apprehended for raping his brother's fiancée on the eve of their wedding, and he agrees to them. Except he's not going to go to the wedding, he says. He's going to leave right that minute. Because if he stays through the next day, if he goes to the wedding, if he has to dress himself up as your best man, he'll tell you himself. Which"—Will's father makes what his mother calls his Abe Lincoln face, pained by human failings and more or less resigned to everything turning out badly.

"Which is probably what should have happened. But, well, we . . . I . . . I thought I could just get rid of it. Him. That Carole could tell you when and if she wanted to. And I was disgusted. Didn't want to look at him, wanted him out of, out of the picture, so to speak. Out of the frame." He shakes his head. "I didn't have much of an idea what would happen down the line, but I didn't imagine he'd never contact any of us again. I thought he'd just go off for a while and by the time he came back we'd've had time to figure out a, a . . . well, we'd've figured something out.

"End of story," Will's father says. He covers his face with his hands. "Christ, I'm sorry. What a mess." He takes his hands away, looks around the restaurant. Ten or twelve of the waitstaff are gathered around a table in the back, talking quietly and eating. Otherwise the place is empty.

"But why?" Will says. "Why?"

"Why what?"

"Why did he? How?"

"For the obvious reason, I assume. I don't have any other explanation. What else is there besides your unmarked face? The ease with which you moved through life when he was unhappy, struggling. He hid his anger—hid it from all of us. I think he must have been about six when he became self-conscious, aware of it—the thing—like he hadn't been before.

"You protected him, tried to make friends for him. Any situation, you always went on ahead of him, told other kids about his face and not to tease him or you'd make them sorry. At school, you'd pick out a few, bring them home to play. Punched a couple, the ones that said anything. But I don't know that any of that mattered to Mitch. Or that he noticed how you worked to save him from being hurt. How you loved him. Maybe all he saw was that you had a face that was perfect and he was a monster."

Will shakes his head. "I never understood why you and Mom were so complacent about the whole thing. Why you never tried to get it fixed. Why you didn't take him to New York, or even Albany, to see if you could get something—anything—done about it."

"We did! For God's sake, Will, of course we did. Your mother took him to a plastic surgeon in Albany for a consultation. Took him down to New York as well."

"When? When did you?"

"Well, the first time you would've been two. But she kept trying, after that she kept trying. The time you and I went fishing—you must remember, I know you do, because it was such a bust, we didn't catch even one fish and you just about got sun poisoning—that was the time your mother and Mitch went to the doctor in Albany. Then, another time, you and me at Saranac, and your mother with Mitch in New York City seeing a different plastic surgeon, guy that specialized in scars, birthmarks—cosmetic stuff. The thing was so extensive, he said, the vascular involvement, and at the time lasers were so rudimentary, that if he'd undertaken to fix it, the result would likely have been just another kind of disfigurement. We got as far as considering replacing that whole area of skin with a graft from his buttock, but it was a whole series of operations, too expensive, frankly, for us to manage. Long, painful, and it's not as if the result would have been a normal face.

"If we could have bought him a face that looked the same as yours, well, then we'd have mortgaged the house, the practice, whatever it took, but while it might have been better, it wouldn't look like a face someone was born with. And because you're twins, the injustice was that Mitch would always see an ideal version of himself, across the playground, the classroom, the dinner table. He couldn't escape you. We thought about boarding school, separation, but . . . I don't know. You were so protective of Mitch that we were afraid to send him out into the world by himself. We made mistakes. Probably we made mistakes. Hell, of course we did. But they weren't from lack of trying. Or for lack of seeing and caring about what was happening."

Will shakes his head. "My brother fucked my girlfriends, and he fucked my wife on the night before we got married. And my father and mother and wife keep this secret from me. For fifteen years. I have . . . I don't even know what my response to this is. Right now, I don't feel a thing. I'm too . . . too . . . I don't know what I am."

On the subway, Will isn't thinking of Jennifer, or of Mitch and Elizabeth, or Mitch and Lisa, or even Mitch and Carole, but of the first Halloween that his brother refused to wear the mask he'd chosen for himself. Their mother had never dressed them in matching clothes or encouraged them to regard their being identical—nearly—twins as special or even interesting, and they'd never worn costumes that were even slightly similar. Typically, Will was the grotesque of the two—not the kind of monster whose external ugliness cloaked virtue but one whose face represented a malignant soul. That year he wasn't any recognizable miscreant, not Mr. Hyde or Count Dracula or Dr. Frankenstein's terrible mistake, but a freak of his own making. Hunchbacked under ragged clothes topped by a repellent werewolf mask guaranteed to frighten the smaller children, he had green rubber gloves covered with putrescent warts and lumps.

Mitch was to be Clark Kent, not yet Superman but the earnest reporter on the verge of becoming Superman: the phone booth moment of transformation. He had on a suit that was a little too small (it had been purchased for a cousin's wedding the previous year) and a white shirt torn open to the waist to reveal the superhero's big red-and-yellow *S* emblazoned on his true-blue chest. Over his own face, Mitch wore a mask with Superman's blandly handsome countenance, with its cleft chin and iconic squiggle of black hair, hair too filled with vigor to remain tamed by brilliantine or whatever it was that supposedly kept the rest of it in place.

"I want to trade," Mitch suddenly said.

"No way."

"Come on. Please."

"No," Will said. "I hate being the good guy."

"I'll rake tomorrow."

"Unh-uh. No deal."

"Come on, Will, please. Did you see how many leaves there are? It'll take all afternoon."

"No."

"I won't go unless you trade."

"Fine. Don't go. What do I care?" Will took off his gloves to tie a shoelace that had come undone.

"Come on, Will. Please."

"No."

"All the raking, then. Not just tomorrow, but after, when the rest of the leaves come down."

"No," Will said. "No, no, no." Stalwart until Mitch cried, something Will couldn't stand and on which he tried and failed to turn his back. The sight of his brother giving up against his grief, the suddenness of Mitch's losing the ability to hide it: this had always had the power to dismantle Will. When Mitch cried, Will felt guilty and cornered and like he had to do something—anything—to stop it.

"Okay," he said, "here." He handed Mitch the mask, the gloves, the hunchback from last year's Igor costume, a cushion to which their mother had sewn two loops of elastic, one to go around each arm and hold it in place, and the ragged, grave-moldered cloak inherited from another year's vampire.

Will put on the Superman shirt and over it the dark suit; he adjusted the plastic do-gooder face. Without talking, he and Mitch went downstairs, stood patiently and listened to the usual cautions, and received quick hugs, each getting the embrace meant for the other brother. Will felt something different in his mother's arms, a communication that wasn't meant for him: an extra little squeeze of protective love and what was almost a tremble of maternal hope, the bodily equivalent of a prayer—please, please don't let them tease him. That's okay, Will told himself under the mask as the two of them went out the door and down the walk. That's okay with me. I don't mind because he needs that. Mitch needs more—more love, an extra cookie, a longer good-night kiss—a little more of everything. Still, he was stung—jealous enough that he knew he wouldn't have been able to hide it, and grateful his face was hidden.

They joined the neighborhood boys on the corner. As if by agreement, neither of them told the other kids that they'd traded costumes but continued under their masks to pretend to be each other. For Will it was a night of silent watching; he learned how seldom other children interacted with his brother. And it must have been, he imagines, a night of discovery for Mitch as well, jostled amiably, joked with, spoken to.

Later, at home, they dumped out their pillowcases to compare hauls, made a few trades, and argued with their mother about exactly how much candy they were allowed to eat that night, only Mitch complying with the limit she set. Then Mitch went up to their room, probably to sort through his baseball cards, shuffle past one after another hearty, handsome face, while Will stayed up with his father, watching *Creature Features*'s Halloween Marathon, and making his way steadily through his candy, methodically unwrapping and chewing what seemed imperative to get rid of and yet was too valuable to just throw out. It took until midnight to make himself good and sick.

"Well, that's a first, just about," his father said, holding Will's head over the downstairs toilet. "I can't remember the last time you threw up."

Will wonders how old he was that fall. He remembers that he'd felt very sorry for himself, so much so that he cried before he got sick, cried because he knew he was going to be sick and that it was his own fault. He didn't understand what he'd done to himself, or why.

The following year Halloween fell on a Friday, and the school held a party in the gymnasium. Will went; he convinced Stacey Davis to come with him to the stairwell, where she poured the contents of a red PixieStix onto her tongue and then let him lick it off before it melted away. Mitch stayed home and handed out candy. He wore a rubber political mask—Richard Nixon, Will thinks it was.

Mitch, his twin, the solitary swimmer, champion of the rights of manatees and hair seals, a man who can withstand whole days in the ocean. Does he remain the boy who traded ten or fifteen hours of raking and bagging leaves for one night of wearing the ugly mask instead of the handsome one? Did he hate Will already by that Halloween, or did that come later, the next year, when he stopped going out in costume, seemingly content to stay home?

Will's parents had done what his father called "their level best" to offset Mitch's antisocial nature. They pushed him into chess club, debate, Young Scientists of America, anything the A- and B-list kids, who filled the yearbook staff, football team, pep squad, and band, left to the losers and dorks, unfortunates who Will and Mitch's parents assumed would be less likely to focus on Mitch's face. Neither of them anticipated that the pariahs might be crueler than their pretty, popular classmates. They didn't understand that one untouchable resented being forced to make do with the damning company of others, that they were all venomous in a way that the luckier, more likeable kids never were. Always, Mitch capitulated to their mother's relentless goading—she called it "enthusiasm." He'd go to these gatherings once, only once, and then refuse to return.

And now, a new picture to add to the others, the image of his brother masked and slipping through the night to steal not just another girlfriend but his wife. An act of hatred? Of desperation? Would it even be possible to parse out one from the other?

So we've both lost a son, Will thinks, referring to himself and to his father. Scenes flash through his head like snapshots—or maybe they are snapshots, images he remembers from the old family albums. The three of them, Will and Mitch and their father, playing touch football in the backyard. Sitting together on the beach, shading their eyes with their hands. Will mugging from behind the wheel of the old station wagon and Mitch sitting on the hood, his turtleneck sweater pulled up so that only his hair showed.

W ill drops his briefcase on the table by the front door. "Hey," he says to Carole, who's sitting on the couch, her arms folded, the current issue of *Yoga Journal* in her lap. At the sound of his voice, she uncrosses her arms, picks up the magazine, and starts flipping through it.

Will glances up the stairs toward their daughter's room. "Where's Sam?" he asks. He doesn't know that he's ever seen Carole take the time to sit and read a magazine before their daughter was in bed.

"Watching a movie."

"Upstairs?"

Carole nods, but she doesn't look up.

"She okay?"

"Why wouldn't she be?"

"I don't know. She doesn't usually watch TV on a weeknight. I thought maybe she wasn't feeling well or something."

"She's fine." Carole comes to the end of the magazine and then starts again at the beginning, licking her index finger and using it to flick past the pages, not so fast that she doesn't quickly scan each one.

"What are you doing, Carole?" Will asks her.

"This is what I hate about *Yoga Journal*," she says. She sounds so fed up, it's as if she's at last voicing a serious complaint of many years' standing. "Every issue, every single issue, there's something on the

cover that you can't find inside. Look." She thrusts the magazine at
Will, talking faster than usual. "Seven Steps for Turning Bad Habits
into Good Ones." She opens the magazine to the table of contents.
"Look. Just look. Do you see 'Seven Steps for Turning Bad Habits
into Good Ones'? No. No you do not. That's because it's not there.
Page by page, I've gone through the entire issue, trying to find anything that might fit the description—'seven steps for turning bad into
good'—and there's nothing. Not one paragraph." She slaps the magazine down on the coffee table. Will sits carefully in the chair opposite the couch.

"You don't have any bad habits, Carole."

"That is not the point. The point is—"

"Carole?" he interrupts.

"What?"

"Is something going on?"

"You tell me," she says. He glances upstairs.

"How long's the DVD going to last?" he asks.

"What?"

"I need to talk to you."

"Yes, I guess you do."

"What's that supposed to mean?"

She closes her eyes as if there's no expression, no other gesture
that could possibly convey her exasperation. "Will—"

"Wait. There's something I have to tell you, Carole. I had lunch
with my father and—"

"Will, I don't want to talk about anything until you listen to—"

He holds up one hand, as if directing a driver to stop. It's the kind
of communication—wordless, and, in her opinion, appropriate only
for animal trainers or airport ground crews—that has in the past pro-
voked her to walk out on an argument. She makes a little huff of
protest.

"We have to talk now," he says. "If we don't . . . if I don't say this now . . ." He shakes his head.

"What is it?"

Will takes a deep breath. "How . . ." He takes another breath. "Carole?" he says, after allowing the silence to grow uncomfortable. "I've, uh . . . something bad's happened. My fault. I did something stupid, and then I made it even worse. Not on purpose. I had lunch with my father. I . . . God, I'm telling this all backwards. I'm trying to go in the right order, but it's not—it's hard to make sense of. I asked him why Mitch left when he did, why he skipped out before the wedding. I had . . . I'd always suspected there was something. Why didn't you tell me, Carole?"

She takes her hands from her face but she doesn't look at him. "I . . . I don't know," she says. "We . . . I . . . I didn't plan to keep it a secret."

"But you did. You kept it a secret for fifteen years. And now, now I've done something terrible. And it's all related, it's all tangled up in the same . . ." Will trails off, watching Carole shake her head, her eyes downcast.

"After he . . . after Mitch . . . there wasn't any way to get back to how it was before," she says. "How I was. Because it was one of those things that—it just divided everything. Me. It divided me into before and after. And how could I change that?" She looks up at him, speaking faster than usual, and more loudly; her voice has lost its characteristic calm. "I mean from the outside would anyone even think I was raped? It was all messed up. Everything was. The person who I, who . . . the, the person was someone I invited into our room. And now there was this ugly, this dirty thing that would play out in front of everyone we knew, everyone we cared about. Our families, people from work, guests from out of town, friends from college. It would . . . I was afraid it would always be, 'Oh, you remember them, don't you? She's the one who was raped, or, or tricked, or . . . or whatever it was, by the groom's twin brother.'" Suddenly Carole is on her feet, pacing and waving her arms as she speaks. Will didn't even see her get up from where she was sitting; she moved that fast.

"I wanted to save face. Or I guess what I mean is, I didn't want to lose face. I was *scared*, Will. And I tried to tell you. Later, I did. But whenever I mentioned Mitch, you changed the subject. You were . . . I felt like you were avoiding the topic. So, I quit. I quit trying so—"

"No!" Will says. "I have no memory, none, of your trying to tell me anything."

"But I did. And how it turned out—that wasn't calculated. I didn't intend for you to not ever know. Maybe . . . maybe that was what your father wanted. Or maybe it was what they both—your mom and your dad—wanted. Or what I thought they'd want. Or vice versa, what they thought I would. I mean, Jesus, Will, you don't know how many times I've gone over this. Anyway, they're all after the fact, these interpretations. I can't remember what I was thinking then, that night, and that's because I wasn't thinking anything. Except I wanted us to get married and everything to be okay." She looks at Will, waiting for him to speak, but he says nothing, and she goes on.

"I didn't have any idea of how . . . how emotionally costly it would become. That wasn't something I even considered in the moment— why would I?—I never planned to keep it a secret. Not indefinitely. But the longer I didn't tell you, the more difficult it got. Once I'd said nothing for a day, since it was our wedding day, and then for all of our honeymoon—because I didn't want to wreck that. It was, you know, our *honeymoon*, and I wanted to protect it, that little bubble of time. And after, when we were back home, it just got . . . it got harder and harder to imagine myself introducing the topic. We'd be apart from each other all day, both of us working, and I'd have scripted a dialogue in my head, rehearse how I was going to begin it, but whenever the chance presented itself, I . . . I didn't. It got to be as if it never happened. Sometimes it seemed so unreal, it was as if it had been a sort of, oh, I don't know, some overwrought fantasy about myself and a famous person, someone who doesn't even exist outside the media. The way a teenager might dream about having a date with Brad Pitt or someone. Since that's what Mitch had become, a person who isn't even real. Not anymore, not for us."

She looks at Will, who leans forward, his elbows on his knees, considering this idea: Mitch's transformation from flesh to fantasy. He tries to imagine the comforts, and the cost, of what would amount to a kind of amputation, the erasure of a distempered part of himself, a version of himself he'd be better off without. Wouldn't the loss leave him desolate, prey to the psychic equivalent of a ghost limb—pain where there is nothing? Pain generated by nothingness. Has this happened already? Has Mitch been removed? Excised?

As if the words *bubble of time* were a tranquilizing spell, Will finds that he has panned back from the argument. Sees himself and Carole grow smaller and smaller, watches their living room shrink to the size of a shoe box. As he ascends, he listens to something like a voice-over inside his own head. A voice too refined to ever—even in extremis— grow loud or shrill, a voice with Alistair Cooke's British accent, the measured tone of one of his PBS program introductions, it talks to Will, making reasonable suggestions like "Let's look at the big pic- ture, Will. Take the long view."

His arrival on this Zen peak, a height to which he's aspired but never even come close to attaining, with its atmosphere too thin to allow the waste of oxygen on untamed emotion, leaves him not only detached but with a clear head. It's as if, after an eternity of fiddling, he's at last managed to tune in his own thoughts without the interfer- ence of static or the indistinct mumbling of other channels.

"The other thing is," he hears Carole say, "do you remember

how fast we got pregnant? How happy we were? I was happy and you were, too, and I . . . I asked myself, why tell you now? For what?" She frowns, shakes her head.

Will sees movement on the stairs. "Samantha!" he says to alert her mother. Carole turns around.

"Hello, sweetheart." There is nothing in her voice to suggest the two of them might be involved in a conversation of any importance. "You must be ready for dinner, no?"

Sam doesn't answer. She stands in the middle of the staircase, looking from her father to her mother and then back. "The movie's over," she says, finally.

"How about another?" Will offers, and she shakes her head.

"I'm not allowed."

"Oh, we can break the rules. Every once in a while we can."

"No," she says, "we can't."

"Aren't you hungry?" Carole asks.

"It could be anything," Will says, "anything you want. It could be ice cream." Sam looks at him, at first with suspicion and then with a peculiarly grown-up expression, a miniature rendition of her mother's men-just-don't-get-it look, one delicate eyebrow raised, her mouth puckered in a wry, little twist. She turns to her mother.

"The thing is," Carole says, "Daddy and I are talking. We have something we need to figure out and—"

"What? What do you?"

"It's not . . . it's something . . ."

"Is it money?"

No, Will is about to say, but then he reconsiders—if ever an occasion excused a white lie, this would be it. "It is, Sam," he tells her. "It is about money."

"Grilled cheese?" Carole asks. "Or how about an omelet? There are apples from the green market, and I'll slice them the way you like." Samantha nods and pushes her hair behind her ears as she follows her mother to the kitchen, showing Will the pale, almost transparent skin of her temple.

"How do you know?" he asks Carole as soon as Samantha has eaten and gone back upstairs. "How can you be sure Luke isn't—wasn't—Mitch's child instead of mine? Because I do remember, and it was fast. Barely nine months from the wedding."

Carole is shaking her head before he stops talking. "I know," she says, "I know because he . . . because I made him pull out before it got to that point."

"You—"

"You don't think he could have—you can't think I wouldn't have known. That I didn't guess who it was. I knew right away it wasn't you. It just . . . I just didn't believe it. Myself. It took me that minute to convince myself that I wasn't crazy, that it really was him instead of you."

Will nods slowly. "My dad had it wrong, then. He thought it was the same as with the others. That Mitch didn't pull off the mask until the end, after . . . that he didn't reveal himself until it was done."

"The same as with . . . what others? What are you talking about?"

"It wasn't the only time. He'd done it before, with other girls." Will watches Carole's expression.

"Before? He did it with other girls you . . . girls you knew before?" She's speaking with her face in her hands, the way someone might cradle an aching jaw.

"Yes. That's the part that's . . . that's how this is connected to the . . . to the mess I've made. I saw a woman, an old girlfriend, at the reunion and . . ." He trails off. The two of them watch each other from across the coffee table.

"Elizabeth?" Carole says, finally.

"How did you know?"

"There's a message. On the machine." Will raises his eyebrows. "You'd better just listen," she says, and he gets up, goes to the kitchen phone.

"Hey there, Dr. Moreland," drawls a familiar voice. "It's Jennifer. I'm, like, looking at a lab report. Because guess what? As it happened, I found this little hair of yours glued to my thigh with spooge. So I guess we, like, traded—a long one of mine for a short, curly one of yours. And, so, hey, I'm interested in sharing my news with you if you're, like, interested enough to call me back. Or even if you aren't." The machine announces the time and date of the call, then clicks off.

"Shit," Will says. That Jennifer has left such a message for his wife to hear is a surprisingly destructive act, even from her. He hits the play button and listens to the message once more.

"This isn't from today, Carole. It's from . . . it says it's from Tuesday. Last Tuesday, when I was out of town." He comes back to the living room. "Unless the date thing's screwed up?"

"No," Carole says, her face expressionless.

"So . . ." Will shakes his head. "You've . . . you heard this before? Before today?"

"No. You know I always fast-forward through the ones from your patients. But, the . . . the person who left that, that message, Jennifer, her mother called today, just before you got home. After I talked to her, I remembered that before I skipped past one message, I'd heard someone identify herself as Jennifer." It isn't only her face. Carole's voice, too, is without affect.

"Elizabeth?" he says. "Elizabeth called here?"

"She asked me to tell you something."

"What is it?" Will says when she doesn't continue.

"I . . . I want to make sure I get it right." Like a student trying to summon a lesson committed to memory, Carole closes her eyes while she speaks. "A DNA analysis that Elizabeth's husband, Paul some-body, insisted be made, confirmed that Jennifer is not your child. Apparently, Jennifer told him—Paul—about the . . . about whatever's going on among you three, and he was angry enough to force the issue. One that Elizabeth considers is now closed, never to be re-opened. Jennifer is Paul's biological and legal daughter. If you at-tempt to contact Elizabeth or any member of her family, any colleague or associate, any friend or acquaintance, 'even the fucking paper boy'—that's a direct quote—you'll be in violation of the re-straining order she's filing tomorrow." Carole opens her eyes.

"That's it?" Will says. "That's all she said?" He's so flooded with relief he starts to laugh, just for a moment. The look on Carole's face sobers him up. She's furious, her teeth clenched so tightly that a band of muscle stands out in her cheek. "See, I thought . . . I wasn't laugh-ing because anything was funny. For a month, almost, I've thought she, Jennifer, I thought she—"

"You slept with this person. You had sex with her."

Will sits down; then he stands back up, puts his hands in his pockets. "Yes," he says.

"She's . . . she's a patient?"

"No," he says. "Was. She was before."

"Before what? Before you fucked her!" Will doesn't answer. "Why!" she says. "Why!"

"Why?"

"All right, how? How could you!"

"I—"

Abruptly, Carole's voice has acquired an edge. "I want a way to understand."

"I'm sorry. You remember I told you about the girl, the one who came on to me?"

"I think you may have understated the case," Carole says, "in that you told me she kissed you." The venom in her voice more than compensates for whatever expression her face lacks.

"She did," he says. "And then I did what I said I was going to. I told her we couldn't continue working together and referred her to another therapist. But she came back. Came to the office, refused to leave. Told me she was sorry and carried on. She even cried, or I thought she did. Anyway, I believed her. I believed her enough to let down my guard. I turned my back for a minute—just to disengage while I tried to come up with a way to convince her to leave without exacerbating the whole mess—and when I turned back around she'd taken all her clothes off. Threatened to, well, to make it appear as if I'd tried to rape her unless I . . ."

"Unless you?"

"Complied."

"Complied."

"Yes. With her intention to have intercourse with me."

"Come on! Am I supposed to believe that—"

"Yes! You are. Because she did. And as it turns out, she was looking for a . . . for revenge."

"Revenge! For what! Revenge for what!"

"I . . . it started when I ran into Elizabeth at the reunion." Will looks away and then back at his wife. "The fact is, when we broke up, Elizabeth was pregnant, and I . . . I wondered was there a chance of her—the daughter—being my biological child. We talked. I said something that offended Elizabeth. I didn't mean it the way she took it—I'm not even sure exactly how she took it, other than badly. Whatever she thought, I just wanted to know, not to interfere. As soon as I read her page in the reunion book and saw the date of her daughter's birth, I . . . I needed to get a fix on it. Needed to know one way or the other. So I asked would she give me a hair sample, so I could have it tested."

"You wanted proof?" Carole says.

"Yes. Something definitive. Otherwise, it would be open-ended. Alive. I wanted to put it to rest."

"But how? How could you if she turned out to be yours?"

"I don't know. I'd have to deal with it, obviously. But it wouldn't be as—I don't think it would be as disturbing as not knowing. Anyway, the conversation got combative. I didn't back down; she got more and more defensive. Clearly, she imagined I was going to . . . to intrude on her life. Or Jennifer's. She even said I was looking for a surrogate for Luke. But, honestly, I don't think that was my intent. Not even unconsciously. I've thought about this a lot. Maybe if the child had been a boy, but I can't see myself drawing an equation—I just don't think that was what I wanted."

"Well, what did you want?"

"I don't know. I'm not sure. It was a mistake to press her, Carole, and I apologize. I was . . . I don't know what I was. Lonely, I guess—at loose ends. And she . . . she went ballistic. Must have then misrepresented my request to Jennifer. Characterizing me as . . . as an asshole, evidently. And Jennifer, who is, well, she probably tends to sexualize every transaction, but in this case she must have determined to possess me in return. In response to Elizabeth's saying I had possessive feelings for her. Jennifer, I mean. Possess me sexually." Carole stares at him, arms crossed, mouth closed. "And I, uh, I couldn't . . . didn't . . . stop it. She didn't tell me who she was until it was over."

"Why!" Carole says. "Why! Why didn't you!"

"I don't know," he says. "After she'd refused to put her clothes back on and leave, I just was . . . I don't know what I was. Struck dumb, basically."

"But not unaffected."

"Not unaffected?"

"As in not unable to perform. I mean, come on, Will, it's not as if a woman can sexually . . . can sexually engage a man without a certain degree of . . . cooperation. A physical willingness."

"Yes. You're—well, you're right. That's true. But that isn't within my conscious moral control. It's not something I can decide whether or not to do."

"So this would be a case of the, the flesh being weak? Is that what you're saying?"

"I guess that's one way to put it."

"Well, do you have anything to say about that?"

"No."

"No?"

"What can I say, Carole? I'm sorry. I'm sorry I was aroused. I didn't do it on purpose."

"Fine. Fine. Great. Swell. That makes it all okay, right? Will can't help it if he has a hard-on, can he?" she says to the wall, the chair, an invisible witness or referee. "Do I get to ask why? Why did you, or a part of you, want to have sex with her?"

"Come on, Carole."

"Why you wanted it enough that you didn't manage to, to control your physical response?"

"I don't know."

"You don't know."

"No."

"Well, think of something! I think you owe me the courtesy of trying to explain, don't you?"

"Well, she was . . . she was attractive. Physically. I said so. She elicited a physical response."

"It's not as if you're deprived at home."

"No." Will shakes his head. "Well, I am. I am in that I never get to make love to someone with a face. Leaving me, what, well, alone, I guess."

"Alone? You? What about me?"

"What about you? Are you lonely, Carole? Because how would I know? You're not exactly a person with her heart on her—"

"Will, you're so involved with, with Luke that—"

"That's too easy! You're projecting your feelings onto me. I don't think I'm any more involved with him than you are."

"He can't . . . Luke can't . . ." Carole shakes her head. "He can't be the end of every argument. He can't be the cause of every problem we have."

"Of course he can't! He isn't. In fact, it's become suddenly clear that from the beginning—long before the accident—my brother was—"

"I never didn't forgive you, Will, for the accident. I forgave you from the beginning. No—that's not right. Forgiving you would imply I'd weighed what had happened and decided you weren't—"

"Carole, you can't just have been automatically saintly. No one is. You've repress—"

"I never blamed you! And I am so sick of this stupid, stupid argument. I always thought of it, and I still do think of it, as something that happened to us. Both of us. All of us."

"So why? Why then? You do have to admit something happened, Carole, something inside you. It wasn't me who, who . . . our sex life wasn't the same as it had been. Right away, it wasn't. The very first time we made love after Luke drowned, it was different. And you were the one who made it different."

Carole opens her mouth, and he sees a tremor in her chin and her bottom lip. "It's not you," she says. "If the accident is anyone's fault, it's mine. Not yours. *Mine.*" She says the word with one hand splayed over her breastbone.

Will throws his hands up over his head. "Yours! How is that possible? What kind of upside-down thinking could lead you to believe any of it was your fault?" Carole looks away, her lips compressed into a tight line. "What?" he says. "What!"

She gives up trying to stop the tears. "I can't make myself . . . I know this sounds like what you'd call estrogen logic, but I . . . I can't help feeling that it was, it had to have been a kind of . . . of correction. A realignment. Because of me."

"What are you talking about! I have no idea what you're talking about!"

"Luke was"—her voice catches—"he was perfect, he was good. He was a . . . there was nothing wrong about him. And I'm . . . I was afraid I was being corrected. Punished for, for—"

"For Mitch?" he says. "For my brother's . . . out of some kind of, of cosmic readjustment?"

Carole nods as if what Will said does in fact add up.

"And what about Luke? What about our little boy? In this line of reasoning, why should it be Luke who pays for the realignment?" Will stops pacing to look at Carole. "I mean, unless you have a whole different moral scale for yourself. Unless the rest of us—me, Sam, your friends, your clients and their, their well-meaning, unenlightened parents—unless we all get measured with the mini moral yardstick, the one for regular mortals and their mini virtues and vices. Is that why you forgive me, Carole? Or why forgiving or not forgiving isn't even an issue for you? Because you're on a different plane, a whole other body of water, sailing along smoothly, no waves, no capsizing?"

He stops ranting when he notices the look on Carole's face. An outrage he's never seen before—it's blanched her cheeks and flared her nostrils, so narrowed her usually round eyes that, were he to see this face outside its context, he might not identify it as belonging to anyone he knows. He's so surprised, so intent on her expression, that he doesn't even register that she's seized something from the coffee table, doesn't see her hurl it at his head. Maybe she should have been the one who coached Little League, he thinks absurdly as he stumbles back and trips over his own feet. Then he's on the floor, looking at her through a foggy pink veil.

"Oh God, I'm sorry, I'm sorry, Will. I think I . . . I split open your, your, right above your eyebrow." She has a wad of paper towels and is pressing them to his head. "I think it needs stitches."

"Here," he says. Will uses his own hand to hold the paper towels against his head, pressing harder than she was willing to, to try to stop the bleeding. As he gets to his feet, he sees what it was that hit him, the jar of peanut butter he left on the coffee table when he was talking on the phone with his father, asking him if he was okay with changing their lunch date, seeing each other a week earlier than usual. While talking he'd wandered away from the kitchen, forgotten he was in the middle of making a sandwich. The jar is lying label up, intact. After the Fall is the name of the brand Carole buys, and this strikes him as funny, enough that he starts to laugh.

"Maybe you should start buying Skippy," he says when he can speak, "in the nice plastic jar. Instead of that organic stuff. Then the next time you throw it at me, this won't happen." He's still laughing, he can't help it.

"Shit," she says. "Sorry, sorry, I'm sorry. I'm going to pull the car around. Sam!" she yells. "Samantha! Do you think you can go up and get her, Will?"

The emergency room is its usual purgatory. Will tries not to think of what Samantha might be catching from the little boy next to her, the two of them staring at the overhead TV on the other side of the waiting area, the one tuned to Cartoon Network. Each time the child exhales, a bubble of mucus extrudes from one nostril. He inhales, the bubble deflates, disappears, then reemerges. What it never does is pop.

"I wish you'd thrown it harder," he says; "then I could have been triaged to the front of the line."

"Hmnhh," Carole answers. CNN is on and Will strains to see the time in the lower right-hand corner of the screen, but it's too small to read from where he's sitting. It must be at least midnight, though, because this is the third time they've seen the same tape feed of a distraught Middle Eastern woman holding a man's photograph up to the camera.

"Carole?" Will says. She yawns.

"What is it?" She sits up straight to stretch her arms over her head.

"Marry me?"

He still can't read the time at the bottom of the TV screen, but he can see the digits change before she answers. "I haven't divorced you yet," she says.

Perhaps this is a function of the length of the pause, but Will can't tell whether or not she's being serious. He can't see her face without getting up and walking around in front of her. *You're not serious, are you?* He tries out the question in his head.

"How long do you think it'll take to go through?" he tries instead. Both of them are looking up at the screen rather than at each other.

"That depends."

"On what?"

"Whether it's no-contest or nobody's fault or whatever they call it."

"Fault," Will says. "Fault's tricky."

"Very." Carole retrieves a tissue from her purse and blows her nose.

"You'll think this is ridiculous, but I tend to make pie graphs when I'm assigning responsibility." Will switches the hand holding the paper towels to his head from right to left. "In this case, my brother would get the biggest slice, but then I'd get some, too, and my parents. Jennifer. Maybe Elizabeth. Then there's you."

"Which case?"

"The thing with Jennifer."

"Why am I in there?"

"Because anything that has to do with me and sex automatically involves you."

"Wouldn't there have to be more than one pie?" Carole says after a minute. "One labeled Mitch, the other Jennifer?"

"There could be three. Mitch, Jennifer, and Luke. Drawn on transparencies, so they could be superimposed one over another."

She shakes her head. "Too complicated. Everyone—Mitch, Jennifer, Luke—they're all both pies and slices in other pies."

"Are they?"

"Of course. Take Luke, his drowning I mean. He's a pie, with responsibility apportioned among you, for sailing the boat; Luke himself, for not leaving his vest buckled; me, for renting the house on the
lake; my friend, the one who gave me the joint, just in case you were
a little hungover, less focused—although I never agreed with you
about that. I mean, I didn't notice anything. Then there's the boat-
rental company, for not, I don't know, issuing warnings, or whatever;
the sailing instructor, for not stressing the importance of paying attention all the time; the weather, for being so beautiful; and so on. I
mean you can go on slicing smaller and smaller pieces of causation.
And aside from being a pie, Luke would also be in the Jennifer pie,
if it's true that by drowning he left you vulnerable to involvement
with . . ." She trails off.

"It's funny," Will says. "How much of my time is dedicated to
helping other people to stop assessing themselves, or situations in
which they find themselves, in terms of blame. Judgment. Who did
what, and who said what, and what it might mean as far as his or her
culpability in the given conflict."

"But?"

"But I do it to myself. To us. I can't let go of the idea that I can
figure things out."

"With pie graphs."

"I said it was ridiculous."

Carole looks at his forehead. "Maybe I should go to the restroom
for more paper towels."

"No, don't."

"But it's seeping through."

"It doesn't matter. Stay here. Talk to me."

Carole leans her head against his shoulder. "You were sort of
right about the different moral yardsticks," she says. "Except you
made it sound so smug, and I don't think I am, really. Saying I have

two standards—one for me and one for everyone else—it could just as easily be that I give other people the benefit of the doubt, which I don't do for myself."

"Why?"

"I don't know. Maybe because I'm in my own head. With other people I have to correct for not knowing their private experience. As in that old supposedly Native American proverb, the one about having to walk in someone else's moccasins."

The triage nurse comes to the ER door. "Hernandez!" she calls. She crosses the name from the list on the clipboard resting on the counter of the locked service window. Will sees that Samantha has fallen asleep, her legs stretched across the seat where the little boy had been sitting.

"Do we really have to get divorced before I propose?" he asks.

"I guess I might settle for a pre-nup, instead."

"How much?" he says. She's so deadpan, he can't tell what's a joke and what isn't.

"It wouldn't be about money."

"What then?"

"Well, first off, you have to skip your thirtieth college reunion. And your thirty-fifth. Fortieth, forty-fifth. I guess if you haven't kicked the bucket by your fiftieth—you'll be how old, seventy-something?—we can maybe negotiate."

Will holds out his free hand as if to shake hers, but she's not finished.

"You throw out all your ties. Wear only the ones I buy for you."

"Even the paisley ones?"

"Especially the paisley ones."

"Is there more?" Will asks, when she doesn't continue.

"A new dishwasher before you buy even one more antique map.

Also, I think I really do want cable so I can begin my career as a TV watcher. I'm not giving up yoga, but I want to pursue some vacuous activities, practice wasting time. I must be the only person in New York who never saw even one episode of *Sex and the City*. I might even start, I don't know, drinking a glass of wine or two on weekends."

Will nods. "Is that it?"

She shakes her head.

"Well?"

"No more birth control."

Will looks at her. He says nothing, preoccupied with feeling how it feels, their eyes on each other's. Reminded of the old childhood game: Who'll be the first to blink or laugh? Who will turn away?

The idea of Carole pregnant doesn't summon images of a new baby so much as it does a series of fragments, like flash cards, pictures of Luke mostly, Luke before he could talk. Grabbing the cat's tail and laughing when she hissed. Shoving his pacifier into Will's mouth. The way he slept on his stomach, knees drawn under, butt in the air.

"I can't," Will says, finally. "I don't think I can do it again."

Carole pulls up one corner of the wad of paper towels to look at the gash. "What if I can't stand not to?"

"I don't know. Is it a deal breaker?"

"Maybe."

He takes her hand in his. "I'm . . ."

"What if I can't stand not to?" she asks him again, before he can figure out what he's trying to say.

"Moreland," the triage nurse announces from the door. Will stands up.

"Aren't you coming with me?" he asks.

"Just let me grab Sam." Carole manages to gather their daughter into her arms without waking her. Her legs dangle down as far as her mother's knees. "Ugh," Carole says. "I never get why it is that kids feel heavier when they're asleep."

They follow the nurse into a small examination room, where she takes his blood pressure and his temperature before saturating the wad of paper towels with hydrogen peroxide in order to peel them away from his forehead. As soon as it's uncovered, the gash opens and begins bleeding again. "Whoa," she says, "what happened here?"

"I threw something at his head."

"I bumped it on the mantel."

They speak at the same instant, and the nurse looks back and forth between them, her plucked eyebrows raised.

"It was a joke," Will says.

"Domestic violence is not something we find funny here in the emergency room."

"I'm sorry," Carole says. "I get a little punchy when I'm tired."

The nurse frowns and turns to Will. "Well," she says, "you picked a good night for a facial. Dr. Cunningham came on at eleven." She tears the paper from around a pad of sterile gauze and tells him to hold it against the split flesh, lifting his hand to his forehead. "You don't have to push so hard," she says.

"A facial?" Carole asks.

"Facial wound." The nurse stands, and they do, too, Will pulling Carole to her feet when she can't rise under the weight of their sleeping daughter. All of them file down the hall, the nurse, then Will, Carole and Samantha lagging behind. "Eyebrows are tricky. They heal up crooked if they're not sutured just so. Dr. Cunningham's a plastic surgeon."

She leaves the three of them in an enclosure made by a white curtain hanging from a U-shaped track in the ceiling. Inside are a bed and a chair. On the orange Formica counter are bandages, alcohol preps, and emesis basins. Carole arranges Samantha facedown on the bed to keep the light out of her eyes. There's only the one sheet, tucked around and under the mattress, so she pulls it out and wraps what she can of it around her.

"Wow," she says, shaking her head. "A good night for a facial."

"I didn't know it went through my eyebrow." Will tries to find his reflection in the stainless steel paper-towel dispenser.

"Hello," someone says, and they both jump, turn around. "Let's take a look."

"Are you Dr. Cunningham?" Will asks.

"Last time I checked." He pulls on a pair of gloves and motions for Will to sit in the chair. "Close your eyes," he says. "Deep. How'd it happen?"

"A jar of peanut butter," Carole says. "Glass. Kind of heavy."

"Didn't break?" he asks mildly, not seeming to infer anything from her answer.

"No."

"Looks clean. Have to trim the dermis. Minimize scarring." He flips up the magnifying lens he's wearing on his own head. "Back in a sec."

"A little weird," Carole whispers to Will after the doctor has left the enclosure, "don't you think?"

"You mean the ponytail? The red clogs? The vampire pallor?"

"His lips are so—he looks like he's wearing lipstick, but I don't think he is, really." Carole strokes Will's hair back, away from the gash. "I am sorry," she tells him. "Does it hurt?"

He shakes his head. "It's going to make a distinguished-looking scar. Dangerously sexy. I can see there'll be times I'll have to cover it with a low-brimmed hat to keep you from going wild." She smiles, but it's not because she thinks what he's said is funny: he can see she's humoring him.

The surgeon returns with a tray of instruments, looks at Samantha sleeping. "Let's go next-door." He grabs a handful of curtain and pulls it aside.

"Numb you up," he says to Will after he's settled him under a light so bright that Will can't help but close his eyes, seeing what looks like lightning striking through a red sky, the veins in his eyelids, he guesses. The doctor's latex-sheathed fingers are cool and sticky on his skin, and the antiseptic smell of Betadine jolts Will back to the delivery room: the white flesh at the top of Carole's thighs stained dark orange, the stuff running down into her pubic hair and onto the white sheets.

The doctor covers Will's face with what feels like paper, a disposable cloth, no doubt. There's a hole in the center, though; he can feel air against his skin, cold where the Betadine is evaporating. "Feel a pinch," the doctor says.

Despite the warning, Will flinches when the needle goes in, and Carole squeezes his hand. "Is it okay if I watch?" she asks, but if the doctor answers, it's with a nod or a gesture, something Will can't see.

"It's not quite as big as I thought," Carole says, narrating what's going on for him. "Maybe an inch and a half. He's not doing the skin yet. He's stitching the muscle together underneath."

Will draws a deep breath, so deep that he feels the cloth lift off his mouth when he exhales. "Carole?" He gives her hand a little shake.

"What is it?"

"I'll try." He waits for her to answer, or even just to squeeze his fingers in return, anxious enough that he forgets to pay attention to the tugging of the sutures.

"Are you . . . do you mean what we were talking about before?" she says at last. He startles at an unexpected ring of metal against metal. The doctor must have dropped an instrument into the tray.

"I'm not . . . I can't promise, but I don't want you to think I'd dismissed the idea. It's just that I—"

"Had to shave some hair," the doctor says, "so I could see. Don't want a jig in the brow."

"I didn't think you dismissed it," Carole says. "I just can't figure out how not to want what I want, you know?"

"I know." Still holding her hand, Will strokes her knuckles with his thumb. "I know."

Suddenly, the cloth flies up off his face. "Want to take a look before I put the dressing on?" the doctor says.

"Can I?"

He points to a door across the hall, on it a little blue sign with the outlines of a man, a woman, and a wheelchair.

Will leans over the sink to inspect his face. Now that the two sides are stitched together in a line, the gash is a little anticlimactic, he thinks. He can count at least twenty stitches, but they're tiny, made with very fine nylon thread. He cups his hands under the faucet for a drink of water, aware of a slight throb as he bends his head down. Whatever was in the needle is wearing off.

Someone knocks on the door, and Will turns off the water. "I'll be out in a minute," he says.

"Can I come in?" Carole's voice asks.

"It's not locked." Will watches in the mirror as she closes the door behind her.

She stands beside him at the sink, and he watches their two reflections. "I wasn't serious," she says, "about the pre-nup."

He nods, starts to rub his eyes, but a stab from the stitched eyebrow stops him. "That blue-colored cloth, the plastic basins. Smell of Betadine. Like being back in the delivery room," he says.

Her reflection nods. "We had that great window when Luke was born. Remember? We could see the top of the Chrysler Building, the sun shining on it."

"I just remember him, and you. Cutting the cord."

Her hair spread on the white pillowcase. One of her feet in his hands, the other in the labor nurse's. After—Luke was in her arms—there was the placenta in its plastic dish. Not formless and Jell-O-y, the way he'd imagined it, but a different thing entirely. Impossible to have predicted so rich a color, or so violent a beauty. The elegant tree of its veins, a perfect symmetry, and the way it gleamed, spilling over the sides of the dish. What is this I'm feeling? he remembers thinking, wondering at the prickling sensation behind his eyes. Then he realized he'd been holding his breath as he stroked a finger over its surface. Hot to the touch, slippery smooth. Something she'd made with her own body. A part of her that felt as she did inside, when he put a finger there, when he touched her.

Carole leans against Will's chest. She puts her arms around him and slips her hands into his back pockets. "Let's go home," she says.

"And go to bed?"

"And go to bed."

"Do you think, in honor of my injury, we could try it face-to-face?"

His hands are on her shoulders, and she looks up at him. "In honor of your injury? Or in apology for throwing things at you?"

"For whatever reason you say. For old times' sake. Because we want to. For the good of the cause."

She puts her arms around him again, pulls him into her, hard, so her pelvis presses up against him. "What cause?" she asks. "Is it a worthy one?"

"It's us. Our cause."

She pushes her face into the front of his shirt. "Okay," she whispers. "Okay, okay," a whisper he knows because he's heard it before.

Overheard it, really, because it isn't an answer; it's the way she talks herself through an unfamiliar task, a challenge she's determined to meet, even if she doesn't know how. *Okay, okay,* he's heard her whisper on the floor of their bedroom, twisting herself into a new yoga puzzle. Or at her desk, computer on, fingers poised over the keyboard, *JavaScript for Dummies* open in her lap. In the kitchen, frowning at the piecrust on the floured butcher's block.

Okay, okay, Samantha watching her mother as Carole advances, step by confusing step outlined by the deceptively titled *Origami Made Simple,* her fingers turning a square of gold paper into a frog, a crane, a tiny cup that, if folded correctly, promises to hold a sip of water.

"Okay?" he says again. She nods against his chest.

"Okay," she says, still whispering. "Okay."

ACKNOWLEDGMENTS

For their generosity in discussing the work of a speech therapist, I thank Hillary Bogert, Karen Louick, and Heidi Volosov.

For her gracious response to disruptive (even when amusing) questions, I am indebted to Kera Bolonik. For the plunder of her vocation, I owe Janet Gibbs. For her wise and graceful editing, Kate Medina. For pushing me that much harder, Courtney Hodell and Christopher Potter. For reading between the lines, Gila Sand. For her own art, and more, Joyce Ravid. For her patience, Danielle Posen.

For her friendship and support since the beginning, Amanda Urban.

For as long as we both shall live, Colin Harrison.

ABOUT THE AUTHOR

KATHRYN HARRISON has written the novels *Thicker Than Water, Exposure, Poison, The Binding Chair,* and *The Seal Wife.* Her autobiographical work includes *The Kiss, Seeking Rapture, The Road to Santiago,* and *The Mother Knot.* She has also written a biography, *St. Thérèse of Lisieux.* She lives in New York with her husband, the novelist Colin Harrison, and their three children. *Envy* is her eleventh book.

ABOUT THE TYPE

The text of this book was set in Janson, a typeface designed in about 1690 by Nicholas Kis, a Hungarian living in Amsterdam, and for many years mistakenly attributed to the Dutch printer Anton Janson. In 1919 the matrices became the property of the Stempel Foundry in Frankfurt. It is an old-style book face of excellent clarity and sharpness.

CHAPTER 19

SALT PEANUTS

I was sitting at the bar when Stan Kenton's joyous big band came on the sound system, eased into Ella and then Sinatra. "Someone to watch over me," Sinatra was singing, the Gershwin tune of wit and longing that was just right for the time of day.

I asked Keith what was on the playlist in the late afternoon, the early evening, at cocktail time, the beginning of the evening. "Charlie Parker, Thelonious Monk, Sonny Burke, Sonny Rollins, Hank Mobley, Dizzy Gillespie, John Coltrane, Gerry Mulligan, Ray Charles, Sinatra, Duke Ellington, Miles Davis," Keith had said. This was my music, the musicians I loved best, Sinatra especially, and Ray Charles, Miles, and Monk. I loved Anita O'Day, who was on the playlist, and Benny Goodman.

Ella sang "Lady Be Good." I had always loved Ella. She never took a lesson, never could read music; at an Apollo Theater talent contest when she was sixteen, she simply opened her mouth and everyone went silent; one woman who was there recalled, "You could hear a rat piss on velvet." Like Mozart's, Ella's was a gift from God; even if I was not a believer, I believed that.

Around Christmastime, there was a seasonal playlist, and I could almost always pick out Dean Martin. At Christmas, when Balthazar was at its most celebratory, lovely, festooned with greens and tiny white lights, Dean Martin crooning a carol was just right.

Early evening was a good time any time of year, and before the crowds swarmed the bar, you could hear the music. Later, there would be more noise and more people, though the crowd had changed since the early days. After *Sex and the City* filmed a scene at Balthazar, girls in four-inch Manolo heels and little skirts crammed in to drink pink cosmos and look at the other girls, the baby giraffes who seemed to sashay in direct from the catwalk. Everywhere the *Sex and the City* crowd went, the tourists followed, of course, no matter if it was to Magnolia Bakery on Bleecker Street for pastel cupcakes so sweet you felt you wanted a shot of insulin. And to the bar at Balthazar in late afternoon.

Jimmy Norris was still on duty at the bar, and he made me a martini with Hendrick's gin. He knew I liked the martinis mostly for the gin-soaked olives; he gave me four. The truth was I had always loved sitting around at bars, but I was a lousy drinker; more than a single martini, and I felt like death. This was of real sadness to me because I loved the taste of booze, of dark mysterious spirits and bright fizzy cocktails.

Secretly, I loved cocktails that tasted like soda pop, and the garnishes, the olives in the martini, the cherry on a whiskey sour. Best of all were the fresh pineapples in the caipirinhas I'd drunk in Rio, sitting on the terrace of the Copacabana Palace. Also, and friends told me this was shameful, I loved Miller Lite. And I loved the schmoozing between bartender and customer.

What was it between them? I asked Jimmy. "It's this," he said, and gestured at the space across the bar from him to me. This was what mattered, the single best talent a bartender could have, and he meant the relationship, of course, the connection, the thing that spanned that space of a foot or two. "It's not about being a mixologist or how fancy you can make the drinks, it's this."

Like the best kind of good-looking men, Jimmy Norris was not a bit vain. He was an uxorious sort of guy, though he finally admitted that plenty of ladies (guys, too) would have been easy pickings if he were not utterly faithful. He was crazy about his two kids, and sometimes, if pressed to talk about himself, he told me a little about their gymnastics and football, or about his wife's trip to Paris, but he had perfect pitch for his job: he made you want to talk, and he was talkative, but it was always about you, about the customer.

I leaned on the bar and talked to Jimmy about his kids, about his vacation and mine, nothing in particular; he had the gift of a great bartender, not just the gift of gab, but something else that was more elusive. He made you feel comfortable; he could talk about anything, pretty much. He gave you the sense that in this bar, in this little space, you could expect a good time.

Of course I was always looking for dish, for gossip about Balthazar and the customers, but Jimmy was reticent; he clearly had the old-fashioned idea that the relationship between bartender and customer had an element of the priestly. Jimmy Norris could have been a good priest, the kind that got you through bad times and was charming; but maybe I was thinking of a priest in a movie.

Dizzy blew "Salt Peanuts" on the sound system, and I could picture him, cheeks puffed out, the bent horn, the thrilling, impossible bebop noise I had always loved.

The crowd was wailing its own tunes: the chatter and greetings and gossip, the orders called out, all the convivial noise that set the evening in motion. I ordered some frites with mayo. There was a clatter of glass as a young barback lifted two cases of sparkling water over the bar down at the end near the kitchens.

Along with Rebecca Banks, Jimmy Norris had indulged my desire to make a brand-new cocktail. On three or four mornings we'd held impromptu sessions at the bar discussing it, and tasting it, and pondering what the ingredients would be. It should be French; Balthazar was French. Spirits first, said Jimmy, and we settled on vodka because it was easy to mix and Grey Goose because it was French vodka. There were quite a few sessions where Jimmy lined up French liqueurs—a liqueur was an important element in a cocktail—blue, green, yellow, pink. Eau de vie de poire with the yellow pear floating in the bottle; more eaux de vie, made from plums and cherries; dark blue Chambord, and Grand Marnier, the color somewhere between burnt orange and burnished copper.

"I remember when we served Liza Minnelli Grand Marnier in a teapot," one of the bartenders told me. "She was supposed to be on the wagon, and she didn't want anyone to know, so we poured it in the teapot and she drank it from a teacup."

A cocktail required a topper, a sort of finisher with the elegance and brio of Mariano Rivera, the Yankees' great closer. Champagne seemed nice. So we sat and sampled, dipping straws into the mix, asking strangers to taste it, changing the proportions of Champagne and Grand Marnier, which we had settled on as the liqueur.

The bar snacks came out, the thin, crisp slices of bread toasted with olive oil and Parmesan, olives, and hard-boiled eggs. Soon the night crowd would start arriving. At the end of the bar, a couple was necking feverishly. A pair of hedge fund types in suits appeared, one with his hand in his pocket. Maybe he thought this was dashing; to me, it looked like he was protecting the dough.

A familiar-looking Englishman—who else would wear highly polished and neatly tied brogues with his jeans?—was slumped over a gin and tonic. Just arriving was a woman in a loose black garment that hung over her skinny body. It was loose enough you could peer in and see her "little cone-shaped boobs," as the Englishman announced later. Her Frye boots were tucked under her.

Before the rush, the bar had felt intimate, inviting, private, an old-fashioned downtown place where the bartender who knew you made you a fine martini and had time to chat, and in the burnished light everyone looked swell and the music was good. Jimmy mixed the drink we had named Le Balthazar. When he poured out the Taittinger, the drink frothed up and turned the color of the restaurant's walls: an old gold with a deep patina. With the citrus zester Mark Mason had brought him from downstairs, Jimmy carved a beautifully thin orange peel to float on the cocktail.

The color of the cocktail had been our *eureka* moment. Now, I asked the woman next to me at the bar if she'd like to taste it. "Of course, yes," she said. "I should be happy to taste this drink." Jimmy served her Le Balthazar and she drank it. "Very nice," she said, adding dreamily, "I always come here. I love Balthazar, and I booked for New Year's Eve months early and I brought a friend—it was worth every penny. The food was delicious, and the staff—" She gave a delighted shake of the head. "The staff, you had only to raise an eyebrow and somebody would come, and there was a French woman and I knew French and we chatted. So lovely."

Outside, the light was dying—it had been a gloomy day—but inside it was a sweet time, when there were only a few of us at the bar. Cocktails and Ella Fitzgerald.

It made me think of *The Great Gatsby*, where F. Scott Fitzgerald celebrates the idea of the cocktail hour. "The bar is in full swing, and floating rounds of cocktails permeate the garden outside, until the air is alive with chatter and laughter, and casual innuendo and introductions forgotten on the spot, and enthusiastic meetings between women who never knew each other's names."

CHAPTER 20

BAD TIMES

I t has not always been unalloyed good times at Balthazar. There were arguments and a lawsuit or two; there were people who fell out, who didn't fit, who felt embattled or entitled. Customers who did not pay always caught Erin's eye if she was on the floor; she had a sixth sense about it; usually it was somebody on his own. She could always call a friendly cop from the Fifth Precinct if there was trouble; Erin had the right friends.

There had been unhappy customers.

"I remember when all hell would be breaking loose," said James Weichert, who had been the morning manager and also worked at night later on. "The guy's drunk and the wife is crying," James said. "I would go over and would put my hand on the table and interrupt and say, 'How is everything over here?' And if the man was really drunk and said, 'None of your fucking business,' I would look at the woman and say, 'Is everything OK?' I would ignore the man and make sure that I was doing right by the restaurant. It's a very, very dicey situation. Thank God, it was rare, though we once had a guy who was a movie executive, and he was kicked out of the restaurant because he tried to stab a bartender with a steak knife."

"Where did he get it?" I asked.

"He was eating steak," said James. "He said, 'I'm going to cut your balls off,' or something like that. Keith personally called him and told him he was no longer welcome at the restaurant. Six months later he showed up. What are we going to do? So we sit him down. Nobody will wait on him. The waiters are terrified. He just wanted somebody who would push back, so I said, 'Hello, Mr. Whatever-His-Name-Was,' and I seemed very obsequious the whole entire evening. 'How are you this evening?' Kept my voice nice and low, remained very much in control, and when he started going off the rails, reminded him where the rails were. And it was a little S&M game. It was a bizarre little S&M game," said James. "I loved that."

None of it was unusual in a big restaurant. And Balthazar had also survived death and grief and floods, had done it as a community often with tenacious determination and even a sort of grace. Balthazar, at its best, was like the city itself.

There was nothing, is nothing, in New York that remained unchanged by September 11. By 2001 Balthazar was a dazzling success, in its youthful prime, a place where everyone came and ate and drank pink cocktails and there were nine-foot models at the bar and the staff was still young; that morning, none of it mattered.

It was during that hot September just after 9/11, the black cloud still hanging low over Ground Zero, when, looking for some kind of safe harbor, for something to hang on to, I became a regular at Balthazar. The sense of community that can be crystallized by a place, by the simple universal ritual of breaking bread with others, was a kind of necessity during that awful time.

Most of downtown Manhattan in those sad days felt like an outpost in the middle of the city. A thin coating of black dust had settled on our windowsills. In the streets, we were shepherding our kids to school where a few days earlier they had gone on their own. We all looked up at the sky too often.

That morning of September 11, I had been on a plane coming

home from London, where I had casually stayed an extra day. A few hours out, the pilot said we were turning back, that there was a little problem in New York, that it was thought a Cessna had smashed into the World Trade Center.

The flight attendant mumbled something about all American air space being closed. I knew you didn't close all air space for a Cessna. I knew it was bad.

It took me a week to get home from London. On every level I felt bereft, but the oddest thing was this: I was devastated not to have been in New York, as if I could somehow have helped. This was nuts. Everyone was nuts then.

For a while I sat and stared out of my window, the kitchen window, which had framed the towers. The Twin Towers were gone. As soon as it reopened, I went to Balthazar with a friend from the BBC who was in town covering the disaster. It had opened almost before any other place in the neighborhood. People trickled in, looking for relief from the heat and the stink and the black cloud a mile to the south. Kevin King, who was a waiter back then before he became the maître d', hugged me, and said, "Welcome back. We're so glad to see you. Have a glass of Champagne." I knew this was code for *Thank God you're alive, thank God you weren't down there. Have a glass of Champagne. Welcome.*

From the other regulars and from the staff, I began to piece together what happened there. James Weichert, who was still the breakfast manager then, had been working the morning shift that day. Now I just let him talk.

"On the morning of 9/11, I got to work as I did every morning. I had to open at seven a.m., so I think I was there at five-thirty. It was one of those funny early-September days where you feel fall begin but it was bluebird gorgeous, clear, crisp, cool, and really a lovely day." James, who was usually preternaturally cheery even early in the morning, a good-looking young guy full of enthusiasms—for his friends, for music, for his sailboat, for New York City—was pensive. He spoke with a kind of reflective precision about the events, as if all the details mattered.

"I went in through the back door on Crosby Street, let everybody in, made sure my whole staff was there, and waited for the pastries to come from New Jersey from the bakery. I put them out on the bar just before seven-thirty. It was a gorgeous presentation, those sticky buns glistening in the sunlight. And we would even sometimes dust them with a little bit of confection sugar. There were the bowl of fruit and the bowl of yogurt with the ice underneath the yogurt. There was the egg boiler that used to zap me every time I walked by it. The newspapers were on the round table up front." James shook his head.

"I was the maître d', too, then, so I was standing at the front door, wearing my orange Helmut Lang shirt and wishing people 'Top of the morning,' and in walks this guy and he says, 'You won't believe it, some asshole has flown their Cessna into the World Trade Center.' I wasn't that worried if it was a little plane like that, but I went to the security guard in the back and I asked him to turn on the radio and to keep an eye on it." He looked at me. "Should I go on?"

I nodded.

"Of course everybody is chatting and saying, 'Why do these fucking idiots fly their private planes down the Hudson River?' It escalated. Somebody said it was a Learjet.

"So finally, after about what felt like twenty minutes of banter with me walking around the restaurant making sure everybody's coffees were hot and their butter soft—those were my biggest concerns—I went out to Broadway and Spring Street. Have you ever heard of the term 'foehn'?

"Foehn is, if you're in Munich and you look up at the Alps, some days there's a certain humidity in the air that creates a magnification effect, and so the Alps feel like they are right at the outskirts of Munich. And it was that kind of day, so the towers were magnified and felt closer than they normally are. So you're looking at it like it's a part of the city and at the same time like you're watching a film. All of the sudden I see a 737 hit the other tower." James stopped. Waited. Began again.

"Then I turned around and went back in and said, 'Something's wrong.' I brought the radio out and put it at the front desk, and you know how beautiful it is in Balthazar in the morning, the sun streaming in, but the news came then that one of the towers had fallen, then that the police closed all Manhattan borders so you couldn't get in or out because they knew it was an attack.

"It was very, very quiet in Balthazar—the music was still playing as if that perfect classical world still existed, but the notes seemed off-key," James said. Like so many of us, in talking about that day, he had to stop to collect himself over and over; the memories came back, and it was, for a moment, overwhelming. For James's generation—he had only been thirty then—9/11 was what JFK's assassination had been for mine, the event by which they would mark time.

"You know, we wanted to keep open as much as possible because we felt it's so important for a focus point, a community point, you know, to have a place to go and just sit down and talk," Roberta Delice said. "I remember when I arrived up from the subway, I looked and it was like the air in SoHo was yellow."

Erin had just come back to the city. "I moved back to New York after 9/11," said Erin. "There was a customer, her husband was killed in the World Trade, and she would come here, they used to come together before. She would come and sit in a booth with whoever, and just sit there sobbing, night after night after night, with various people."

It was a time when everyone needed a community. Everyone in New York talked to strangers. I remember a woman in a deli saying to me, "Do you know what's a good flavor of ice cream? I haven't eaten ice cream in ten years, but I figure now, what the hell." *Here Is New York* was an exhibit of photographs that opened around the corner from me on Prince Street. I went to work selling photographs taken on 9/11 for charity. The exhibit lasted a year and a half, with people lining up by the hundreds every day. New Yorkers huddled together more than any time I could remember, the need for community was powerful, and for that I went to Balthazar for breakfast every morning.

In 2003, more tough times came with the death of Lyric Benson.

"Lyric was just on the cusp of everything," remembered Erin. "She was a lovely girl. We were aware that she had a crap boyfriend and was breaking up with him, but nobody knew exactly what was going on. That night, Lyric, who was working as one of the hosts, went home to Chinatown, to the apartment she was sharing with Cheutine Fong, one of our managers. The boyfriend was waiting, he confronted her, he shot her I think through the right eye, in the vestibule. The ex-boyfriend turned the gun on himself," said Erin. "She was twenty-two, to my understanding, she had gone to Yale, on the cusp. There was a real outpouring."

All over town, people told me, Lyric was on billboards, because she was the face of American Express for that year's Tribeca Film Festival. Tribeca itself, just a few blocks south, between SoHo and Ground Zero, had only just emerged from the nightmare of 9/11.

"We were in bad shape that night," Erin said. According to Nicole Hopson, a waiter who remembered everything, "Keith came to Balthazar, drove everyone to the hospital where Lyric had been taken." On the way they stopped to look at the billboards with Lyric's picture—she had been chosen as the young star of the American Express campaign during the Tribeca Film Festival (which was started in 2002 to help revitalize downtown in the aftermath of 9/11.)

"In our business," said Erin, "it was rare that owners did that kind of thing. As a result, there is a loyalty to Keith that a lot of people don't hear about, don't get."

For Erin, Lyric's murder was a turning point from the carefree early days. "There was a moment where anything went, and now we needed security at the front," she said. "After 9/11, after Lyric and things, people getting older, getting married, having kids, I had my son in 2004. He was born with Down's syndrome. We all had to grow up."

Growing up was something Erin got good at over the years, and when Superstorm Sandy hit, she went into action. Superstorm Sandy hit the East Coast in 2012 with the kind of ferocity few remembered. Whole sections of coastal New York and New Jersey were devastated; people tried to swim out of their houses to some kind of safety. Homes were wrecked. People died. Water poured into the subways and the Brooklyn-Battery Tunnel. When the downstairs at Balthazar flooded knee-high, computers were found floating in the filthy water, the way Erin remembered it.

Sandy struck on Monday, October 29, and by that night, much of New York had lost power. I was sitting at home when I heard a strange pop, a kind of bang, like lightning, or a bomb going off. The lights went out; so did the computer and the television. The pop had been from the Con Ed plant only a mile or so away. The blackout in SoHo lasted until Friday night. To charge your cell phone you had to walk a couple of miles to Thirty-Fifth Street.

"We had to get rid of the food before it spoiled. Shane and I drove up to Home Depot," Erin said. "We bought two big barbecue grills, we made steak sandwiches au poivre, we just cooked, we did it for five bucks. A guy said, 'I'll give you a hundred dollars for a lobster.'

"At the end of the day we were giving it all away from the bakery. You'd be amazed how many cooks showed up just to help. I stole a generator from Pastis, brought it over here, drove all over looking for gas, started the generator, pumped up the water, and we cleaned and we cleaned," she said. "We went around and made sure everything was locked up, and at the last minute, I think I'm going to board up the windows, we're all glass, we boarded up everything. I locked the front and the back door, sent the security guard home. The next day, we all tried to get in. The Holland Tunnel was a river, I had to go to the GW Bridge. Down here, it was a ghost town. We had to break in the back door. There was no power, it was pitch-black, three feet of water in the basement."

All this time I had no idea what was going on because I was uptown at a friend's apartment. There were two cities: one with power where people went on as normal; one without electricity or phones, where everyone made do as best they could, huddling under blankets for warmth, lighting candles, stopping by to see if neighbors were OK, getting a lobster sandwich from Balthazar.

Balthazar made sure locals ate; so did Sherpa at Russ & Daughters. The Lower East Side shop famous for its smoked fish was also caught short by the blackout.

Sherpa was, indeed, a true Sherpa. His full name was Chhapte Sherpa Pinasha, and when he arrived in New York from his village in the eastern Himalayas, he got a job slicing salmon. "I'm from Katman-Jew," Sherpa liked telling regulars. It was easy, then, for him, delivering food to people stranded by the storm in high-rise apartments. Climbing twenty-four flights was nothing to a guy who had trekked partway to Everest in flip-flops.

This was New York at its best, the New York that was worth saving, the city that, when I got back from London just after 9/11, I wanted to put my arms around, as if I could somehow protect it.

CHAPTER 21

—◆—

ERIN AND
THE MACHINE

—◆—

All of New York seemed to stream through Balthazar's front door on Thursday afternoon. By four, Erin was settled at a round table near the door. Zouheir Louhaichy was the maître d' that day, and Erin said to him, "Give me five minutes." She wanted coffee before the supplicants filed through the door.

Every Thursday was an open call; anyone who wanted a job showed up. In the early days of Balthazar, Judi Wong told me, she and Keith would do the hiring. "He wanted to know if this person had character. I think because he was an immigrant, he identified with the people at the table, and wanted them to feel it didn't matter where you were educated or what your experience was. It was who you were as a person. Would I want to have coffee with this person? Can I have a conversation with this person? It set the style."

"The thing you should know about Erin is she only hires good hearts. She never hires nasty," said James Weichert.

"I can find ten million people, but they might be jerks," Erin said. "They might not smile when they walk into the room. I can tell before they sit down."

And they came: short, tall, black, white, brown, men and women, boys and girls—some of them were still in high school. A few were ambitious for a career in the glamorous food business as they perceived it and had been to these hiring sessions more than once. Some were simply desperate for any job at all, as a porter, a dishwasher.

The restaurant was still crowded, people lingering over lunch, on their phones making dates for dinner, talking to the office. A guy I knew from around and whose name I could never remember stumbled in, hoping for a bite from the afternoon menu, a sandwich, a plate of oysters, a tarte and coffee to see him through the rest of the day. Four men, chums who obviously did this regularly, piled onto barstools and ordered beer, and when the big glasses of lager came, they chugged them half down without talking.

There was the bright tinny noise of excitement from tourists. Runners weaved elegantly through the crowds with trays full of food hoisted overhead.

Of the job seekers, as they presented themselves to Erin, a few spoke no English. *"Parlez-vous anglais?"* she said, and then called over to Zouheir to translate.

"I'm Patrick," said a slim, sweet-faced young man who stood politely in front of Erin until she asked him to sit down. Erin offered her hand. Patrick had a nice firm handshake.

"Hi, Patrick. Erin. What are you looking for today?"

He sat down tentatively. "I'm looking for work in the bakery."

"Do you want to make croissants or sell them?"

"I'll do whatever you need."

"Where are you working at now?"

"Burger King."

"Tell me," Erin said with a grin and also with real curiosity, "is everything frozen at BK?"

Patrick smoothed out his jacket. "Everything," he said.

"Are you looking for part-time or full-time, Patrick?"

"Part-time, I'm still in school. I came here five times already."

"I see on your résumé that you're on the honor roll at school," Erin said. "What subjects do you like?"

"I really love math."

"Keep loving math," said Erin. "What do you want to do later on?"

"I want to be an accountant."

"Good," Erin said. "I'm gonna talk to Pablo"—Pablo Basi, the bakery manager—"and you'll hear from me by Monday."

Did Erin intend to hire Patrick?

"I will. I have a tendency to push through people who have a focus. The way I hire is very instinctual. I can see as they walk towards me, are they smiling? Are they alert, interested, curious, polite?"

Erin interviewed anyone who showed up. She never hired on the spot in order to give everyone a chance. Never asked about ethnicity because this was forbidden by the Department of Labor—and by her own decency.

The applicant screening forms, in a stack at her side, included a checklist. It included Appearance (poorly groomed/dressed inappropriately; appropriate attire and grooming; very well groomed and dressed) as well as Self-Confidence, Communication Skills, Job Knowledge, Motivation. The section marked Personality had notes that ran to: did not smile; indifferent, appeared smug; polite, pleasing manner, friendly, courteous, very pleasant.

Almost all the job seekers knew somebody, somebody who already worked as a busser, a bartender, in the bakery, as a dishwasher, and they told Erin this with varying levels of confidence; if they were arrogant, her eyes narrowed; her mind turned to her cup of coffee. She was not interested.

Sizing up an attractive young woman, long black well-groomed hair, elegant gray sheath, Erin said, "What do you do, Shannon?"

"I'm an actress, also a professional organizer, I'm also helping a friend of mine who is pregnant."

"Are you looking for full- or part-time?"

"I'd prefer nights, but I'll do anything," Shannon said, and I thought: *Bingo*. She was willing, she was eager.

"When we do hire hostesses, they come in at around thirteen an hour, but if they want to progress up, we are constantly reviewing."

Shannon said, "I've been excited about switching to the restaurant industry."

"I'll be in touch soon." Erin shook hands with Shannon.

"Is she in?" I said.

"Probably. She's well groomed, she smiles, she's friendly."

The next candidate for a job was Guillermo, a good-looking young guy with a charismatic smile. He was looking for work as a bartender while he started an EMT course. Erin told him there was a bartender whose brother was a fireman at a local house, thought he might combine his EMT training there with working at Balthazar.

Inside the Balthazar family, there was always somebody who was related to somebody who could help with a connection; at the center of the network, as if running a giant metaphorical switchboard, was Erin.

Finally, a round-faced man who did not speak English sat down. Shy, needy, he adjusted his cap. One of the waiters translated for him. He didn't want me to use his name. He would take "anything, whatever you have," he said. "I'll take it, please."

Erin was kind to him, and she listened and made notes carefully. But suddenly I was outside the gilded purlieus of Balthazar, its contented patrons drinking Gironde and martinis, examining each other in the opulent lighting, talking into phones, laughing, making plans. Perhaps this shy man—from his accent, I thought he must be Haitian—across from Erin had originally come to the United States on an inner tube and had somehow made his way to the enormous Haitian community in Brooklyn, and now he had been riding the train all day, looking for a job. Again he said, but without much hope, "I'll take anything."

I asked Erin what she thought. "I'll try," she said.

For new staff members, the Balthazar manual always seemed pretty daunting. Everyone who went to work at the restaurant was issued this enormous compendium that had grown over the years and that contained just about everything you had to know. It was big and it was detailed, and it ran to behavior, the rules of good service, and right down to which flavors of jam were available at breakfast.

I read through it. It was a lulu. It was a humdinger of a manual. It was also revealing, not so much because of details about learning the names and origins of oysters, but because it was like a little key to what made Balthazar's service so good. A few points included that the customer was always right and the only reason the place was in business; that if a guest didn't like a dish—no need to give a reason— it was to be changed; that every table was a VIP table. No waiter was ever to argue with a customer, at least "until they touched you or don't pay." Honesty, it was written, was better than bravery, and also that a waiter must learn at least six types of oysters and their origins.

Longtime staff had internalized everything in the manual years ago, but rules in a book were only a guideline; as the general manager, Erin was responsible for keeping the spirit of the place intact, and that depended on her emotional style and her connection to the staff. When Erin was in a sentimental mood, which wasn't often, she revealed that Balthazar had part of her heart. I had once seen her glance around the restaurant, heard her mumble under her breath, "This is a gorgeous room." Still, she spent most days worrying about everything from the needs of the staff to replacing espresso cups.

Generally, there were two sorts of general manager, according to people who had worked around in various restaurants.

Erin's predecessor had turned Balthazar into a military force, an ex–staff member told me. With customers, he had a certain charm and I had liked him, but he intimidated the staff, some of them told me.

The autocratic style went back to the day of the brasserie overseer who tyrannized the staff. He paid homage only to the owner. "The job was to keep the owner in profit, and to remember to order the new silverware," a disaffected ex–Balthazar manager said.

Inevitably Erin Wendt belonged to the second category; she was den mother to the staff: maternal, but tough. She had hired most of the current staff anyway, and she knew them as well as she knew her own kids.

New Orleans. Theater. Stand-up. Bartending. Guts. Erin's rare ability to organize and perform, to read behind the rules, to get the meaning of what was not said, added up. These were real assets for running a big restaurant like Balthazar, with rigorous standards, open eighteen hours every day, with a thousand moving parts. To Erin, the unforeseen, the unexpected, whatever hit her out of the blue, was routine.

Erin Wendt grew up in Gretna, Louisiana, across the river from New Orleans. "My family had three things that they did: construction, working for Chevron oil, and running restaurants and bars," she said. "That's what you did in NOLA, you were either blue-collar or you fed people." She picked up her coffee cup, and we went to a quiet table near the bar.

Her ambition was to act, or to do stand-up. With *Saturday Night Live* in her mind, Erin replied to a want ad in the *Village Voice* for a room in New York City. "I sent cash to this woman for the sublet, and prayed to God. I can't believe I did something that stupid. I actually had traveler's checks." Erin was laughing and sipping at her coffee, recalling how the room turned out to be on 207th Street, the last stop on the A train.

Looking around, she was lost. Inwood was the neighborhood

where Manhattan ran out, the last stop on the train before you stumbled into the Harlem River. It was where Irish and Jewish immigrants had settled and where Dominicans had moved in more recently. Inwood Park was also where as a child I had gone on field trips to look for Indian arrowheads. There were caves at Inwood, and sometimes you found old pieces of metal and could claim they were the real thing.

The neighborhood, with its shabby old Art Deco apartment buildings and storefronts, most of the signs in Spanish, in no way resembled the New York of Erin's imagination—no theaters, no bright lights, no way to make real contacts. All she had was ferocious determination.

A friend got her a job at Balthazar Bakery. Erin worked, and she auditioned for the theater and for stand-up and she cashed her check at the bank because she couldn't afford a checking account. After she paid her bills, she had twenty bucks left every week. "I was fishing for dimes in the pay phone. I was excellent at that," she said.

She got to know her way around New York while she wrote a screenplay, bartended, and waited tables at Capsouto Frères. When she heard Keith McNally was opening Pastis, she applied as a waiter, but it didn't work out. "He thought I'd be better suited here, so I started waiting tables at Balthazar, then I became a captain."

Acting kept its grip on Erin, she couldn't quite extract herself from the ambition. *One more shot*, she figured, and went to Los Angeles. "I auditioned for this dumb movie with Vince Vaughn, and it came down to two of us, and I didn't get it, and I thought, fuck it, I'm done." McNally asked if she'd be the general manager at Morandi, but before she actually got back to the city, he asked her to take over as GM of Balthazar.

Getting home after work kept Erin going, allowed her to manage the mountain of stuff that she climbed every day all over again because in a restaurant these were things—laundry, staff, plumbing—that required fresh attention daily. For Erin, getting home at the end of each day was like returning to base camp. Those who thought women were incapable of running two lives, of working at big jobs and caring for families, had not met Erin; Erin was a poster girl for how to do it all and with humor, even grace.

I asked how she managed her worlds; she said she didn't sleep much, just lay awake organizing things in her head, then got up before dawn to see the kids.

"My greatest support in this job are my kids and my wife. You've met them. A hug from Leo, kisses from the twins—Lucy and George—and a long conversation with Ellie will fill your well any day of the week. And Maya is my person." Whenever Erin talked about her family, she lit up, and you could tell from the way she talked that this was her real solace, her purpose, her passion.

Maya Kukes, Erin's wife, who is a journalist, told me that Erin moved effortlessly between their laid-back New Jersey suburbia and the pressures of Balthazar; that though Erin loved fine food, "she is also just as happy barbecuing chicken and hot dogs in the backyard with a Corona in her hand."

"OK." Erin put her coffee cup down and got up. "Come on." It was past five. Still, she had something to show me, and we went back through the swing doors into the kitchen, where the cooks were working on dinner, into the dishwashing area, down the metal stairs, past the prep and the chef's office, and all the way back to the far end of the underground world.

In a small room was a container for oil and grease, which was stored and recycled for bio-diesel. "We try to recycle where we can—rather than pay somebody to take it away, we get paid." In a storage area she showed me cartons of dishes. "Bargain prices," she said, almost giddy.

Finally, we arrived at a small room about fifteen by twenty, lined with huge plastic bins.

"Take a smell," said Erin, breathing deeply, a little theatrical.

"This is one of the most beautiful things on the planet. This is a re-frigerated garbage room in New York City," she said, as if she had just encountered a particularly fine piece of art. "By the end of the night, the room will all be filled to the ceiling.

"What do you smell? Nothing. Only the sweet smell of air-conditioning."

In one of the corridors, as we made our way to Erin's office, she noticed a waiter whose shirt was rumpled. She looked at him and, with the mix of consummate tact and maternal irritation, said, "Go iron your shirt," adding to herself, "Give a shit."

CHAPTER 22

WAITING AROUND

The staff room downstairs at Balthazar was where most of the waiters changed clothes—the men into freshly pressed white shirts, bistro aprons, black ties; women into the black frocks and white aprons; everyone into sturdy shoes. Waiting tables was hard on the feet, and there was plenty of standing and waiting around, and it would go on until eleven or twelve at night. A few more waiters would come in at five-thirty, and they would close the restaurant after midnight.

It had surprised me how crummy the staff room was; the peeling paint, the dull lighting, the metal lockers. A couple of tables had been shoved against the wall. The cooks ate their meal here. Rebecca Banks taught her wine classes here. Sometimes I saw one of the waiters or cooks changing his shirt.

Around three-thirty, the underground at Balthazar, which had been quiet in the few hours after lunch, sprang into life with the sound of metal locker doors banging. On one locker was a large Greenpeace sticker. It belonged to Nicole Hopson, and she was just tying on her white apron and chatting in French with Moustapha Konte, a tall Senegalese man in little round wire-rimmed glasses.

Moustapha had been a Balthazar waiter for years, though he resembled a French professor—one who specialized in Roland Barthes, I thought. "*Alors, Maman,*" he said to Nicole; this was a term of endearment and respect for her, and they put their heads together and laughed at some private Francophone joke.

It had been tough for Moustapha in the beginning, arriving in America. "I was like, oh, you know, wonderful country, no suffering, everything is fine," he told me. "You just step inside and you're set. It was harder. I found out it was harder. It was so different. It even smelled different."

To Nicole Hopson, who had been at Balthazar for eighteen years and knew her way around every inch of the restaurant and had a line on most of the staff, Balthazar was family. Every year she sent money to the fund set up by Lyric Benson's family. She remembered the good and bad. Wistfully she recalled the parties Keith once held for the staff at Nell's (the club he owned), which were, she said, "beautiful." "And the ravishingly pretty invitations" that were sent out when he married Alina Johnson. "Alina was the most lovely young woman," said Nicole, who adored the young staff she had taken under her wing. She was a generous woman.

No matter how delicious Shane's food was, it was the waiters who were center stage every night, the actors who sold the play to a new audience. As with the theater, the play was always different and always the same. Like actors, the waiters could make or break an evening, could sell it and make it swing.

The rewards of a contented table, especially one that ordered a second bottle of wine, were also the tips that went with it; the more you sold, the bigger your tip pool.

The best of them actually enjoyed the hours on the front lines, rose to the performance. This was where they got the applause, and they fed on it like everyone else in this business. Like Shane McBride, who had told me how, as a young chef, the instant gratification was in a guest liking something you had made. The best advice I ever got on how to have a good time at a restaurant was from a London maître d', who said, "You know, if customers treat it like a party and they treat us—the staff—like we're at the party, too, they get the best out of it." The long-serving waiters knew exactly how to make customers feel good; they'd had plenty of practice, they knew the tunes.

I thought of Nicole Hopson as a "guest whisperer." I had seen her in action; she could turn even that aggressive guest who had arrived furious into a pussycat. She had worked at Balthazar for nearly twenty years.

"I consider people sitting in my section as my personal guests," Nicole said. "I have to pay attention that they leave happy—they make a reservation, they take a taxi, they may have to wait at the door, they sit down, they have basically somebody sitting on their lap when it's crowded and the noise level is high. So you have to be nice to these people, because they deserve a medal, and then it's not cheap," said Nicole. "Sometimes I can make it a special occasion. You know somebody is coming in unhappy or somebody is having an argument, a couple, maybe, and you think about how you are going to walk around this. It's a lot of psychology, you have to read people, basically."

"Nicole is a great pro," said Erin. "She works four nights a week all year long, with two or three months off in the end of summer and fall when she goes to France to visit her mother, and she can come back, and go right to work. She is one of the great characters in this show."

Still, sometimes there was a slight sadness about Nicole, a faint melancholy, the sense of a tough history she had put behind her and never talked about. Over the years, she had been offered management jobs at Balthazar. She turned them all down. "I want my freedom," she said. "When I finish my shift, I'm done. Keith is very demanding of management."

"True," said James Weichert when I mentioned this to him. "But if Keith thinks a guest is wrong, or was ugly with one of his staff, he will call them and tell them to fuck off, so to speak. He's pretty goddamn loyal."

Fiercely intelligent, skeptical, tough, Nicole's face was like a little map of France. In her late fifties, a small, curly-haired woman, she was gamine, too, which made her look younger than her years. She had bright curious eyes and a sense of humor. Her kindly, open expression, though, was tempered by a fury from time to time whenever she thought there had been an act of cruelty of any kind, to people, to animals, or kids.

After studying American literature at the Sorbonne, she had come to New York, worked at a variety of jobs, and found herself at Balthazar. She was on her feet for eight or ten hours at a time. She worked four full shifts every week and went to the gym most days. Nicole was fit. We weren't far apart in age, but I would have been dead on my feet if I worked as hard as she did. Nicole was kept going by her inexorable will. This was what she did, and she was a pro.

Art was Nicole's passion—a trip to the Met was her greatest pleasure—and often she bought interesting postcards and sent them to friends.

Born in a village outside Paris that had been gobbled up by the urban sprawl near Charles de Gaulle Airport, on one side Nicole was French, on the other Armenian. She marched for Armenian rights and for recognition of the genocide in which a million and a half of her people had been slaughtered by Turkey; some of them had been her own ancestors.

She was also passionately devoted to animals, and it got her into trouble; in the history of Balthazar, Nicole was infamous for the broken-egg affair.

It all started with Evolution. Evolution had been a shop on Spring Street—it finally moved last year—that sold skeletons and fossils and other oddities. Nicole was sure they were also, at one time, selling bears' paws and elephant-foot wastebaskets, that sort of thing, and this may or may not have been true, but the very idea enraged her. This was a woman who kept a bird feeder outside her flat in the West Village; she took particular care that no bird went hungry or cold.

Before she left her apartment one afternoon, she checked on the bird feeder outside her window, then got an egg from the fridge and put it in her purse. After her shift, probably around midnight or later, she walked west on Spring Street to Evolution, where, furtive but determined, she smashed the egg against the window. Removing dried egg was a lousy business, she knew.

This went on for some time—every night the egg, every morning an enraged proprietor scraping the sticky crap off the plate glass—and then he laid a trap. He stayed late in the shop and caught Nicole red-handed; she was taken to the local precinct by the cops. Keith rushed down to bail her out.

Fierce and very funny, Nicole was once summoned to Balthazar to work a Sunday brunch because somebody had called in sick. She went in, did her work, and left a message on the staff bulletin board for "he who called me." It read: "Tell him I'm going to nail his balls to his thighs."

In the staff room, Nicole chuckled and sat down briefly on one of the benches. Next to her, handsome with his sleek black hair, was Sazzad Islam. He loved clothes, and before he had changed for work he was wearing fashionable pants and studded biker boots. The outfits, the love for going out, his slightly knowing smile, Sazzad had become a quintessential New Yorker.

At home in Bangladesh, Sazzad had been studying accounting when quite suddenly he found himself in New York almost overnight. The visas came faster than expected, and Sazzad's dad packed him off to his mother, who was already settled in Queens; the rest of the family followed. You could never tell when the visas would come, and when they did, you just picked up and went to America.

"So I tried to educate myself when I was very new in New York," said Sazzad. "Me and my friend, we both liked city life, you know, liked to have fun, go out, look around, eat, see what was happening."

It was Christmastime when Sazzad walked into Balthazar almost by chance. He had no real experience, but it was Christmas and therefore busy, and there was a gig. He loved it. His first focus was getting to know what Sazzad calls "the alcohol life." In Bangladesh, a Muslim country, he had never touched wine.

"When he first started he was drinking a shandy, beer and a little Sprite on top," said Moustapha, kidding around. The two men were pals, though Moustapha sometimes treated Sazzad a little like a younger brother.

"I was drawn to the restaurant business," said Sazzad. "I enjoy spreading my love and knowledge of food and wine to my customers and watching them engage in a pleasurable dining experience."

Every month Rebecca offered a prize for whoever sold the most wine, and Sazzad Islam almost always won. He reveled in knowing it all, in explaining why certain French wines were comparable to those from the United States, Australia, Italy, or Argentina, and which were his personal favorites. He had never tasted wine until he was twenty-three, but he had fallen in love with it. Most of his holidays were spent exploring the wine-producing regions of France and other countries.

"This transcends itself with each new country I visit," he said. "From Paris to Champagne to Istanbul to the Greek islands, I've always enjoyed immersing myself in the culture of food and dining."

Sazzad stopped talking. The high, the euphoria of talking about places he loved disappeared. His voice went flat. He slumped down next to Nicole. A faint look of concern crossed her face. Sazzad's mother had died not long before. Nicole had been there for him